NO PLACE TO REST

Forced Removals and the Law in South Africa

edited by

Christina Murray and Catherine O'Regan

CONTEMPORARY SOUTH AFRICAN DEBATES

1990
Oxford University Press
Cape Town

in association with the Labour Law Unit
University of Cape Town

Oxford University Press
Walton Street, Oxford OX2 6DP, United Kingdom

OXFORD NEW YORK TORONTO
DELHI BOMBAY CALCUTTA MADRAS KARACHI
PETALING JAYA SINGAPORE HONG KONG TOKYO
NAIROBI DAR ES SALAAM CAPE TOWN
MELBOURNE AUCKLAND

and associated companies in
BERLIN IBADAN

ISBN 0 19 570580 7

Cover
Detail from a painting by Willie Bester entitled *Forced Removal*

Maps by Rosemary Kovats

Published by Oxford University Press Southern Africa,
Harrington House, Barrack Street, Cape Town, 8001, South Africa
in association with the Labour Law Unit, University of Cape Town,
Private Bag, Rondebosch, 7700, South Africa

DTP conversion by the Centre for Applied Legal Studies,
University of the Witwatersrand, Johannesburg

Printed and bound by Clyson Printers, Maitland, Cape

Contents

Maps

Photographs

Contributors

Laurel Angus is a researcher at the Centre for Applied Legal Studies at the University of the Witwatersrand.

Geoff Budlender is an attorney and Director of the Legal Resources Centre, Johannesburg.

Colin Bundy is professor of History at both the University of Cape Town and the University of the Western Cape.

Aninka Claassens is a fieldworker for the Transvaal Rural Action Committee.

Alan Dodson is a Cape Town attorney practising in the field of human rights.

Kathy Eales is the publications officer at the Centre for Applied Legal Studies at the University of the Witwatersrand.

Moray Hathorn is an attorney at the Legal Resources Centre in Johannesburg.

Nicholas Haysom is an attorney and senior research officer at the Centre for Applied Legal Studies at the University of the Witwatersrand.

Dale Hutchison is professor of Roman-Dutch and Private Law at the University of Cape Town.

Raylene Keightley is a lecturer in the Department of Roman-Dutch and Private Law at the University of Cape Town.

Gilbert Marcus is an advocate and senior research officer at the Centre for Applied Legal Studies, University of the Witwatersrand.

Christina Murray is a senior lecturer in the Department of Public Law at the University of Cape Town.

Susan Ogterop is a librarian in the African Studies Library at the University of Cape Town.

Catherine O'Regan is a senior lecturer in the Department of Criminal and Procedural Law and a research associate in the Labour Law Unit at the University of Cape Town.

Clive Plasket is an attorney practising in the field of human rights law in Johannesburg.

Michael Robertson is Director of the Centre for Socio-Legal Studies at the University of Natal at Durban.

Michael Sutcliffe is acting head of the Department of Town and Regional Planning and a member of the Built Environment Support Group at the University of Natal at Durban.

Alison Todes is a lecturer in the Department of Town and Regional Planning and a member of the Built Environment Support Group, University of Natal at Durban.

Norah Walker is a town planner and on the full-time staff of the Built Environment Support Group, University of Natal at Durban.

David Unterhalter is an advocate and a part-time lecturer in law at the University of the Witwatersrand.

Preface

One of the notorious acts of inhumanity of the twentieth century has been the forced removal of at least three-and-a-half million people by the South African state. These removals have been implemented under sweeping powers conferred upon officials by a compliant legislature. But the policy of forced removals has not been a monolithic one, nor has it been uniformly implemented.

The early months of 1990 have seen the promise of political change, but the new State President, F W De Klerk, has as yet failed to announce the suspension of the practice of forced removals, or the repeal of legislation empowering them. Even if forced removals are suspended in the future, the fundamental question of how to redress the injustice of centuries of dispossession will remain. This question cannot be answered without a full understanding of the way in which people were dispossessed.

This book seeks first to examine the changing political and socio-economic context of forced removals. Secondly, it describes some of the struggles communities have waged to resist removals, and the role of law and lawyers in these struggles. Finally, it provides an accessible guide to the legislation enabling officials to carry out forced removals, identifying possible avenues for litigation to prevent further removals.

Language in South Africa is always contested. It is impossible to analyse government policy without using racist terms, abhorrent as they are. The convention used in this book is that the groups defined in the Population Registration Act are referred to as African, white, 'coloured' and asian or Indian. Black is used to refer to all people who are not classified as white. The words homeland and bantustan have been used interchangeably to refer to what the government now calls national states.

Some of the contributions in the book originated as papers presented at the Conference on Law and Forced Removals in South Africa held by the Labour Law Unit at the University of Cape Town in April 1989, with the financial support of Lawyers for Human Rights. The photographs were selected from an Afrapix exhibition at the conference.

Many people have co-operated to make the publication of this book possible. In particular we wish to thank Zaida Dinaully who typed the manuscript, and Kathy Eales who did the DTP conversion. The birth of our sons, James and Daniel, while this book was being edited, renewed our hope that for all young South Africans apartheid will soon be a lesson of history.

Christina Murray
Catherine O'Regan
Cape Town
March 1990

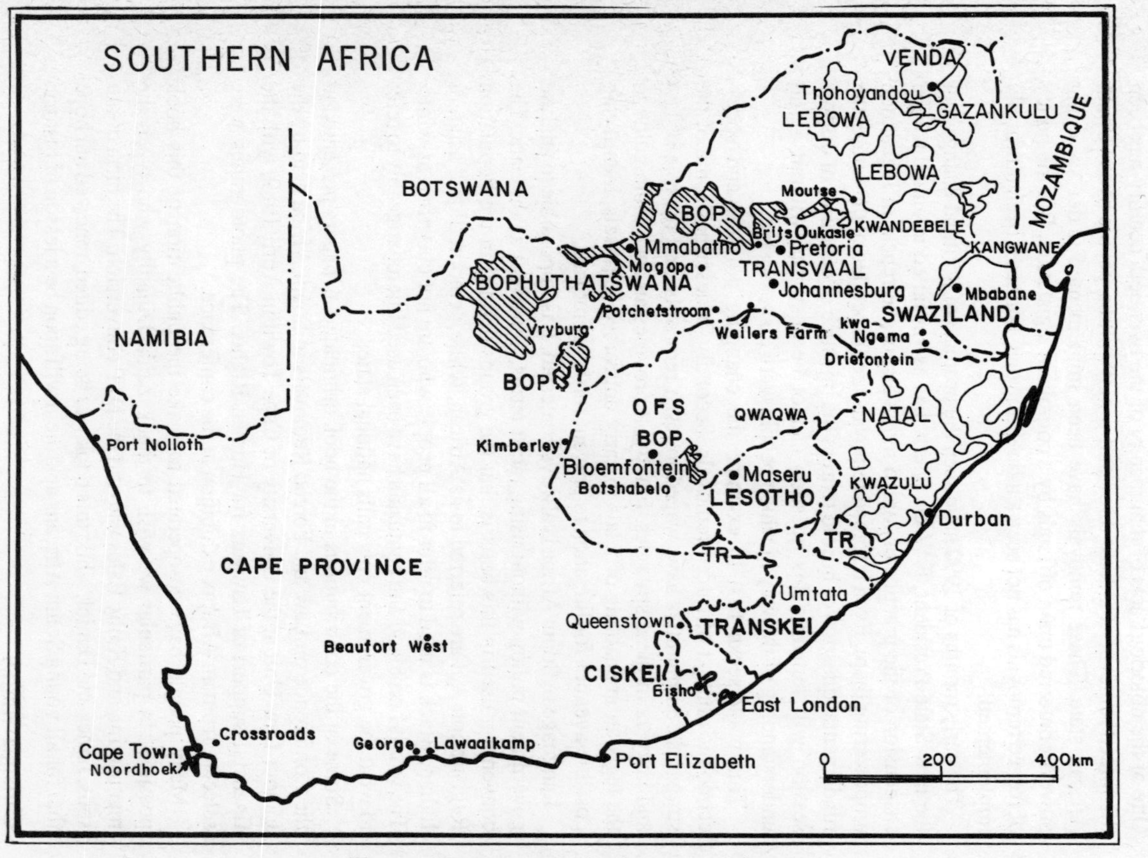

Forced Removals in South Africa

Part one: Social and Historical Context

Leaving Mogopa
(Paul Weinberg, Afrapix)

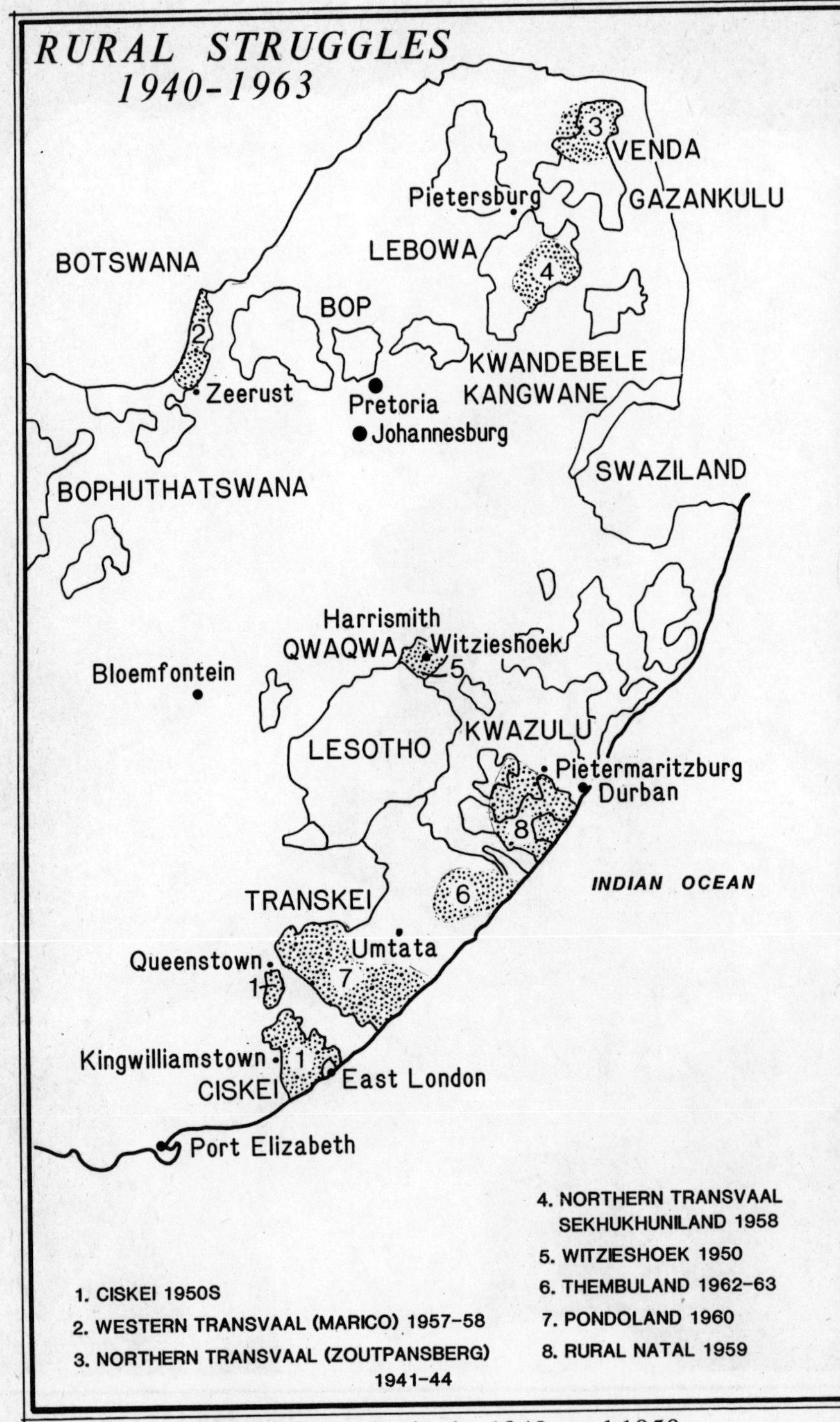

Rural Struggles in the 1940s and 1950s

COLIN BUNDY

Land, Law and Power: Forced Removals in Historical Context *

Seventy-three years ago, an African witness (one Reverend Mtinkuli) gave evidence to a Commission of Enquiry chaired by Sir William Beaumont. He was asked about the 1913 Natives Land Act which had been in force for three years:

> There are many natives who have already been removed from the farms on account of this Act. There are some being removed from the farms today. There are others who have farms but titles are refused them by the Government.... This Act therefore, seems to us like a one-edged knife – it cuts a big piece off the native and is very gentle with the European. The white man is told: 'If the natives do not carry out the landlord's wishes, chase them off the farm' but the natives are not told where to go to.... When the white man threatens to remove us from off his farm we have nowhere to run to; we would be obliged to stay and work for him at 2s 6d a month as we have to accept his conditions.

Senator the Honourable G G Munnik also gave evidence to the Commission. What, he was asked, was the intention behind the Land Act?

> The object of the Government should be, as far as possible, to force the natives, of course peacefully, into agriculture. The great object therefore should be to get him to work for the white men on the farms at a wage.[1]

Both of these witnesses, it seems to me, accurately perceived the relationship between land and power. They understood that certain forms of land ownership – private property rights in land – confer and concentrate economic and social power in the hands of one group or class of people, giving them the ability to subordinate and exploit another group or class. Both men were also aware of how the law defined and perpetuated these property and power relations. From their different perspectives, Munnik and Mtinkuli both described a central process in our history: how unequal access to land, ratified by statute, has underpinned the domination of the majority of South Africans.

They referred to a particular, and very important, moment – the 1913 Land Act – which was, however, part of a much longer and broader process. That process, in South Africa as elsewhere, is one whereby small-scale cultivators are not only dispossessed of land, but also deprived of the ability to provide for themselves. This process is common to all societies that modernize, that industrialize, that become capitalist. Pre-industrial, pre-capitalist societies consisted predominantly of peasants or petty producers – people who had direct access to a portion of land, who owned some livestock and who, with the prevailing technology, were able to provide for the subsistence of their families.

For such societies to modernize, to make the transition towards capitalist societies, this basic pattern of production had to be recast: self-sufficient cultivators were transformed into wage labourers; rural populations flowed into towns and cities; individuals, families or larger groupings were stripped of the ability to provide for themselves. This historical process – divorcing small-scale producers from their land and their means of working it – could take different forms, could happen quite gradually or with great rapidity.

In England, the crucial mechanism was the enclosure movement, where over a period of about 300 years land that had been held in common – land to which all had access – was enclosed or privatized, so that increasingly the rural population sedimented out into landlords (the farmers) and labourers (the farm workers). A speedier version of the process took place in eighteenth-century Scotland, where the Highland clearances forcibly removed crofters, or peasants, off ancestral lands to make way for profitable herds of sheep. The savage enslavement of Central and Latin America by the Conquistadores was even more rapid, and considerably more brutal; but in each case the outcome was the same. A majority of people who once had access to land no longer did.

What form did this process take in South Africa? How were rural producers stripped of their land? To simplify a complex process, let me suggest that there were three major mechanisms:

- The first was forcible dispossession, by colonial conquest. The Khoi and the San lost their grazing and hunting lands to Dutch settlers by force of arms; in the Frontier Wars it was the combination of British and colonial troops that broke Xhosa power and seized Xhosa lands. The 1811-12 Frontier War (its savagery memorably recreated by Ben MacLennan)[2] witnessed the first large-scale removals in South African history.

- Secondly, new economic forces and pressures severed people from their land. Peasant producers became involved in new economic obligations, such as paying rents and taxes; they fell into debt – and paid off their creditors with their land. A cash economy provided new goods – and new pitfalls: as a descendant of the Kat River settlement told historian Jeff Peires: 'those lands went for sugar and coffee and things like that'.[3]
- The third mechanism was the role of law, or intervention by the state. Law is not neutral: it reflects existing interests and the distribution of power in any society. The law in nineteenth- and twentieth-century South Africa favoured the propertied and employing classes: there was precious little neutral about the Masters and Servants Acts, vagrancy laws, the 1913 Land Act, the Urban Areas Act, the Group Areas Act, or the Prevention of Illegal Squatting Act. These, and many others, expressed in statute form the asymmetrical property and power relations of a colonial society: relations that one might sum up as 'I am an owner; you are a tenant; he is a squatter'.

Each of these three elements – the military, the market and the magistrate – is a major topic in its own right. I shall concentrate upon the third: upon the particular way in which legislation has been shaped by struggles over land and labour. It is impossible, in the space available, to survey that history in detail; instead, this paper will look at two decisive aspects of it: the 1913 Land Act and the phenomenon of social engineering on a mass scale in the 1950s and 1960s, and more briefly, it will sketch some of the developments between those moments.

The Natives Land Act of 1913

The 1913 Act had, of course, been preceded by a vast number of land laws in the British colonies and the Boer republics before 1910: laws controlling squatting, regulating tenancies, imposing taxes and rents, and escalating the penalties and punishments for their transgression. But the 1913 law – while it echoed details from earlier legislation – went much further.

It provided the statutory basis of territorial segregation, by dividing South Africa into areas where Africans could own land (the reserves) and the rest, where Africans were prohibited from 'purchase, hire or other acquisition of land or of any right thereto'. In 1913 these reserves constituted 8 per cent of the land – with provisions to increase their area to 13 per cent of South Africa's surface.

Most people think of the 1913 Act in terms of this territorial segregation. But it included other crucial elements, which in many ways had a more immediate impact upon people's lives. These provisions determined the circumstances in which Africans might live and work on white-owned farms.

In the early years of this century, enormous numbers of Africans lived on the land which technically belonged to white proprietors. Many different forms of land tenure permitted this. There were Africans who lived and farmed on white-owned land as cash-paying tenants. Others 'farmed on the halves' – that is, paid rent to their landlords in the form of a share of the crop that they raised. Sharecropping arrangements in the Orange Free State had seen the emergence of a relatively prosperous stratum of black peasant farmers. A third category, called labour tenants, lived on farms and received a portion of land for their own use, paying for it by working for the landlord for a stipulated number of days each year.

What the 1913 Act attempted was to legislate out of existence the more independent forms of tenure and to perpetuate instead the most dependent. Its intention was to outlaw cash-paying tenants, and in the Orange Free State to forbid all sharecropping agreements. The Act was intended to reduce cash tenants and sharecroppers to the status of labour tenants or wage labourers. As the magistrate of Heilbron put it: 'This Act is one by which a man is reduced from being a farmer in his own account to being a servant at one stroke.'[4]

In the Orange Free State, the Act had an immediate and devastating impact upon the lives of black people. The forced removals of 1913 – in the shape of evictions of better-off peasant families from Free State farms – are memorably described by Sol Plaatje in his classic *Native Life in South Africa*. The African National Congress – formed the year before – embarked upon opposition to the Act as one of its first campaigns. A spokesperson for the Transvaal branch of the ANC told the Beaumont Commission:

> It causes our people to be derelict and helpless .... Another reason why this Act oppresses is that the farmer refuses to engage the average native who is in possession of livestock as he says the native is a baas himself. In the latter case the native is compelled to sell his stock for whatever he can get in order that he may obtain employment as he has no place of refuge. There is winter in the Natives Land Act. In winter the trees are stripped and leafless.[5]

And let me quote from the Beaumont Commission once more. When it took evidence in the Soutspansberg, a number of chiefs and headmen gave evidence. They were eloquent in the acuteness of their distress and graphic in their analysis of how pressures and problems intermeshed. Mphephu complained of high taxes: 'I am all by myself because little children have been made to pay taxes. They have to go out to work ....' Mapafuri told of how economic losses had weakened Africans politically: 'We have lost our herds and the only thing you can do is to say "Do this! Take that away!" and we obey your orders.' Mayemo and Senthimula denounced the unfairness of the legislation: 'I do not think this Act is quite in order, because land and money are just the same.'

One of the commissioners, Colonel Sir Walter Stanford, then scolded these witnesses:

> I can judge by your answers that you did not quite understand. You have talked about your children at work, about the punishments inflicted upon them, about dog taxes and other taxes – all matters to which Sir William Beaumont made no reference whatsoever. He told you we were here about land.[6]

Sir Walter was blind to connections which the peasants perceived perfectly clearly: connections between land and money, between land and power. They saw precisely that their poverty and their impotence were linked to land loss. They also glimpsed something of the longer term significance of the 1913 Land Act: that it laid down the conditions and terms upon which the struggle between landlords and tenants would be waged in the future. The law loaded the dice heavily in favour of landlords and employers.

A decade later – in the latter half of the 1920s – the South African countryside became the arena of intense struggles between white proprietors and their workers and tenants. Scores of localized grievances and conflicts were linked to broader demands for land and liberation; hundreds of activists distributed literature and made speeches; many thousands of rural Africans glimpsed deliverance. The catalyst to all this was the Industrial and Commercial Workers Union (the ICU), which between 1926 and 1929 became the first black mass movement in South African history, signing up between 100 000 and 250 000 members – predominantly from the platteland. This story has been told recently[7] – and the defeat of the ICU is of the utmost importance if we are to comprehend how the balance of power was tilted decisively in that decade in favour of landholders and employers.

In the 1940s and 1950s, the focus of rural protest and resistance shifted from white-owned farmlands to African reserves. By the 1940s, the reserves had become overpopulated and less agriculturally productive: their inhabitants were locked into migrant labour on a massive scale. If the reserves were the source of migrant labour, the mining compounds and the squalid urban townships were its destination: the system as a whole was propped up on the Land Act, the pass laws, influx control, and political exclusion. Denied access to land elsewhere, the inhabitants of the increasingly crowded reserves were condemned to a sphere of existence simultaneously distant, debilitating and deteriorating.

In the 1940s, the central state was forced to cope with this mounting crisis in the reserves. The policy that evolved had three main thrusts. First, economic intervention (variously stabilization, rehabilitation, conservation, and betterment) was designed to halt the decay of food production. Secondly, political intervention (successively Bantu Authorities, homelands, and national states) was intended simultaneously to restructure local political authority and to balkanize African nationalism. Thirdly, after 1948, controls over the movement of African workers were tightened and extended.

In response to these treble pressures – new clamps on how people farmed, how they were governed, and how they were employed – reserve inhabitants mounted a series of desperate struggles between the mid-1940s and early 1960s in the Ciskei, western and northern Transvaal, in Witzieshoek, Thembuland, Pondoland and rural Natal (see map on page 2). The defeat of these struggles (which involved savage repression and the accelerated promotion of the bantustan collaborators) helped to usher in the phase of mass social engineering.

Social engineering: mass forced removals in the 1960s

'Social engineering' might be defined as social and economic restructuring according to politically defined objectives. More brusquely, but equally accurately, it means pushing large numbers of people around, forcing them to do things they don't want to do. Its most dramatic expression in South Africa has been the forced removal of 3,5 million people. (See Table A.) There is a sense in which these appalling figures have been cited so often that we are used to them: that we cease to realize their import, their horror – what they mean in terms of degradation, misery, and psychological and physical suffering.

The legislation providing for forced removals does not date from 1948 only; but it was sharpened and amplified after the National Party came to power. Forced removals on a large scale have been a reality of the past half century; but they reached their most concentrated and colossal form between the early 1960s and mid-1970s. These years form a distinctive period in South African history: they saw the apex of economic growth, the nadir of organized resistance, and the swaggering dominance of the strong state.

International capitalist confidence in South Africa reached its height: between 1962 and 1972 the dollars, pounds, francs, marks and yen poured in, doubling the total of foreign investment. White South Africans – especially home-owners, investors in the stock exchange, entrepreneurs and professionals – had never had it so good. 'At some point around 1970', writes Bill Johnson, 'white South Africans overtook Californians as the single most affluent group in the world'.[8] From 1962, under the new Minister of Justice, Vorster, new security legislation swelled the power of the police, shrank that of the courts, and shredded the rights of people under arrest. A generation of political leaders was banned, jailed or exiled.

*Table A: Estimated Numbers of Forced Removals, 1960-1983**

Farm evictions	1 129 000
Black spots and consolidation	614 000
Urban	730 000
Informal settlements	112 000
Group areas	860 400
Infrastructural/strategic	103 500
TOTAL	3 548 900

* *Source:* Platzky & Walker *The Surplus People* at 10.

This was the context of social engineering in its heyday. This was the period in which the ruthless implementation of the Group Areas Act transformed our urban geography and in which clearance of 'black spots' wiped out islands of peasant tenacity. These were the years symbolized by the notorious General Circular 25/1967 of the Department of Bantu Administration, which defined as 'surplus' the 'aged, the unfit, widows, women with dependent children' – and which promised to leave no stone unturned in making the bantustans the rural receptacles of the nation's unemployed. This was the era that could dream up bureaucratic solutions like rezoning bantustans so as to create the new category of commuter migrants – workers who have been dubbed 'a nation of sleepwalkers' – dream up *and* implement the scarcely credible odyssey of thousands who are bused from bantustan to business centre. These years called into being areas like kwaNdebele – which Joe Lelyveld described as 'a squalid rural ghetto, besmeared with metal shanties and mud houses in an almost unbroken sea of resettlement sites'. Such sites, he added, 'can be seen in other countries, usually as a result of famine or war. I don't know where else they can have been achieved as a result of social planning.'[9]

Above all, the social engineering worked. It achieved, by and large, what it was meant to achieve. Broadly speaking, during the first half of this century, bureaucrats and bosses favoured policies which would gouge workers out of the reserves, as migrant labourers, while setting up barriers to permanent African urbanization. By the 1940s, it seemed that the flow of Africans into the cities as permanent residents was an irresistible tide: you might as soon 'sweep the ocean back with a broom' said General Smuts in 1942, as stem that tide. 'Aha' – the social engineers might have responded – 'if a broom won't work, we'll use bulldozers.' And mass forced removals were precisely that: the ruthless bureaucratic machinery used to fight the human flood and to force it, against the laws of social gravity, back into the reserves.

Table B: Results of Social Engineering
*(Distribution of the African Population in South Africa, %)**

Year	Urban Areas	Rural Areas	Bantustans	Total
1950	25,4	34,9	39,7	100
1960	29,6	31,3	39,1	100
1970	28,1	24,5	47,4	100
1980	26,7	20,6	52,7	100

* *Source:* Platzky &Walker *The Surplus People* at 18

Between 1960 and 1980, the proportion of Africans living in urban areas fell from 29,6 to 26,7 per cent – even though these were years of massive industrialization. The proportion of the African population living on white-owned farm land fell from nearly a third of the total to one fifth, as farmers mechanized and pushed 'non-productive' people off their land, and as the category of labour tenants was all but expunged from the platteland. The reserve-based population rose from under 40 to nearly 53 per cent – but if one adds to the census totals of those who were absent from the reserves as contract labourers, the true figure would be over 60 per cent. In these statistics one confronts one of the most staggering realities of recent South African history.

Behind the arithmetic are whole dimensions of experience and suffering and pain that lie beyond the reach of the sociological imagination. Let me be clear: I do not suggest that we are wholly ignorant. On the contrary we know a great deal of the human cost of forced removals thanks to Cosmas Desmond, the Surplus People Project (SPP) collective, the National Committee Against Removals, the Farm Labour Project and the Carnegie Inquiry into Poverty, amongst others. From them we discover the details of broken promises, shattered communities, desolate camps and shallow graves; and how these translate into trauma, frustration, grief, dull dragging apathy and surrender of the will to live. Equally important, we learn from them something of the ingenuity and determination and courage that have enabled women and men to survive, to resist, and above all to envisage a different future.

Even their accounts are in a sense preliminary. They are told by sympathetic observers, committed reporters, and relief workers. They are probably most vivid, most poignant, most horrifying when they capture first-hand experience, with individual life histories and direct quotations. But the full picture is not yet available. The case studies offer mere glimpses: the voices are fragmentary echoes. What is still impossible to convey is the cumulative, collective, *epochal* character of the experience. None, yet, can convey the totality of the impact of social engineering under racial capitalism. Nor do we yet possess a theoretical understanding of exactly how forced removals, in all their forms, meshed with other social processes. And we are perhaps too close in time for an analysis of mass removals as contradictions, as an element feeding into popular resistance from the mid-1970s and deepening the crisis of legitimacy suffered by the state. That task demands an epic of empathy, a vast historic reconstruction, and a moral passion.

Let me conclude with a final reference to the three components in the title of this talk: land, law and power. I hope, firstly, that some sense has emerged even in a sketchy overview like this, of the centrality of the land question to the South African past, present and future. An entire history of colonial conquest and dispossession, of cheap labour and systematic exploitation, and of segregation, apartheid and white supremacy has created a society in which 60 000 capitalist farmers own 12 times as much land as over 14 million rural poor. Fundamental to the construction of an unjust, inequitable, repressive and brutal social order is an unjust, punitive and untenable allocation of land and rights to land.

Secondly, this entire edifice is buttressed by law – by statutes, regulations, circulars and government gazettes. As Platzky and Walker remind us:

> People are driven from their homes, loaded onto trucks and transported to relocation sites, their sites are numbered and expropriated, their houses are demolished by bulldozers and they are prevented from entering certain areas, all in terms of the law. Legislative sanction exists for every one of these procedures.[10]

Thirdly, such laws exist because of the way in which political, economic and social power is concentrated in the hands of a minority. The relentless exercise of that power – by politicians and policemen, by armies of bureaucrats and armies of soldiers, and by bankers, farmers, stockbrokers and courts of law – is the central, constant, definitive experience of the vast majority of South Africans. This is why they are so properly sceptical when those who monopolize power speak of 'power sharing'. What this really means is the preservation of power. Power, dribbled down from above, has about as much significance as the consolidation of the bantustans has to the land question. Political power is not participation in tricameral racism or in local government elections based upon votes for squirrels.[11] Political power – real power, the capacity of people to play a part in shaping their own lives – will only be attained in a new South Africa. In that South Africa, land, the law and power will all be distributed on fundamentally different terms.

Notes

* This paper was prepared as a talk, and not intended for publication; the text appears here in its original form – and perhaps should be read with that in mind.

1 *Report of the Native Land Commission* (Beaumont Commission) U G 22/1916 at 256.

2 B MacLennan *A Proper Degree of Terror: John Graham and the Cape's Eastern Frontier* (Johannesburg: Ravan 1986).

3 J Peires 'The Legend of Fenner Solomon' in B Bozzoli (ed) *Class, Community and Conflict* (Johannesburg: Ravan 1987) 82.

4 Beaumont Commission at 36.

5 Ibid.

6 Ibid. at 378-81.

7 H Bradford *A Taste of Freedom: The ICU in Rural South Africa, 1924-1930* (Johannesburg: Ravan 1988).

8 RW Johnson *How Long Will South Africa Survive?* (London: MacMillan 1977) 28.

9 Joseph Lelyveld *Move Your Shadow* (London: Jonathan Ball 1986) 125. (The phrase 'nation of sleepwalkers' is also his.)

10 L Platzky & C Walker for the Surplus People Project *The Surplus People: Forced Removals in South Africa* (Johannesburg: Ravan 1985) 138.

11 This is a reference to the government's advertising campaign for the municipal elections in 1988.

GILBERT MARCUS

Section 5 of the Black Administration Act: The Case of the Bakwena ba Mogopa

The law regarding the removal of a native from place to place in the Union is at present in force in Natal, and it is an excellent provision.

General J B M Hertzog (1927)[1]

The most notorious power granted to the government by Parliament to carry out forced removals was contained in section 5 of the Black Administration Act 38 of 1927.

In matters of race and security, the legislature has frequently seen fit to vest state functionaries with powers which are evidently intended to give them a free hand to do as they please, unhindered by judicial control. This philosophy underlies much that was contained in section 5.[2] It is sometimes argued that those possessed of special powers can be trusted to apply them reasonably and humanely. This is a dangerous supposition as the experience of the exercise of powers under Section 5 so strikingly illustrates. It is under this section that successive heads of state have ordered the forced removal of countless people. The full horror of these removals is not yet known. The Surplus People Project (SPP) estimated that between 1960 and 1982 approximately 3,5 million people were the victims of removal under various laws.[3] Faced with the 'shattering evidence' contained in this report, one newspaper offered a 'despairing' suggestion:

> [O]pponents of this Government and its policies should begin now to compile a register of those who have, in the name of the nation, committed these atrocities.
>
> We need to begin to work towards our own redemption by recording the names of the politicians who have made these policies, and their

> words. We need to compile a register of the names and pictures, and a record of the specific acts of the officials and the policemen who have carried out these mass removals. We need to begin now to record who did what to whom so that, one day, when South Africa is put on trial for its actions, the guilty will not be able to hide in the ranks of those who were merely indifferent.
>
> For surely, as there is justice under heaven, there will be a day of reckoning.[4]

This editorial was read in Parliament by Mr D J N Malcomess. When he suggested that there might one day be apartheid trials, he was told by the Minister of Mineral and Energy Affairs that his speech bordered on treason.[5] Only months later, the State President ordered the forced removal of the Bakwena ba Mogopa tribe. The circumstances of the removal were particularly callous and brutal.

This chapter examines the genesis of the State President's powers of removal under section 5 of the Black Administration Act, with particular reference to their use in the Mogopa case.

The Native Administration Act 38 of 1927

The Native Administration Bill was introduced to the Union Parliament by the then Prime Minister and Minister of Native Affairs, General Hertzog. It was an attempt, amongst other things, to impose a uniform system of black administration throughout South Africa. An examination of the parliamentary debates reveals that the proponents of the measure had several aims in mind. On the one hand, a crude paternalistic attitude emerges from many of the speeches. General Hertzog, in proposing the Bill, saw the role of the 'European' as a civilizing influence over the primitive 'native' population:

> We cannot expect any guardian over minor children to make a success of his job if we insist upon it that he should treat his youngsters just as he would treat his equals in life. It is impossible and unless we take the necessary opportunity in time of dealing with the subject, tremendous injury is going to be done to the native. I do not speak of those natives who can look after themselves, but we must never forget that of the 6 000 000 natives, 5 700 000 at least are not in the position of really digesting ... what is being passed, unless they are protected properly.[6]

General Smuts, one of the drafters of the Charter of the United Nations and often hailed as the greatest South African statesman, entertained similar views:

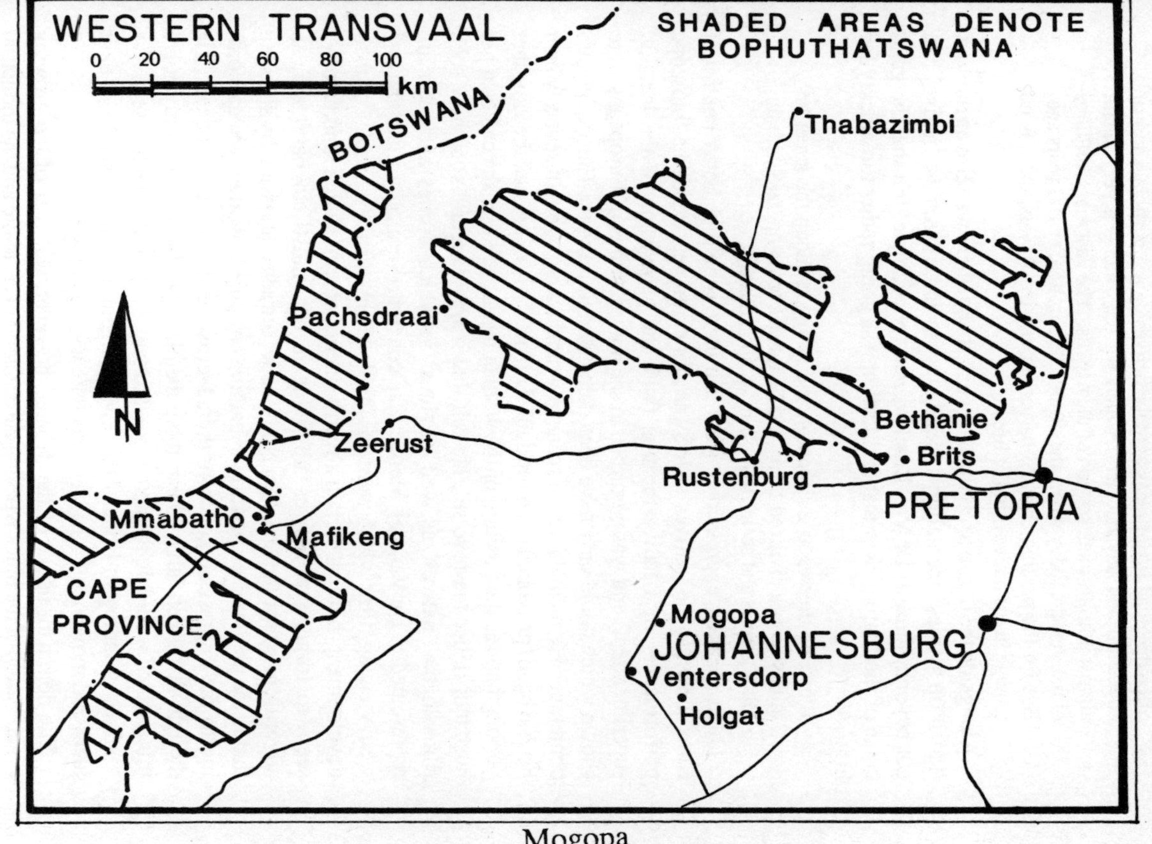
WESTERN TRANSVAAL
0 20 40 60 80 100
km
SHADED AREAS DENOTE BOPHUTHATSWANA
BOTSWANA
N
Thabazimbi
Pachsdraai
Zeerust
Bethanie
Brits
Rustenburg
PRETORIA
Mmabatho
Mafikeng
CAPE PROVINCE
Mogopa
JOHANNESBURG
Ventersdorp
Holgat

Mogopa

> The Native mind is very immobile and does not respond to the changes and advances which move whites. I am afraid that we are often deceived in our ideas as to the natives by a superficial show of education and advancement, which we see among a very small, almost infinitesimal, portion of the natives. The vast mass, millions of natives, are today where they were 20 years ago, or 100 years ago. But for the passing away of barbarism and tribal wars, there is no change in the native mind or life.[7]

Alongside the desire to civilize the uncivilized, there was also an obvious 'kaffir op sy plek' mentality; a feeling that in some cases the 'native' had got beyond himself. Dr Van Broekhuizen, for example, felt that the great curse of the 'native' was that civilization was going rather too quickly for him:

> When he dresses as a European and swaggers along the street he thinks he is a civilized being and he refuses to co-operate with the other natives and seems to look down upon them.[8]

Other speakers expressed concern that there should be better control of films shown to the 'natives'. Mr Swart, for example, attended a 'bioscope performance' in a native location (with the permission of the location superintendent) and was perturbed to see how 'pictures of Europeans were shown which could only have been calculated to bring the Europeans into contempt'. He recalled how a scene in which a white woman severely beat her husband 'provoked uncontrollable laughter'. He expressed the view that 'among natives the position of the woman is not such that she can beat her husband, rather the reverse'. He felt that it was dangerous to show such films to the 'natives' as well as films 'in which crimes and theft are represented'.[9] Dr Van der Merwe was concerned not only that 'natives' were viewing films which were unsuitable given 'the present stage of their development' but that certain advertisements were of such a kind that 'we seem to forget that natives are living in our midst'. In particular, an advertisement for the play 'No No Nanette' attracted attention by showing that in the play women perform in bathing costumes, 'women who, according to the impression got from the advertisement, are nearly naked'. He thought that given 'all we hear about the black peril it was certainly not a thing which would do the native good to see'. He said that he had seen five 'natives' standing in front of the advertisement and could 'see from their faces and movements what remarks they were making'.[10]

The dominant theme of the debates, however, was fear of the growing organization of the black working class. Clements Kadalie and his Industrial and Commercial Workers Union figured prominently in the speeches of most speakers. The mobilization of the working class and the articulation of opposition to the government were perceived to constitute a real threat to the white way of life:

> There is an insidious and poisonous propaganda based upon a gloomy hatred of the capitalist or landowner which is artificially being pumped into the natives through most unclean pipes of socialism and bolshevism. The spirit of lawlessness and communism is being engendered throughout South Africa amongst the native races. The doctrines of bolshevism and socialism find among the natives a very rich soil. It is growing far more rapidly than people realize. These red flaggers are allowed without let or hindrance to carry their objects throughout the country, and the time has come when a stop must be put to it .... And unfortunately they are using this propaganda amongst a people who might be called a child race. Is it fair? Does the true native, who has not been contaminated by these doctrines, believe in these doctrines? Every one of them is totally opposed to this sort of propaganda; in fact, many of these natives have asked me why the big Government does not put a stop to this sort of thing.[11]

Stemming the spread of noxious doctrine was principally to be achieved by three methods. The primary force of control was the creation of the criminal offence of fomenting feelings of racial hostility between 'natives and Europeans'. Secondly, the Act sought to bolster the power of chiefs and headmen in the hope that these people would exercise discipline over dissident elements. Finally, the Act created the power of forced removal. This power was conferred on the Governor-General in his capacity as the Supreme Chief.

Segregationist policies and the creation of labour reserves for mining and agricultural needs were firmly entrenched in South Africa by 1927. The containment of the black population in manageable units was obviously advantageous to the needs of industry and the ability to effect population shifts was essential to ensure a steady supply of labour. The stifling of dissent, however, was also regarded as essential. In justifying the conferral of the powers of the Supreme Chief on the Governor-General, the Minister of Justice, Tielman Roos, made the following observations:

> I regard it as of the greatest importance that those powers should be conferred upon the Governor-General, not only in respect of natives who are living under the tribal system, but also over detribalized and exempted natives. Now take the power in regard to detribalized and exempted natives, who, in many cases are the principal agitators in South Africa today. If you have the power to remove them from one place where they do mischief to a place where they do not do mischief, what a useful provision that would be. Just imagine for a moment. I am going to a certain extent into the realms of fancy. Imagine taking a farm and placing upon that farm all the agitators who are going about

> the country and letting them hold meetings with each other on that farm. In three months time how many of them would survive? Just think what the result would be of that sociological experiment .... I believe that powers of this kind are essential in South Africa, and that they are going to do more good to the natives than any other portion of the community.... It is quite obvious, I think, that these powers would be used for the benefit of the natives.[12]

By 1982, three-and-a-half million blacks who had been forcibly moved had 'benefited' from the Minister's 'sociological experiment'.

Forced removals

The power to forcibly remove black tribes was contained in section 5(1)(b) of the Black Administration Act. In its original form, the section provided:

> The Governor-General may whenever he deems it expedient in the general public interest, order the removal of any tribe or portion thereof or any Native from any place to any other place within the Union upon such conditions as he may determine: Provided that in the case of a tribe objecting to such removal, no such order shall be given unless a resolution approving of the removal has been adopted by both Houses of Parliament.

These were awesome powers of the sort usually reserved for times of war. Yet, they were enacted with little debate. Commenting on them in *Rex v Mpanza*[13] Watermeyer CJ stated:

> One of the fundamental principles of our South African law is that, except possibly in times of national emergency, the individual citizen, provided he obeys the law of the land, is not liable to have his personal freedom restrained by executive action, and the idea of a Supreme Chief, at his discretion and without trial, directing an individual to move his place of residence from one part of the country to another is foreign to that system.[14]

These sentiments were reiterated by Centlivres CJ in *Saliwa v Minister of Native Affairs.*[15] Notwithstanding the expression of distaste at these harsh provisions by no fewer than two Chief Justices, the legislature proceeded to turn an already harsh provision into one which was positively draconian. The section was amended a number of times over the years. In the form in which it existed before its eventual repeal, it provided:

> The State President may, whenever he deems it expedient in the general public interest without prior notice to any person concerned order that, subject to such conditions as he may determine after consultation by the Minister with the Black Government concerned, any tribe, portion of a tribe, black community or black shall withdraw from any place to any other place or to any district or province within the Republic and shall not at any time thereafter or during a period

> specified in the order return to the place from which the withdrawal is to be made or proceed to any place, district or province other than the place, district or province indicated in the order, except with the written permission of the Secretary for Plural Relations and Development: provided that if a tribe which is resident on land referred to in section 25(1) of this Act or in section 21(1) of the Development Trust and Land Act, 1936 (Act No 18 of 1936), refuses or neglects to withdraw as aforesaid no such order shall be of any force and effect unless or until a resolution approving of the withdrawal has been adopted by both Houses of Parliament ....

The power to order a removal 'without prior notice' was a direct result of the decision in *Saliwa v Minister of Native Affairs*. In that case a removal order was set aside on the basis that the individual concerned had not, in advance, been acquainted with any prejudicial allegations against him, nor was he given any opportunity of submitting any defence to such allegations.[16]

The 1973 amendment to section 5 was proposed by the high priest of bantustan consolidation, M C Botha.[17] This amendment assumed particularly sinister dimensions. It involved a tampering with the safeguard of parliamentary approval in the event of a refusal by a tribe to move. Previously, where a tribe neglected or refused to move, the order could not be implemented *unless* it was sanctioned by Parliament. The amendment proposed by M C Botha provided that in the event of a refusal to move, the order could not be executed *unless or until* there was parliamentary approval. In justifying the amendment, M C Botha told Parliament that with the consolidation of the homelands,

> population shifts will inevitably have to take place. According to existing legislation the State President may order a tribe to move from its dwelling place, but if the tribe refuses, such an order cannot be executed before both Houses of Parliament have approved the move, and this leads to considerable delay. It is now envisaged that the approval of Parliament, where suitable, be obtained prior to and contemporaneously with the approval of consolidation plans.[18]

On 16 May 1975, the House of Assembly, by 99 votes to 26, adopted a resolution accepting the recommendations contained in the First Report of the Select Committee on Bantu Affairs.[19] The Select Committee recommended that the House approve:

> the withdrawal of the Bantu tribes, Bantu communities and Bantu persons residing in the areas set out in Schedule B, in terms of the provisions of Section 5 of the Bantu Administration Act, 1927 (Act No 38 of 1927) as amended by Section 1 of the Bantu Laws Amendment Act, 1973 (Act No 7 of 1973).

Schedule B listed scores of areas which were probably together occupied by hundreds of thousands of people. One of the areas designated in the schedule was occupied by the Bakwena ba Mogopa tribe.

The Mogopa case

The Bakwena ba Mogopa tribe had resided on two farms in the Ventersdorp area since the early part of century. On this land they had built houses, schools and churches. Members of the tribe conducted farming operations and produced their own food. They also owned cattle and sheep as well as farming implements including tractors and ploughs. The land held by the tribe was rich in minerals, particularly diamonds. The community was entirely self-sufficient. The land and the improvements to it constituted the investment of a lifetime for many members of the tribe.

During 1983, officials of the Department of Co-operation and Development, as it was then euphemistically called, embarked upon a series of measures designed to coerce the Mogopa to move 'voluntarily'. These measures included the demolition of houses, schools, churches and clinics; the removal of water pumps; the termination of the bus service; the refusal to grant official assistance with pensions and the refusal to issue endorsements in terms of influx control legislation. These measures failed.

Thereafter on 18 November 1983, an order in terms of section 5 of the Black Administration Act was served on members of the tribe at a special gathering convened for this purpose. In terms of this order the tribe was ordered to move to Pachsdraai in the Groot Marico district within ten days. The district commissioner for Ventersdorp, Mr J A de Villiers, informed members of the tribe present at the gathering that if they had not moved by 28 November 1983 they would be removed summarily and with violence ('met geweld') the next day. The order bore the signature of the State President, Marais Viljoen, and was countersigned by Dr P G J Koornhof, then Minister of Co-operation and Development and subsequently Ambassador to the United States of America. Upon receipt of the order, the tribe, through their attorneys, notified Dr Koornhof that in terms of section 5(1)(b) of the Black Administration Act, they would refuse to move until the necessary resolution authorizing the removal had been approved by Parliament. The letter called for an undertaking that the removal would not be executed pending compliance with the procedures prescribed by the section.

On 25 November 1983 and after no undertaking had been furnished, an application was brought against the Minister of Co-operation and Development in the Transvaal Provincial Division of the Supreme Court, seeking an interdict preventing the forced removal of the tribe. An order directing the Minister to comply with the provisions of section 5 of the Black Administration Act was also sought. The district commissioner for Ventersdorp, Mr J A de Villiers, was cited as a second respondent in the application.

The matter came to court by way of urgency and it was necessary to dispense with the usual rules for service of documents. Phillip More, one of the members of the tribe, attempted to serve a copy of the application on De Villiers. From the affidavit of service which was filed in court, it appears that this task was more difficult than anticipated:

> At approximately 10.30am, I found the second respondent, who is known to me personally. I attempted to obtain acknowledgement of receipt of the application from second respondent. Second respondent refused to accept a copy of the application. The second respondent informed me that there was no one at the magistrate's offices by the name of De Villiers. He told me to get out of his office. In the presence of one Anita Kromberg and George Rampou who accompanied me, he kicked me on the calf of my left leg. I left a copy of the application at his feet.

In an answering affidavit filed on behalf of the Minister, it was stated that the necessary parliamentary resolution had in fact been passed on 16 May 1975. The applicants argued, however, that the 1975 parliamentary resolution did not comply with the proviso to section 5(1)(b) because it merely authorized the withdrawal of the tribe from the farms in question without any reference to the place where the tribe was to be moved. It was argued that 'withdrawal' must be construed to mean a withdrawal from one place to another place. This contention was rejected by Van Dyk J who relied upon the case of *Steven Sihewula v The Minister of Bantu Administration and Development.*[20] In that case Solomon AJ held:

> It is clear that what was intended was that Parliament should have the power to decide the area from which Bantu communities should be withdrawn, and that when the time came to implement the withdrawal, the State President should specify the area to which such withdrawal should be made.

Van Dyk J accordingly refused the interdict.[21]

In December 1983, representatives of the tribe met with Dr Koornhof to plead that he allow them to remain at Mogopa. Dr Koornhof requested them to visit Pachsdraai before taking a final decision not to go there. They visited Pachsdraai on 9 December 1983 and in a letter dated 12 December 1983 set out their objections to moving. Among their many objections was the fact that Pachsdraai was 150 kilometres away from Mogopa and 69 kilometres away from Zeerust, the nearest town with proper shopping facilities and work opportunities (see map on p 15). They regarded Pachsdraai as unsuitable from an agricultural point of view. They noted that they were shown fields which looked as though 'they were covered with ash' and that the little grass they saw 'was dead and dry'. They thought 'the place looks like the middle of winter, not the middle of summer'. The letter concluded with a desperate plea:

> We hope and trust that it is possible to negotiate this matter in a way that befits human dignity. We have faith that you as a Christian will approach this matter in a way that takes account of our terrible suffering.

Dr Koornhof never replied to the letter. An application for leave to appeal against the refusal of the interdict was dismissed by Van Dyk J. The tribe then instructed their attorneys to petition the Chief Justice for leave to appeal, and on 10 February 1984 the attorneys made a request to Dr Koornhof not to execute the order of removal 'until this avenue of seeking legal redress has been exhausted'. Four days later, on St Valentine's day, the tribe was forcibly removed. The removal was executed without warning by an armed contingent of policemen who first sealed off the farms, preventing entry by the tribe's lawyers, journalists, diplomats and priests. In the ensuing panic members of the tribe suffered substantial losses through breakages and the forced sale of their cattle to white farmers who appeared on the scene.

The petition for leave to appeal was subsequently granted by the Chief Justice, and the appeal was ultimately successful. In its judgment,[22] the Appellate Division held that the 1975 parliamentary resolution did not comply with the requirements of Section 5(1)(b) of the Act:

> The necessity for both Houses to review the State President's decision only arises once the tribe has refused or neglected to withdraw as directed in the State President's order.... And ... a tribe may have perfectly reasonable and legitimate reasons for not wanting to withdraw to the place or region specified in the order. It follows, as a matter of logic and common sense, that the two Houses cannot possibly fulfil their role meaningfully unless they are apprised of the terms of the order and the reasons for the tribe's refusal or neglect to withdraw. If the two Houses had the right ... to approve of the withdrawal without due regard to the terms of the order and the reason for the tribe's attitude, the whole purpose of the proviso would be thwarted. The sole safeguard provided to a tribe against consequences of the exercise by the State President of the drastic powers conferred upon him would in effect be bypassed. As far as the tribe is concerned, it would be pointless and futile to offer it an opportunity of considering whether or not to withdraw if its fate has already been sealed by a prior resolution of both Houses of Parliament approving of the withdrawal.[23]

The demise of section 5

The judgment in the Appellate Division was a hollow victory for the Bakwena ba Mogopa. Determined to ensure the removal of the tribe at all costs and regardless of the legality of the removal, the state expropriated the farms in question before the matter came before the Appellate Division. Dr Koornhof went so far as to attempt to introduce legislation intended to nullify the tribe's right of appeal altogether.[24]

The expropriation of the farms followed Dr Gerrit Viljoen's dramatic announcement of the government's decision to suspend all forced removals of black communities pending review of its resettlement policy. He stated, however, that the government would continue to resettle black communities 'if their leaders agree'.[25] In April 1986, the government published the *White Paper on Urbanization* outlining its strategy 'for the future management of the social, economic and physical problems which may follow in the wake of rapid urbanization'.[26] In setting out the government's points of departure and general policy framework, it noted that, 'in the interest of planned development, the effective management of urbanization or in aid of an improvement in their own living conditions it will sometimes be necessary for individuals and groups to move. However, all such moves will always be negotiated with the individuals and groups concerned'.[27] It specifically stated that section 5 of the Black Administration Act would be repealed 'since the government has announced that no further forced removals will take place'.[28] The repeal was effected by section 1 of the Abolition of Influx Control Act 68 of 1986. Little attention was paid to the repeal of section 5 in the parliamentary debates. Ironically, it was singled out only by Professor N J J Olivier of the Progressive Federal Party (as it then was) who welcomed the repeals as 'concrete implementation' of the government's announcement to suspend forced removals.[29]

All of this was of little consequence to the Mogopa tribe. Notwithstanding an Appellate Division judgment effectively declaring the order of removal to be invalid, and despite the repeal of the law used to effect their removal, they remained dispossessed of their ancestral lands. However, they never gave up hope of returning to Mogopa. In December 1986 Dr Gerrit Viljoen agreed to meet the tribe. Over the next two years the tribe and the Minister explored various options including the reversal of the expropriation and even the repurchase of the land by the tribe.[30]

With the lapse of time the graveyard at Mogopa became overgrown and fell into a state of disrepair. Towards the end of 1988 it was agreed that members of the tribe could move temporarily onto the farms to clean and maintain the graves. In February 1989 Dr Viljoen launched urgent proceedings in the Supreme Court for the eviction of those members of the tribe who were on the farms. It was alleged that the dispensation to clean the graves had been abused and the tribe was surreptitiously reoccupying the farms which were now the property of the South African government. An undertaking made by Dr Viljoen not to sell the farms while negotiations were underway was unilaterally revoked. Indeed, one reason advanced for the urgency of the matter was the government's intention to sell the land to farmers within the next few months. The application for eviction was defended on the basis that the government was not in fact the owner of the farms as the expropriation was effected in bad faith and for an ulterior motive and was thus invalid. It was argued that the expropriation was not for 'public purposes' as required by the Expropriation Act 63 of 1975 but was in effect a forced removal in disguise. The only use to which the land had been put since the purported expropriation was to lease it to the Koster and Ventersdorp Agricultural Union for emergency grazing. Neither this nor the proposed sale constituted a 'public purpose'. Although the defence failed on a technicality[31] the matter is on appeal to the Appellate Division. For the time being, therefore, those members of the tribe presently on the farms may safely remain there. If their appeal should fail, the spectre of another forced removal confronts them.

Amidst the fanfare of the government's announcement that it had suspended its policy of forced removals, the injustice perpetrated on the Mogopa tribe remains unredressed and removals have in fact continued. Old devices are still employed and new ones have been created.[32] As the editorial referred to above observed:

> Cruelty, like any sin or any crime, is easier after the first time, and it becomes progressively easier with each repetition.[33]

Notes

1 *House of Assembly Debates* 28 April 1927 col 2905.

2 Other sections of the Act reflect a similar philosophy. Section 25, for example, confers powers of legislation on the State President which are so extensive that they have been described as being 'equal to those of Parliament' (*R v Maharaj* 1950 (3) SA 187 (A) at 194D). Although the Appellate Division has since acknowledged that powers expressed in these terms are indeed subject to judicial scrutiny (see *Staatspresident v United Democratic Front* 1988 (4) SA 830 (A) at 848E-851I) the grounds upon which such powers can be reviewed are extremely limited.

3 Surplus People Project *Forced Removals in South Africa* Vol 1 (1983) 5.

4 *Sunday Express* 12 June 1982.

5 *House of Assembly Debates* 29 June 1983 cols 10597-10602.

6 *House of Assembly Debates* 28 April 1927 col 2904.

7 *House of Assembly Debates* 28 April 1927 col 2914.

8 *House of Assembly Debates* 28 April 1927 col 2978.

9 *House of Assembly Debates* 2 May 1927 col 3012.

10 *House of Assembly Debates* 29 April 1927 col 2953.

11 Mr Nel *House of Assembly Debates* 2 May 1927 cols 3031-3032.

12 *House of Assembly Debates* 15 June 1927 col 5099.

13 1946 AD 763.

14 At 771.

15 1956 (2) SA 310 (A) at 317.

16 Section 3 of Act 42 of 1956.

17 The amendment was effected by s 1 of Act 7 of 1953.

18 *House of Assembly Debates* 12 February 1973 col 394.

19 SC9/175. On 27 May 1975 the Senate adopted a similar resolution.

20 South Eastern Cape Local Division, 22 November 1977, unreported.

21 This judgment was not reported.

22 *More v Minister of Co-operation and Deveopment* 1986 (1) SA 103 (A).

23 At 115I-116C.

24 Section 9 of the Laws on Co-operation and Development Amendment Bill 89/85(GA) attempted, with retrospective effect and 'irrespective of whether any legal proceeding is pending in any court' to amend s 5(1)(b) of the Black Administration Act by providing that the parliamentary resolution envisaged in the section need not specify the place to which the tribe in question has to withdraw. This section of the Bill was withdrawn following international and domestic pressure.

25 *The Star* 2 February 1985.

26 *White Paper on Urbanization* April 1986 para 2 p 3.

27 Ibid, para 4.3.7 p 7.

28 Ibid, para 2.1.3 p 62.

29 *House of Assembly Debates* 9 June 1986 cols 7670-7671. It is suggested that there was a further reason for the repeal of s 5 apart from a change of heart on the part of the government. The Appellate Division judgment declaring the order of removal in the Mogopa case to be invalid posed a dilemma for the architects of forced removals. It meant that if any of the tribes mentioned in the 1975 parliamentary resolution which had not yet been removed, refused to move, the matter would have to be debated in Parliament. By this time, Parliament was no longer an all white affair. What was previously accomplished by brute force in remote areas far from the public gaze, would henceforth be the subject of debate in the new tricameral Parliament. It is

extremely unlikely that political parties in the House of Representatives and the House of Delegates would have sanctioned forced removals. Although the government enjoys the power to have its way in Parliament, it is unlikely that it would have wished to risk a serious confrontation with 'coloured' and Indian members of Parliament on so sensitive an issue.

30 At a meeting in June 1988, Dr Viljoen indicated that he would consider allowing the tribe to return to Mogopa provided this met with the approval of white farmers in the Ventersdorp area. Despite this possibility, the only reason furnished to the tribe for the refusal to allow them to return to Mogopa was that the Cabinet had so decided. Yet other communities in the Ventersdorp area in identical situations to Mogopa, namely Mathopestad and Matlatla, have been reprieved and allowed to remain on their lands. The tribe also explored the possibility of farming another piece of land at Holgat. This plan was aborted by government action. See Claassens in this volume at 55ff and Haysom at 107.

31 *Die Minister van die Departement van Landbou en Watervoorsiening v Daniel Molefe* (TPD 2 May 1989 Case No 2077/89, unreported). The court did not find it necessary to even consider the defence raised since it held that a challenge to the validity of the expropriation by way of a defence would require the joining of the Minister of Community Development as the person statutorily responsible for expropriation in terms of the Expropriation Act.

32 Old devices include proclamations in terms of the Group Areas Act 36 of 1966 and new devices include land excisions under the Borders of Particular States Extension Act 2 of 1980.

33 See note 4 above.

ANINKA CLAASSENS

Rural Land Struggles in the Transvaal in the 1980s

> Umhlaba, the land.[1] Our purpose is the land, that is what we must achieve. The land is our whole lives, we plough it for food, we build our homes from the soil, we live on it and we are buried in it.
>
> When the whites took our land away from us we lost the dignity of our lives, we could no longer feed our children. We were forced to become servants, we are treated like animals. Our people have many problems, we are beaten and killed by the farmers, the wages we earn are too little to buy even a bag of mielie-meal. We must unite together to help each other and face the Boers. But in everything we do we must remember that there is only one aim and one solution and that is the land, the soil, our world.[2]

Land has always been contested in South Africa. Despite the centuries since the wars of the conquest, the legitimacy of white landownership has not been established.

. . . in a recent trespass case in the Wakkerstroom court, the magistrate became incensed when the accused testified that she had been born on the farm, as had her parents and grandparents. He shouted that this had nothing to do with the charge and asked her if she thought she had the right to go on living there just because she was born there. Didn't she understand about title deeds, about private property? Was she in fact saying that the farmer didn't have the right to get rid of people *off his own land*? When she said she knew no other home and could find nowhere else to go, he asked her how long she planned to stay on the farm in the meantime, one hundred years? 'Yes', she answered, 'one hundred years if necessary.'

Enforcing Group Areas in Hillbrow
(Eric Miller, Afrapix)

And farm workers threatened with eviction routinely answer questions about landownership obliquely. 'A white man called so and so says he owns the farm' or 'What white man tells you his name?'

In 1988 I was part of a delegation which gave evidence to the parliamentary Standing Committee on the Illegal Squatting Bill.[3] Arguments that the Bill removed all normal legal protection from people in 'white' rural areas and provided for large-scale eviction were received somewhat listlessly. But evidence that there are millions of people who have lived in these areas for generations under legal contracts with white landowners and that the bill conflicted with their contractual rights elicited keen interest – especially from the farmers amongst the members of Parliament. What contractual rights? Were we inferring that these people had a right to stay on the land? Is 'birthright' something which is in the law? The questions were not merely rhetorical, they were asked with keen interest.

Apart from being a primary source of wealth, control over land is the measure of political sovereignty. Wars are fought to extend or defend boundaries. Political conquest and land dispossession are intricately bound up with each other. In this country they took place simultaneously. Given this history and given the fact that 73 per cent of the population is restricted to land rights in 13 per cent of the country, it is not surprising that conflicting notions of land rights remain an explosive issue.

The inequitable division of land did not begin with, nor was it caused by the 1913 Land Act.[4] It is the result of the wars of conquest fought by well-armed white settlers against black people armed only with spears, and of transactions where goods paid by the newcomers were accepted as tribute by black kings and recorded as purchase price by the whites.

Ever since whites gained control of the majority of land in South Africa there has been a steady flow of measures to stabilize and maintain this situation. The Land Act was one of these; so was the establishment of the bantustans; so was the forced removal of over 3,5 million people. Intrinsic to this process has been an ideology that blacks be allowed to remain in the 'white' areas as servants only, never as independent producers or owners. But the most pervasive ideological expression of this state of affairs is the notion of the sanctity of private property, a notion generally equated with transactions and title deeds, and seldom with wars of conquest. But sometimes it is: Eugene Terre'blanche has said 'My ancestors paid in instalments of blood for certain parts of the country. We bought land with blood and tears. We have a title deed on it.' He goes on to say '... it cannot be the property of the Indian or a Tswana.'[5]

The Preamble to the Constitution of the Republic of South Africa leaves out both wars and transactions and skips straight to God:

> In humble submission to Almighty God, who controls the destinies of nations and the history of peoples, who gathered our forebears together from many lands and gave them this their own; who has wondrously delivered them from the dangers that beset them.

The process of legitimizing and attempting to stabilize and maintain the racial division of land has not been limited to ideological assertions. The last one hundred years have seen a devastating process of dispossession, removal and destruction. It has been violent because there has been black resistance throughout. Most resistance has been defensive, against further dispossession. But there has also been, on a smaller scale, a struggle to (re)occupy and obtain land by whatever means possible.

In this paper I will look at some defensive and some offensive struggles about land in the 1980s. I hope to show how these struggles have emerged from, and been shaped by specific histories and traditions, and that choices made decades ago have had a major influence on the different forms that struggles have taken in the 1980s.

The topic of 'rural land struggles' is too vast to cover in one paper. I have limited case studies to the Transvaal and also to land struggles in 'white' areas. These are serious limitations; they exclude the important struggles against Tribal Authorities and so-called Development Corporations in the bantustans. They also exclude some of the responses to more subtle co-optive strategies being used by the state in other provinces.

Part I: Defensive Struggles in the Platteland

I will look at two different categories of people: people who have title to the land (landowners), and those who have no legal rights to specific pieces of land. The first category covers the so-called 'black spots', farms bought by black people in areas that were subsequently restricted to white land-ownership. The second covers people who live in the same areas, in many cases also since before the introduction of the Land Act, but who never actually acquired land.

There was a song about the Land Act when it was introduced:

> THE LAND ACT SONG
> We are children of Africa
> We cry for our land
> Zulu, Xhosa, Sotho
> Zulu, Xhosa, Sotho unite
> We are mad over the Land Act

A terrible law that allows sojourners
To deny us our land
Crying that we the people
Should pay to get our land back
We cry for the children of our fathers
Who roam around the world without a home
Even in the land of their forefathers.[6]

The people living in 'black spots' are those who accepted the sojourners' terms – they bought the land back. The others are people who did not, either because they could not or because they chose not to. Since this initial division the two groups of people have used different strategies and different ideologies in their struggles to secure their rights to land.

Landowning communities

The Surplus People Project (SPP) estimates that between 1960 and 1983 475 000 people were removed from 'black spots'.[7] By the early 1980s the inhabitants of most of the farms owned by black people in the white platteland had been removed to the bantustans. There were then fewer than ten 'black spots' left in the Transvaal. All of them were resisting removal.

In the early 1980s the state adopted a softer line on removals than it had in the 1960s and 1970s. It spoke of 'voluntary removals' as opposed to forced removals. The new policy amounted to 'persuading' people to move by means that progressed rapidly from discussion, to withdrawal of health services, to demolition of schools, to withholding pensions and finally, in the Mogopa case, to surrounding the village with armed police in the dead of night.[8] Notwithstanding the quick progression to the use of naked force, the state was in a more defensive position than it had been in previous decades. This was partly as a result of the publicity surrounding the exposure of the terrible conditions in the resettlement camps.[9]

I will give examples from two neighbouring Eastern Transvaal 'black spots' which fought, and won, long battles to avert forced removal: Driefontein and kwaNgema. The stories are detailed and anecdotal because I wish to illustrate some of the many overlapping tactics and efforts which finally combined to challenge a balance of power which had seemed hopelessly stacked against the people.

These two landowning communities were able, by exploiting the excesses of the racial platteland, to turn the contradictions in the dominant ideology to their advantage. They are very different from the non-landowners (described in the next section) who do not have this tactical advantage because they operate from outside the dominant ideological framework, as people without title deeds, they are people without land rights.

One purpose of the Driefontein and kwaNgema stories is to show how the various opportunities for tactical manoeuvres were exploited in preparation for a comparison with labour tenants later in this paper. Another purpose is to show how local resistance grows out of local tradition and style. A comparison of Driefontein and kwaNgema shows how, even in adjoining areas, responses may differ. Often the forms this resistance takes initially appear unexpected and inappropriate to outside eyes. Yet it is only issues which are meaningful and dear to people's hearts that seize their imagination and galvanize community participation. Repeated assaults by the communities at the local balance of power were, in large part, responsible for the ultimate success of these struggles.

I will then look at state strategy to incorporate black landowning communities into bantustans by redrawing bantustan boundaries rather than by physically removing people. This strategy gained increased momentum in the late 1980s as a result of the successful struggles to stop forced removal.

The process of incorporation has caused greater physical violence and loss of life than the process of removing communities from one place to another. Incorporation takes place by the publication of a government gazette; no tangible physical confrontation with the community is involved. Thus there are not the same opportunities for community resistance to avert the disaster.

The communities threatened with incorporation are landowning 'black spots'. Successfully resisting incorporation is often more difficult than successfully preventing a forced removal.[10]

Driefontein: small victories, big changes

In the early 1980s the chances of averting forced removal in the south-eastern Transvaal 'black spot' of Driefontein seemed bleak. The beloved leader of the community, Saul Mkhize, had been shot dead by a young white policeman at an anti-removal meeting. Despite the fact that the unprovoked murder was witnessed by hundreds of people, the policeman was acquitted and the judge, in exonerating him of blame, referred to Mkhize as a 'rude and arrogant man' who 'had it coming to him'.

Piet Koornhof, then Minister of Co-operation and Development, made a concession after Mkhize's death. The people would not be divided along ethnic lines, they would all be moved to one place. But they would still definitely be removed. Legally their position was tenuous: section 5 of the

Black Administration Act empowered the State President to order the removal of any black person, black tribe, or group of black people from any area to any other area.[11]

The Driefontein committee had been plunged into despair and mourning when Mkhize was killed. They were infuriated by the trial which had absolved his murderer. They were especially angry with the local commissioner about evidence he gave of events leading up to the day of the shooting. The committee called their lawyers and instructed them to arrange a retrial with a judge from another country. When it was explained that this was impossible the committee said that, in that case, the local commissioner must be removed.

At this time, in rural areas like Driefontein the commissioner was the repository of all state functions. He heard trials, paid pensions, permitted or prohibited meetings, issued identity documents, authorized maintenance of roads and public buildings, conveyed government policy and communications, and chose which local committee he would recognize as the authorized representative of the community. In Driefontein the commissioner did these things very selectively. He continued to recognize a committee whose period of office had expired and which was in favour of removal. Its members had been expelled from mass community meetings in his presence. He refused to approve pension applications, he refused to issue passes (thereby rendering young people unable to get jobs) and he refused to give permission for community meetings. He held money collected from the community for fixing the roads and refused to allow it to be used for this purpose. He said that pensions, passes, meetings and road repairs would all be forthcoming in the resettlement area after the people had moved.

The Council Board committee (of which Mkhize had been the chairman) decided to challenge the commissioner on each and every one of these actions. Members of the committee called together people who were being refused pensions, or passes, or who had been unfairly treated in the courts. Large meetings were held (without permission) where statements were taken and strategies discussed. Lawyers advised on legal requirements. One strategy concerning pensions was particularly successful. It was planned that various ladies who were clearly old, clearly destitute, and clearly resident in Driefontein (the three requirements which entitled them to pensions) would apply for their pensions for the umpteenth time, but they would be accompanied by a large group of people, including committee members. The arrival of this large group infuriated the commissioner and he responded, as usual, by telling the old ladies to take up with old men who could support them in return for services rendered. Alternatively they should go and ask the Black Sash for pensions.

But the commissioner, as the pension officer, had no right to refuse pensions to those who fulfilled certain legal requirements as all the old ladies did. And the lodging of applications, filled out properly and carefully in advance by paralegal advisors, had been witnessed by the large crowd. So a court order was sought to compel the commissioner to pay pensions. To prevent the matter reaching court, police vans were sent out at high speed to fetch the gleeful old ladies so that they could get their money by special individual payment.

This small victory was greeted with what seemed quite disproportionate delight and rejoicing. For the issue was not just pensions, it was the defeat of the repository of state power and the heady possibilities that this created. These possibilities were quickly exploited.

The Council Board committee had long been ignored by the commissioner, and it was unthinkable that he would grant them permission to hold a community meeting. So the Council Board members went to his office and requested permission for a meeting. They took with them an agenda and a list of speakers which was eminently reasonable. The commissioner responded by refusing them permission and adding that he would never, ever, recognize them nor permit them to hold meetings. But the law requires the commissioner to apply his mind to such applications which he clearly had not done. Another application led to the first of a series of legal community meetings held in Driefontein.

In the meantime the committee was taking up other issues. They organized the election of a clinic committee and then the building of a wattle and daub clinic. They negotiated support from private doctors and funders to open a health service for Driefontein. (The community of 26 000 people had been left without health services apart from birth control and inoculation after the decision to remove them became official.) More and more people were drawn into community activity. All this activity was directed at stopping the removal. It was to improve life at Driefontein in the face of the state's attempts to starve them out.

In the meantime the state continued with removal plans. Buses were sent to show people the proposed resettlement area but nobody went. When officials came to make the arrangements necessary for moving 26 000 people they were met by vast crowds who rudely challenged whatever they said. There was a mood of defiance and aggression. The officials stopped coming over weekends and came during the day to speak to women and old people who were at home. They got short shrift. The majority of people at

Driefontein had always opposed the removal. Nevertheless many had felt that the state was all-powerful and that it was impossible to win. This despair had been entrenched when Mkhize was killed before their eyes. But when the commissioner was forced to back down on issue after issue they began to change their views. He had been the embodiment of state power, just as Mkhize had been the symbol of hope and resistance. He was not invincible.

Whereas previously people had boycotted meetings and been silent and unresponsive when faced with government officials, now they flocked to all meetings, even to court cases at Wakkerstroom. Wherever a government official turned up, there they would be. They would argue with him, contradict him, laugh at him and challenge his views and the morality of forced removal.

The officials' job was to *persuade* these people to move. The state could not afford another murder, nor another forced removal like Mogopa. Both had been too recent, too publicized and had cost the Department of Foreign Affairs too dearly. At one meeting Mrs Mkhize told the presiding officer that he should come with her and she would show him where she had dug her grave, next to her husband's. Then, when he came back to remove them, he should just shoot her so she could fall in neatly. There was a whole big pile of sand so he could cover her up with minimum effort.

The common refrain used to taunt officials was this: 'Don't worry we're prepared to move. You just bring Saul Mkhize back to life and then we'll follow him out of here. But as long as he is in the ground here, we're staying here.'

The officials were having a difficult time. They came less and less often. Driefontein got a reputation for being unreasonable and militant. The commissioner had said at the trial of the policeman who shot Mkhize, that any white person who set foot in Driefontein risked his life. Whether they believed this or not, officials knew that there was no way they could accomplish anything resembling a voluntary removal at Driefontein.

The Council Board was equally vocal at a higher level. Notwithstanding the fact that the commissioner still referred to the pro-removals committee as the authorized committee, the Council Board had won de facto recognition at all levels by the sheer number and volubility of their supporters. They had various meetings with Cabinet Ministers and their deputies. At one such meeting Dr Piet Koornhof had a taste of what his officials were experiencing in less urbane surroundings than his Pretoria offices. Dr Koornhof had answers for every point and expanded at length on issues of religion, authority and benefits of a nomadic life-style. The meeting lasted well into the night. The following extract from the minutes contains one of the numerous biblical references used by both sides:

> *Shadrack Mkhize:* I thank you for what you've said and for what you people have decided. But the people of Driefontein deny and refuse to be moved, let God be our judge. For we truly believe in God, the creator of everything, he placed us in Driefontein. In 1903 our forefathers found this place. There were arguments from 1907 until 1912 when there was agreement that we are belonging in this place, and the Governor General signed that we should belong in Driefontein for generations. All people believe God is there, let him be the judge.
>
> *Koornhof:* I respect what you say, I respect very highly what you say. I am also a great believer of God, it's true that God knows what is best for us. God has placed on you and me responsibilities, he has given us a head to think with, he has told us you must not kick against the tentacles. He teaches us to obey authority, and teaches authority to obey his words, not to place a yoke on the people which they can't bear. I am going extremely out of my way to meet your principles as best I can.
>
> *Shadrack Mkhize:* I have read the Bible and I know it well, the old testament and the new testament. And in Kings we read the story of a man named Naboth ....
>
> *Koornhof (interjects):* This is not at stake – this is not a case of Naboth's vineyard. I know the story of Naboth's vineyard. If it was such a case, I wouldn't want anything to do with it.[12]

KwaNgema: hobnobbing in high places

KwaNgema, the black community adjoining Driefontein, was fighting a battle to stop removal at the same time. The Ngemas are also landowners, but they did not buy their land. It was given to their forefathers in exchange for services rendered to the Boers during the battles against Zulu kings. Although transfer had not yet taken place when the Boers were defeated in the Boer War, the British decided to honour the Boer pledge and transfer finally took place as a grant from King Edward VII.

The Ngemas, when faced with the threat of removal, took some liberties with the exact details of their history and wrote to Queen Elizabeth of England asking her to intervene on their behalf. 'How,' they asked 'can the South African government have the right to take away from us, that which was given to us by your great grandfather?' The Queen gave the letter to Mrs Thatcher who took the issue up with the State President, Mr P W Botha, who happened to be visiting Britain at the time. Mr Botha gave assurances that the Ngemas would be fairly treated and this publicized conversation provided kwaNgema with a protectively high profile.

The Ngemas believed in making contacts and seeing influential people. They invited a Nationalist Member of Parliament to visit them. They were eloquent. He was moved and promised to take up their case. They also contacted the Chief Ministers of both kwaZulu and kaNgwane and asked that they refuse to accept them into their 'homelands'. Chief Buthelezi responded by saying that he could not assist them as this tragic policy was not of his making or implementation. Mr Mabuza on the other hand immediately offered to meet them. He said that Pretoria officials had told him the Ngemas favoured removal, but that since he now had proof that this was not the case, he would refuse to co-operate with Pretoria in any way. He told the Deputy Minister of Co-operation and Development that kaNgwane refused to administer any land to which the Ngemas were removed. This left Pretoria with the embarrassing prospect of a 'black spot' adjoining kaNgwane with no schools, no clinic and no structures of local government.

Mabuza's stand was very important: it meant that the resettlement camp at Oshoek then being constructed for both the Driefontein and kwaNgema communities became a giant white elephant and Pretoria was left with nowhere to put the people.

A matter of style

The Driefontein committee was very sceptical of the Ngemas hobnobbing in high places and almost destroyed the alliance with Mabuza. They initially treated Mabuza in a similar way to any other official or cabinet minister. Mr Mabuza paid a courtesy visit to Mrs Mkhize on his way home from a meeting at kwaNgema. He happened to arrive during a legal clinic and about a hundred people were at the house. Nobody went forward to welcome him and there was an uneasy period of people shuffling feet and looking at each other while more and more people gathered together. Finally an old man said:

> Well, Mr Mabuza, you have come here and found us as we are; people who are being rushed down a swollen flooding river with no control over where we will be dumped. We are assaulted from all sides by bits of debris and now we have put out our hand in this chaotic water and grabbed something. And we don't know what it is; whether it is a stick to help us fight, or a snake to finish us off. The floor is yours to tell us which one you are.

Mabuza didn't turn a hair. He responded by saying that he understood that they, as independent landowners, would suspect that he was trying to extend kaNgwane's sphere of influence over them – but that was not his intention; he had come to make contact and to offer his assistance in whatever form they wanted. Ultimately a very constructive relationship developed which helped to avert not only the removal but also the state's subsequent attempts to incorporate Driefontein and kwaNgema into ka-Ngwane.

The Ngemas have a completely different style from the Driefontein people. They are always charming and courteous. For example, they are on good terms with the very commissioner who is so disliked at Driefontein. When they meet government officials they shake them by the hand and enquire about their health and welcome them into their buildings. This is not to say that they go along with them. They laugh deeply and say 'No, no, no, that is quite impossible, that is most unfair, we will never agree to that'.

During the period when the removal was imminent, the Ngemas asked any officials who visited them to respond to their objections and engage with the issues they raised. Again and again the officials replied that the decision to remove them had been taken at a higher level and they were merely messengers. Again and again the Ngemas asked for those people who made the decisions at the higher level, the people who had the power to enter into debate. And when they didn't come the Ngemas proceeded in their absence. Machinery which arrived to dig up the graves was broken. Numbers put on the doors of houses were painted over. A man who had agreed to the removal, and subsequently been appointed chief by the state, died suddenly. His successor, who also agreed to the removal, died soon afterwards. Things like this were not commonplace at Driefontein.

At both Driefontein and kwaNgema the removal issue was complicated by the construction of a dam by the Department of Water Affairs. The dam was not the reason for the removals; it was a new project, the removal had been pending since the late 1960s. Large parts of both areas were to be flooded by the dam. The Department of Water Affairs had never consulted the Driefontein or Ngema people, even though as landowners they had legal control over the land. This was because the Department of Co-operation and Development had advised them not to bother; they had been that confident of getting rid of the people.

The dam was built. As the waters rose people at kwaNgema found their houses flooded and all their possessions washed away. The Ngema lawyers brought an urgent application against the Department of Water Affairs that they empty the dam. The dam was a crucial part of a multi-million scheme and Water Affairs was furious that Co-operation and Development had placed them in such a legally vulnerable position. Thus they agreed to settle the case by providing compensation so that people could rebuild their houses on higher ground within kwaNgema. Co-operation and Development was furious. They were trying to move people away and here was another government department helping them re-establish their village on higher land in the same place. Water Affairs was not sympathetic; they assured the Ngemas that had they known that the Ngemas had title to the land they would have gone through the proper legal channels before starting work. (In many ways it was lucky that this did not happen; there would have been no way to contest an expropriation for a public purpose like the construction of a dam.)

By 1985 the government was in a very defensive position in relation to Driefontein and kwaNgema. There had been publicized court cases; P W Botha had been confronted in England; kaNgwane had deprived them of a resettlement camp and both areas were flourishing in terms of the balance of power with local officials. It was clear that the majority of people in both places not only opposed removal, but that they would resist it physically and by all means at their disposal.

The communities were called to meetings in Pretoria and told that the government no longer wanted to move them for political reasons; it had changed its mind. But there was still the matter of the dam. Large parts of their land were being flooded and the people affected would have to move. Where to? Unfortunately the government could not give them adjacent land because just as it was now opposed to the forced removal of black people, so it was opposed to the forcible removal of white people. The committees wanted to know whether this was the only reason? Of course. Sure it has nothing to do with politics? Of course. So if there were no whites on the land adjacent to us, you'd let us have it? Yes, that follows logically.

The committees went home and identified various pieces of land around their farms which they said had been expropriated, or were empty, or were state land. Sure enough, searches in the deed's office confirmed their local knowledge. But there was still not enough land. So they approached Barlow Rand who had land in the area, and asked them to make a piece available to them. Then the two committees sat down and worked out a distribution of the available land between the two areas and went back to the government with this information. The government was left with no choice but to give them the land. And so on 27 August 1985, Driefontein and kwaNgema were formally reprieved from forced removal.

Tactics/Maplan

At workshops held afterwards other black landowning communities asked how Driefontein and kwaNgema managed to win – what was the secret of their success? Moses Ngema, the chairman of the Ngema committee explained it like this:

> Maplan, you must always have plans, whatever they do, you must be clever, you must look at it from all angles, you must think of what have they done which is too proud, or too stupid. And you must organize people so they have always got something to do, and answers to give, a step to take. You must never wait to see what will happen next. Try something and know what you will use as a follow up if it doesn't work. And sometimes you must not restrain people, they must act according to what is in their hearts. If you are furious, let it come out or you will get sick and the Boers will win.

There is no doubt that 'maplan', tactics, call them what you will, have been an integral part of the 'black spot' struggles, and also that these tactics grow directly out of local beliefs, concerns and even style. Driefontein and kwaNgema adjoin each other, and yet their tactics were different from each other, although complementary. An outsider can never predict which issue is going to catch people's imagination, unify them and inspire them to take risks and engage in mass action. It often takes months to understand the local histories and past battles which make an issue that seems quite tangential, one which is deeply meaningful to people. Time and again actions around these issues do indeed highlight and challenge the very heart of the removal issue.

The process of forced removal is very physical. It requires the evaluation and numbering of houses, the moving of graves, the quantification of people, goods and cattle. It requires that set tasks be achieved on set dates. It is a process made up of a million arrangements all of which require interaction, at least in terms of obtaining information, with the people who are to be removed. As a result it provides for very concrete opportunities to oppose the process and to confront the actors on the other side. Because it is a tangible process, it is easy for rural people to deal with. The officials often overplay their hand because they are used to having unchallengeable power in relation to black people. Thus, the minimum of legal support can tip the local balance of power very easily.

Any victories, however small, are important in boosting the confidence of the communities and thereby drawing an increasing number of people into active, as opposed to passive, resistance. They are also important in undermining the confidence of government officials. Often the shock of defeat is enough to shake them completely. They retreat, unsure of exactly what went wrong, but not prepared to risk the ignominy of defeat again. This official response occurs at both a national and local level. Instead of examining why the issue was lost and how to avoid the pitfall in future, officials jump to the conclusion that the law is inadequate. They back off completely to wait for Parliament to add some strength to their arm in the form of a new law or an amendment to the existing law. Over the years the body of South African law which governs the removal and dispossession of black people has become an impenetrable forest of racial decrees and orders.

Bitter experience in these areas and other 'black spots' has shown that legal challenges that address laws such as the Black Administration Act are often doomed to failure. Where the legal challenge can be directed at less explicitly racial law, law which is ostensibly common to all South Africans, like pensions, the law of expropriation or the law of contract, there is a much greater chance of legal success.

Finally, both the Driefontein and kwaNgema struggles focussed on the fact that the people were landowners. This was relied on in the various legal strategies, in the case presented to state officials and extensively in the publicity and lobbying. What options are open to black people if even those who own land are subject to arbitrary removal and dispossession? How strong is the protection of private property if it can be negated by political whim, depending on the race of the title-deed holder?

Incorporation: a new state strategy

In 1985 Minister Gerrit Viljoen announced that the policy of forced removals had been suspended.[13] This announcement followed successful struggles all around the country. It took place during a period of political challenge by the unions and by the United Democratic Front, and at a time when popular mass action was forcing the state to make major concessions.

With the introduction of the second state of emergency in 1986 these concessions stopped. A classic forced removal took place at Langa/Kabah in 1986 and then a massive removal at Crossroads. The state plans more. Minister Heunis has given the names of various areas that 'must go'.[14] Notwithstanding these setbacks some of the earlier gains have not been lost. Unusually, rural people have fared better than their urban counterparts. Since 1986 most removals have been of urban people and the areas cited by Heunis are all townships. But this does not mean that the state has abandoned rural removals.

Since Mogopa in 1984, there have been no forced removals of black landowning rural communities. The state has a new strategy for dealing with these areas. They are to be incorporated into one or other bantustan. This does not involve the physical removal of people, rather the redrawing of homeland boundaries to include their land.[15]

Incorporation is not a tangible process. It is something which is done far away in Pretoria at the Government Printer's office. As Chief Pupsey Sebogodi of Braklaagte has said: 'How do you fight the drawings of a pen?' This does not mean that incorporation is necessarily a 'hands-off' process. On the contrary, the recent incorporations of Moutse, Botshabelo, Braklaagte, Leeuwfontein and Peelton have been much more violent than most forced removals. In these cases the bantustan authorities immediately moved in, rounded up people and viciously assaulted them. People are told that they must now realize that they are under the bantustan. They are told to shout pro-bantustan slogans and when they refuse are assaulted. In Moutse over 300 people were assaulted in this way on the night of the incorporation which was New Year 1987. In the subsequent turmoil at least 20 people died. In Braklaagte over 80 people were seriously injured over the Easter weekend in 1989. In Leeuwfontein 11 people were killed on 1 July 1989. Nine of these were policemen. The Bophuthatswana police have instituted a reign of terror in the village in retribution for the police deaths.

These communities had developed an anti-bantustan reputation in the years that they resisted removal and incorporation. Attacks by bantustan authorities are directed at the whole community, so that while certain leaders get particularly vicious treatment, grandmothers, priests, businessmen and village elders are not exempt.

There have been legal challenges to the incorporations. These were won at Moutse and Botshabelo[16] and were major setbacks for the state's independence plans for kwaNdebele and QwaQwa respectively. They were also very important victories for the communities concerned. But legal action at this level does not help provide the tangible victories for local struggle that consolidate organization and tip the balance of power *before* incorporation becomes a fait accompli. As long as the issue is fought in the Supreme Court or the Appellate Division the major actors will remain lawyers. And lawyers for the communities are in a vulnerable position because when presented with the fait accompli of an incorporation they have to challenge the fact in terms of the very laws designed to implement it, the National States Constitution Act[17] and the Borders of Particular States Extension Act.[18] The bush-war advantages of the common-law approach are not available here. Successful legal challenges to action taken in terms of statutes often provoke amendments to the principal legislation.

In Moutse the legal challenge to incorporation was finally won in the Appellate Division on the basis of ethnicity: the incorporation of 100 000 Sotho people into an Ndebele homeland is inconsistent with the (apartheid) legislature's intention of ethnic consolidation. This argument was the only possible way to reverse the hated incorporation; both the lawyers and clients were fully aware of the irony of using apartheid ideology to undo apartheid. But the ramifications of this approach are not yet fully played out. During the period of opposition, unprecedented alliances were developed. The previously conservative tribal authority joined forces with the young comrades and the women and the civic association established by Moutse migrant workers on the Witwatersrand. There was a period of physical uprising which mobilized tens of thousands of people. Then there were years when the population put their hope and faith into the outcome of the court case. Ultimately the case was won. But in those years the practice of working within the prevailing institutions had become dominant. Now a commission has been appointed to address Moutse's future.[19] While comrades and migrants assert that the long battle against kwaNdebele was a battle against the bantustan system and that Moutse should be administered as part of the common area of South Africa, the chief and tribal authority argue that as North-Sotho people they should fall under Lebowa. The traditional Tribal Authority is asserting that it is the established leadership and the other partners in the alliance have played their role and should now retire gracefully. A clever legal point has reinforced an already inherent conflict of interests in the society.

It is to be hoped that local strategies will be developed so that some concrete victories will be won in the arena where rural people are strongest and the law is least biased against them.

Struggles without title deeds: non-landowners

'Black spot' dwellers are not the only people who have occupied farming land in the white rural areas for generations. There are parts of South Africa where black families have lived and farmed on what are now white-owned farms since before the period of conquest. This situation does not apply all over the country. Generally it occurs on poorer agricultural land and in areas bordering land reserved for blacks. In richer, highly-capitalized agricultural zones like the western Cape, the Natal Midlands, and the western Transvaal, capitalist relations of production are firmly established and black people on the farms are wage labourers and their families. Their struggles are for improved wages and working conditions rather than for access to land.

The following section does not apply to these regions, it applies to areas such as the south-eastern Transvaal, northern Natal and parts of the Free State where more feudal relations still exist. My examples are drawn from the south-eastern Transvaal.

There are vast numbers of black people (living on white farms) who are not wage labourers or their dependants. This number is increasing. Charles Simkins has analysed government figures and shown that the ratio of Africans to whites on farms has soared since the 1950s. He found that, in absolute terms, the number of rural blacks outside the bantustans rose by about 2 million between 1951 and 1980.[20] This is despite the fact that the number of people employed in agriculture has dropped steadily since the 1950s and despite the fact that well over a million people have been forcibly removed from white farms since the 1960s.[21]

These figures bear testimony to a process of tenacious resistance in the face of overwhelming odds. A barrage of laws has been directed at destroying black farming on white land, and there has been a violent physical process of ejectment.[22] The Surplus People Project's figures show that farm dwellers have been the largest category of people affected by forced removal.[23] They are also the most legally disadvantaged people in South Africa. This situation is especially significant when one considers that only 20 per cent of the African population lives on white farmland.[24]

The terms

The struggles people have fought to keep occupation of land which is their historical home, but which legally belongs to white owners, have been very different from the 'black spot' struggles.

There has not been the same tactical approach. This may be because black landowners could maximize the opportunities provided by contradictions within the legal system between apartheid land law and the notions of sanctity of private property and equality before the law. Black tenants, on the other hand, have tended to reject the ideological concept of private property within which the law operates. The notion of the ownership of land is always contested, however obliquely. Again and again tenants refer to the white farmers as transient sojourners and to themselves as the permanent inhabitants of the farms.

Questions as to who own the farms often elicit responses like the following one from a person threatened with eviction:

> The whites have not been here for long. This one has been here for six months. The one before was just the same. The one before him was a doctor from Ermelo and he was just like this one .... We are the people who live on the farms, we are not people who are visiting or people who are passing through. We were born here. Another place we have not seen. We were born right here on this farm.

There are individual families who have been evicted from, and returned to, the same farms many times. (One old man, Sergeant Yende, from a farm near Driefontein, did this eight times.) In this process people suffer incredible loss, often their houses are burnt down, their cattle are impounded and they must spend periods in jail. But they persist with a conviction that pays scant attention to the formal and legal mechanisms used against them.

A recent case in the Wakkerstroom Magistrate's Court illustrates the conflict in perceptions of rights to the land between white and black farmers. A young man, Joseph Nhlabathi, lived and worked on the farm Geelhoutboom. He had been born on the farm, as had his father who was buried there. He worked fulltime for Riaan van Wyk in exchange for a wage of R45 per month and the right to keep his cattle, sheep and goats on the farm. (This right was the substantial part of his remuneration.)

Then a new white man (Van Zyl) came to the farm and announced that a new system would be introduced; the people would earn higher wages (R80) but could no longer keep their own stock. Nhlabathi ignored this and continued to work for Van Wyk, who still farmed the adjacent land. Van Zyl then served Nhlabathi with a 'trekpas' or notice of eviction telling him to vacate the farm, with his family, his goods (he has extensive buildings on the farm), and his animals. In response to this Nhlabathi hired another man to work for Van Zyl. He paid this man R100 per month. (This is a common practice in the area.) For several months this man joined the group of labourers who reported for work every morning, although Nhlabathi did not introduce him to Van Zyl or explain why he was working for him. While this man was working for Van Zyl, Nhlabathi was arrested for trespass on the basis the he had not vacated the farm within the notice period of the 'trekpas'.

In court, Nhlabathi testified that he was providing labour for Van Zyl and that he had continued to do this, at considerable expense to himself, throughout the period of notice. He said that this maintained the contract and cancelled the 'trekpas' and the notice. He therefore had the right to remain on the farm, even if he himself continued to work for Van Wyk who had, in any event, never properly explained the change of ownership.

Nhlabathi would not budge from this position despite both the magistrate and the public prosecutor's fury and righteous indignation at his 'stupidity'. Nhlabathi stood in the dock, young and dogged and desperate, and repeated that the farm was his home, his parents were buried there, he had done nothing wrong and he would not leave. Clearly for him Van Zyl's conduct and the entire legal system was irrelevant. He occupied the farm by an age-old contract in terms of which blacks acquire access to land in exchange for providing labour. He was providing labour for *two* masters, he had the right to stay.

The rights Nhlabathi was asserting are not very different from those asserted by the 'black spot' communities; rights won through a contract with the white conquerors of the land. But the position from which they were asserted is infinitely more vulnerable – all alone in a court which dismissed his reality as stupid and perverse.

The isolation and loneliness of tenant struggles has sometimes been broken by group action and legal victories that tip the local balance of power with white farmers. Some recent examples emerged in three different situations:

(i) arrest and eviction of individual families from farms;
(ii) eviction of whole villages from forest land; and
(iii) assault and murder by white farmers.

(i) Individual evictions

When a south-eastern Transvaal farmer decides to evict a tenant family he will generally give them a 'trekpas'. This is a letter which says that the person, his or her family, and all their livestock and cattle must vacate the farm by a certain date. If the family has not left by that date the farmer reports the matter to the police and lays a charge of trespass or illegal squatting. The head of the family is then arrested forthwith and brought to court.

In most cases the only basis for challenging eviction is the unreasonableness of the circumstances of eviction and the shortness of the notice period. Sometimes farmers give only a week's notice and generally not more than two weeks or a month.

Recent legal defences to charges of trespass or illegal squatting in these circumstances have been based on the fact that a contract has existed for decades, and that the tenant has not breached it and thus is legally on the land.

(ii) Eviction of villages or settlements

In the south-eastern Transvaal large forestry companies are buying up land which used to be individual white farms. With the land come people who have lived there for generations on the basis that as long as one or more able-bodied members of the family tender themselves for employment, the rest of the family will be allowed to live there and keep cattle and plough land allotted as their family fields. On some farms there are large villages of black people in this position, especially in situations where the previous 'owners' had been absentee landlords.

The policy of the forestry companies is generally to employ some of the people and evict the others. Those to be employed are to be moved from their 'disgraceful' mud structures and to be accommodated in housing schemes where schooling, water and health facilities will be provided. Only the nuclear family may be accommodated in the family housing and families will be allowed vegetable gardens and perhaps one or two cattle, but not the large herds and extensive lands they presently use.

Again and again these schemes are met with massive resistance. The smart new houses stand empty and people insist on staying in their mud houses with their large families. Crowds of people tender themselves for work every morning and those for whom there is no work refuse to leave the farm. Even the most 'progressive' companies are 'forced to resort' to eviction notices and criminal prosecutions. Their only explanation for the situation is the 'childlike simplicity or perverseness' of the 'rural black'.

Recently the successful defence of criminal prosecutions has opened the way for negotiations between villagers and companies. The villagers have explained the terms upon which they have occupied the land for the past century. They have shown that they were born on these farms and that the extended family is necessary for their survival: there must be enough people in a family both to provide labour for the 'owner' of the land and to farm the area which is theirs as payment for their labour. They have said that their inherited wealth and only real security is the cattle that belong to them and it is no easy matter to dispose of their stock. They have said the new housing schemes have no space for fields, or cattle or decent independent family life. They have stressed that they are more than willing to work in the forest, and they need the cash wages that go with this employment. They have said that the important aspects of the system can be reduced to written contracts which determine the number of cattle, the size of the field allowed, and even the size of the family as it is defined in Zulu custom. Some companies have accepted these conditions and the notion of a contract that regulates the relationship.

In 1987 there was an unusual meeting between the management of Hunt, Leuchars & Hepburn and a group of villagers who had been served with eviction summonses. The meeting took place in a patch of open land in the forest. One after another the villagers stood up in the long grass and explained how they had been born on the land; they gave the names of the white farmers they had worked for as the land changed hands, and explained how, when Hunt, Leuchars & Hepburn bought the land, they had been employed on a seasonal basis depending on the demand for labour. Now, the company was introducing 'progressive' measures such as a permanent fulltime employment and family housing but, they explained, because they were amongst those who had been recently retrenched, they must leave the farm forever.

When everyone present had finished describing his or her life there was a long silence. The management was hidden in the long grass. Only the tops of their heads were visible so no-one had been able to gauge their response. Then the group personnel manager stood up, and he apologized. He said he had been responsible for the new measures, he had thought they would be improvements. Now he saw they would never be accepted by the people if the whole fabric of society had to be forcibly destroyed for them to exist. He said every person present could stay on the farm for the rest of his or her life and the summonses would be withdrawn. He sat down. There was dead silence in the forest, which stretched on and on. He jumped up and said that perhaps they didn't believe him. He told them his name, and his position and assured them that he had the authority to implement what he had said.

The villagers were too amazed to respond immediately. Then one after another they stood up and made tentative speeches of thanks. After he had left there was incredulous wild rejoicing.

Other negotiations have not been so dramatic, nor depended so much on an individual's changed perception. But forestry companies in the area have stopped evicting people on the same scale and with their previous self-righteousness.

(iii) Assault and murder by white farmers

On occasion legal action by tenants has asserted their rights in the face of violence by farmers.

Farmers often act as if they have absolute power and control over the lives of the people who live on their land. Assault and murder are commonplace. Very few prosecutions are brought against whites who assault blacks, even when charges are laid. Those prosecutions that do take place are half-hearted and, even when they result in convictions, whites seldom serve prison sentences.[25]

All institutions in the Transvaal platteland are fundamentally racist; shops, the police, the post offices and the courts. This can be related to the way in which race is functional to the balance of power in these areas. The only real edge that white farmers have over black farmers is that they own the land. The only reason they own the land is because they are white. And by owning the land, they gain control over the black farmers in the area who must work for them on their terms, to keep a toehold on the land.

Political power, access to land, free labour, all these things depend on skin colour alone. So skin colour must be asserted as having meaning; blacks become less than human – a lower species whose inferior position must be reasserted daily.

It is not surprising that black life is cheap in this context. Ensuring that farmers are brought to court, pushing for convictions and, at the least, instituting civil claims for damages become challenges to the balance of power.

Farmers have always been able to rely on the implicit (or explicit) support of the local police and courts and so their absolute power is seldom challenged. As soon as the tenants have legal representation and cases of assault are won the farmers become profoundly disturbed and unsettled.

Legal support – adopting what terms?

Legal support in the three kinds of situations described above often seems to recognize that whites own the land although labour tenants reject this.

In a 1922 Natal judgment this contradiction is illustrated:

> One's knowledge of conditions of this country convinces one that it is difficult for a native to find at a moment's notice new land upon which to settle. To remove his kraal takes some time when he has found the land. The right of occupation of the soil has from the earliest times been a fertile source of social and political trouble, and it is incumbent upon the court to see that the rights of tenants, as regards notice, especially in a country like this, are properly safeguarded, when they are being turned off the land.[26]

To assert that notice should be 'proper', contracts written down and that murderers should go to jail is hardly revolutionary. In fact these are all demands that legitimize and stabilize the present order. For example, lawyers arguing that one month's notice is unreasonable for a labour tenant have been concerned that they are focussing on reasonable notice rather than on other, more permanent rights.

But the tenants and 'black spot' committees do not share this concern. For them the issue, at this stage, is to win by whatever means available. Any challenge to absolute control by the white farmers is seen, by both sides, to be a significant shift in the balance of power. The issues of race, power and land are so inextricable that a challenge to any one aspect is a threat to the entire order.

Yet the victories won are few. Tenant struggles remain essentially vulnerable and isolated. In this context the persistence shown by thousands of tenants who return to their farms again and again, and assert their right to the land seems inexplicable.

However, while each individual act of defiance and resistance may seem suicidal, together they amount to an expression of the permanent instability and pressure that will exist while black farmers are restricted to tiny overcrowded reserves and vast areas of agricultural land lie open and reserved for whites only. Not even the barrage of laws introduced to prohibit black tenancy and the violence of the evictions in the 1960s and 1970s could reverse the tide of black people to this land.[27] In the immediate term, however, the position of tenants district by district and family by family remains very vulnerable. A family threatened with eviction faces terrible suffering whatever choice it makes – whether to resist or move to the bantustans.

There can be no real improvement in the lot of labour tenants until there is general recognition of the positive contribution that they can make as farmers. This would entail an ideological shift to a recognition that decades of occupancy give them the right to some form of security of tenure on the land. It would also entail an acceptance of the notion that blacks on the platteland can be there as independent producers, not just as employees or servants.

Defensive land struggles: conclusion

'Black spot' dwellers have been able to adopt legal strategies to resist dispossession. This is because long ago they were able to enter into the conquerors' terms and buy back their own land. Labour tenants do not have access to the same strategies. All they can do is assert that they have a right of occupancy of the farms on which they were born. In the face of the dominant ideology of landownership this often appears a last ditch stand with no prospects of success. The difference is that the 'black spot' people believe in the title deeds which have been the measure of their compromise and also their flimsy protection in the conquerors' world. 'Tenants' on the other hand have never seen either a title deed or a lease agreement. Their experience is contained within the parameters of birth, life and death on the same land that their families have always occupied.

But there is an underlying similarity far greater than the differences. Most 'black spot' communities were forcibly removed and lost their land in the 1960s and 1970s *despite* having bought it. The two groups of people certainly see themselves as fighting a common struggle and see each other as allies against the 'Boers'. There has always been interaction between them. Evicted tenants take refuge with relatives in 'black spots'. There is a constant stream of tenants consulting the Driefontein and kwaNgema committees about threatened evictions.

This overlap has an objective base. Both groups are fighting for the rights of ordinary contractual relations, the one of sale, the other of tenancy. Both can easily be met within the parameters of capitalism. They challenge platteland society only in relation to racial power and control.

Part II: The Offensive Position – Some Implications for the Future

Empty land – an empty page?

The three situations described so far (Driefontein, kwaNgema and labour tenancy) all exist in one magisterial district, Wakkerstroom. If one drives through this area it looks under-utilized and empty. Driefontein and kwa-Ngema are tucked out of view of the main roads.

It is the kind of area which one can imagine that future land reformers would put down for immediate re-allocation. But how and to whom? Because this land is not empty. There are as many people in Driefontein and kwaNgema as in the town of Ermelo. And the wattle and daub structures scattered on the farms house tens of thousands of people.

Leaving out of consideration the white farmers (a luxury which will never be practically possible) there are at least three different groups of people who have a historical relationship to the land and lay claim to it.

The labour tenants are in occupation of the vast white farms. They are the 'landed gentry' of the area. In many cases they are petty chiefs and healers who are consulted by large numbers of people. They have cattle and extensive homesteads and their children have high status in the marriage market. For them, when the boers go, the farms will be theirs.

Then there are those that live in the overcrowded 'black spots'. These areas have become refugee camps for people evicted from white farms. There is not enough land left to farm or for grazing. People who live in 'black spots' also claim other land in the area for, when their farms were initially acquired, payments were made on other pieces of land which were never transferred to them.[28]

Finally there are the inhabitants of the vast resettlement camps in ka-Ngwane. These are people who were removed from white farms. There is a constant traffic between the farms and resettlement camps with people returning to the farms again and again only to face repeated evictions. These people are the most desperate of all.

All these people have fought courageous battles to retain access to farming land. In some cases their houses have been burnt down and they have been forcibly loaded onto trucks; people have even died fighting for the land.

In this context land is an explosive issue. Battles for land in the 1980s have not been confined to battles to stave off dispossession. There are also constant struggles to acquire land. Sometimes, these struggles have been slow and insidious, in which individuals settle on land or return to farms.

Each family fights tenaciously against overwhelming odds. This process is not negligible, vast numbers of people are involved. State concern about this 'uncontrollable process' has been a major factor leading to new measures in rural areas introduced by the latest amendments to the Prevention of Illegal Squatting Act.[29]

At other times, the process of getting land has not been slow or insidious, but a chaotic scramble:

> Land is a major resource around which racial competition and black anger often crystallize in South Africa. Even small tracts of land become the centre of intense wheeler-dealing if it seems likely that access may be opened up and the logjam of racial apportionment of land eased.[30]

Recent events at Driefontein bear testimony to this.

Driefontein explodes

Driefontein has become a secure area. It has weathered attempts both to remove it and to incorporate it into kaNgwane. In the last decade the vast majority of the population has been drawn into concrete struggles at one time or another. During the course of these the Council Board committee changed from being a group of male landowners dominated by Soweto businessmen, to one where there is an equal proportion of landowners and tenants, with a couple of women playing important leadership roles. There have been no major schisms in the community since the rift with the pro-removal group was healed.

From this point of view and compared with other parts of South Africa it seems a haven of rural bliss and tranquillity. The realities of life in Driefontein belie this. It is very overcrowded and there is serious poverty, but it is relatively fortunate.

Towards the end of 1988 the issue of purchasing a neighbouring farm came up. A group of tenants brought a letter to the Legal Clinic asking the Black Sash to intervene with 'our father, the State President' to give them land. The letter, written in English, detailed the suffering of the Driefontein tenants at the hands of their exploitative landlords:

> We need a Trust Area for our suffering community of Driefontein. At the moment we are oppressed by the landowners (stand owners). Under these people we are not allowed to possess properties such as livestock, free enterprise businesses, modern houses and enough ground or land for crop farming ....
>
> Sir, we are living in squatters and shacks, we are oppressed and there is no way to stretch our arms and legs. How long shall we suffer in our fathers' land? We are your children. We desperately need your

help and your Cabinet. Our products will benefit your people all over the Republic of South Africa even yourself.

We will apply the Free Enterprise System.'

The Council Board committee representative who was assisting the legal worker, and was himself a tenant, asked for examples of instances where landowners had oppressed tenants. The group of tenants were genuinely confused; what was he talking about? Their letter had never said such things. They just wanted land. Their letter was translated into Zulu for them and they dissociated themselves from the parts complaining about the Driefontein landlords. They would not say who had written the letter. They said those parts should be cut out and the letter sent to the State President.

Meetings were held between the Council Board committee and the rapidly expanding group of tenants seeking land. The meetings were tense. A vocal group amongst the tenants accused the Council Board of having failed to procure enough land for all the people at Driefontein. The Council Board accused the tenants of stirring up trouble. The committee's explanations about the legal difficulties of buying white farming land were clearly seen as wilful obstructionism by the tenants. The Council Board committee explained that it had always intervened to stop landlords evicting tenants; indeed half of its members were tenants. The new tenant leader insisted on referring to the committee as a group of landowners.

The ever-increasing number of tenants who attended the meetings shifted from side to side as the argument went back and forth. It was clear that they would support whichever side promised land. Finally the Council Board proposed that a joint committee be set up to identify land and work out strategies for persuading the government to lift the legal restrictions on blacks buying this land.

At the first meeting of the joint committee none of the vocal tenant leaders arrived. But many other tenants did. They were nervous about recent developments and they wanted to check out the legal situation. They said that the tenant leaders had met up with a 'dominee' Van Rensburg who had made a deal to buy the next door farm on their behalf. Anyone who paid R400 would get a share in the farm. The purchase price was R400 000. The Saturday before he had set up a table on the road outside Driefontein and collected R85 000. The Council Board was well aware of this collection. Hundreds of people had swarmed around the table all day long. Armed guards were present while tellers from Boland Bank gathered the money. Mr Van Rensburg declined to explain more than that he was from the Internasionale Christelike Gemeente and that the money was for the purchase of a mission farm.

All that is known about Mr Van Rensburg is that he is the Personnel Manager of the Natal Tanning Extract factory at Iswepe. The Council Board had earlier assisted various workers to take legal action against Mr Van Rensburg for retrenching them after 45 years with 'pensions' of R15 per month.

Enquiries with the NG Kerk offices in Pretoria and Johannesburg drew a blank on a church named 'Internasionale Christelike Gemeente'. The local official from the Department of Development Aid told the Council Board committee that he knew nothing of the project. The Council Board asked their lawyer to investigate and in the meantime warned the people who were flocking to them for advice as to whether to go and pay the following Saturday that the whole thing looked dubious.

In the meantime Mr van Rensburg assured the committee's lawyer that he had the interests of black people at heart, that he had investigated all the legal constraints and had been given the green light by Minister Heunis and Deputy Minister Roelof Meyer of Constitutional Development.

This proved correct as Constitutional Development had approved the scheme. The Department of Development Aid (previously Co-operation and Development) then became involved and assured the Driefontein people that they would stand by and guard their interests. They would insist that each person who had contributed received registered title deed to an individual plot; it would not be a mission farm.

The result of this has been to revive old community divisions. The tenant leaders say that the Council Board committee was jealous of more people becoming landowners and so advised them not to participate. The businessmen on the Council Board committee came home from Soweto and said that this confirmed their previously unexpressed reservations about allowing tenants onto the committee: they should all be expelled and the committee revert to its previous membership of male landowners only.

None of these issues is settled, least of all the purchase and transfer of the new land, but people on all sides are saying that there will be bloodshed before it is resolved. Everyone in Driefontein has a strong and desperate desire for access to land or more of it. The fury at obstacles in the path of this desire is not directed at the state, but at other groups within Driefontein. The tragedy is that Driefontein's present predicament is a result of state action. It is overcrowded because it has become a refugee camp for people evicted from white farms in the area. In court case after court case when people plead lack of alternative accommodation, the magistrate says 'What about Driefontein, or Daggakraal or kwaNgema – there are black farms with lots of space for you'. The Driefontein landlords charge a yearly rent of R20 to R40 per tenant family. This is much less than the return they would get from the land if it were used for crops. The agricultural base of the community has been eroded over time and there is not sufficient grazing for cattle, whether by the landowners or the tenants.

Everyone wants and needs more land. The white farms around are being steadily depopulated by their white owners. The logical thing is that the state allow black farmers to purchase the land. But one cannot blame the Council Board committee for being caught off guard by the government's completely unprecedented decision to allow black people to purchase more of the very land from which they have been trying to evict black people for decades.

Holgat – hopes raised and dashed

It is neither necessary nor inevitable that black people's desire for land should implode self-destructively.

In 1984 the South African Council of Churches passed a resolution that its member churches should make mission land available to dispossessed black people. Generally this land, usually mission farmland, is scheduled or released in terms of the Land Act and so fewer legal restrictions on black ownership apply.[31]

In 1987 the South African Council of Churches raised money to purchase a farm, Holgat, in the Western Transvaal from the Hermansberg Mission of the Lutheran Church. This land would otherwise have been sold to white farmers and its status as released land wasted. It is a beautiful, fertile farm right in the heart of the district from which hundreds of thousands of Tswana people were moved into the Ramatlabama and Marico settlement camps in Bophuthatswana.

A trust was established with three groups of people as beneficiaries: the Mogopa people who were then living under terrible conditions in Bophuthatswana; the Machavie people who had been moved 17 years before, and the farmworkers who lived on the farm, many of whom had been there for more than ten years.

Throughout that year many weekend workshops were held with about 80 people representing the different groups. The workshops discussed questions such as:

- How should the farm be allocated? Kept as one unit or divided into three units for the three groups?
- What kind of farming should be practised? Maize and cattle or mixed farming?

- Where should the housing be established? Three different villages or one village? On richer land for vegetable plots, or on poor land to release the richer land for fields?
- How should production be organized? Who would work, and for what? Wages or the final crop?
- How should the crop be divided?
- What about the herd of Brahmin cattle that was included in the purchase price? Who would own this? Who would care for it?
- What would be the status and role of migrants who worked in Johannesburg, but were members of the community?
- What would happen to the white farmhouses on the farm?
- What did people think about the trust document and the form of ownership?
- How exactly should beneficiaries be defined? Who could be considered members?
- What sort of community committee should there be? How should the different groups be represented in it?
- How should disputes be resolved?

These questions were all very pressing. The farm was to be available from the next ploughing season. It had machinery and cattle. Some money had been raised to finance the first season's ploughing but otherwise there would not be external financial support for the farm. It was not a 'project', it was a transfer of land.

All the participants stressed that the success of the first season's production was crucial. It would enable them to meet their future expenses. It would also show the surrounding white farmers that this was a viable agricultural project and was not the beginning of an invasion of 'squatters'. The three groups were very different. The Mogopa people had farmed their land until 1984. They had never used complex machinery and advanced methods but were very experienced in the general organization and management of their farms. They had a system of land tenure based on share-cropping which led to high land utilization and spread the benefits of the crop between entrepreneurial farmers and old people and migrants who could not, or did not, want to plough their fields themselves. The farmers among them had established relations with the local Korporasie where they ordered their requirements and sold their produce. They were confident and experienced within these parameters.

The farmworkers on the other hand had never had much to do with organizing community resources, or with the ordering and marketing of agricultural goods. However, they had a good deal of experience of the processes of intensive farming. They could use and maintain the big machines (huge tractors and combine harvesters) which came with the farm. They were also experienced in the processes of when and what to plant, how to protect crops from pests and the organization of work necessary to maximize the pressured times of planting and harvesting. (Their skills were probably unusually advanced; the mission farm had run on a participatory model where the workers discussed and allocated the production tasks for the day, week or month.)

The Machavie people had lost their land a long time before. All their agricultural implements were rusted and broken. And many of the young men and women had had to go off and find other ways of supporting themselves. Thus the community was dominated by old people whose whole lives were bound up with the past – the loss of their land.

At first the three groups eyed each other warily. The farmworkers were quiet and observant; they had the choice of participating or not. The Mogopa group was in the majority and also very familiar with the support agencies, the Transvaal Rural Action Committee, the Environmental Development Agency and the South African Council of Churches. They made the first overtures to the others, assuring them that since they were in a clear majority, issues would have to be settled by consensus rather than voting or dominance of numbers. A major factor in breaking down barriers was that people were staying together. Meal times and evening discussions in the bedrooms were where the real negotiations took place.

After days and days of discussion the following decisions were made. There would be one village and no segregated living areas within it. It would be built on the most rocky, least productive land. Each family would have a yard big enough for a vegetable garden and keeping small animals. The white farmhouses would be used for offices and a school.

The farm would continue to be farmed as a single unit. The fields would not be broken down and divided. But mixed farming projects such as pigs, rabbits, poultry and vegetables would be introduced over time to cut down the reliance on the mealie and sunflower crops. The herd of cattle would be kept as one unit and used as the group's 'bank'. Particular people would be put in charge of it and made responsible for proper care.

The farm labourers would be responsible for organizing production, especially in the next season's ploughing. But everybody would be drawn into tasks at certain times of the year – for example planting and harvesting. The migrants must contribute cash to pay for the farm labourer's living expenses for the first year. They would carry the major burden of work, both in putting the crops into the soil and looking after the cattle. Everyone in the community must have a stake in agriculture, whether by cash contributions like the migrants, or by labour at seasonal times of the year. Finally the crop would be divided between home consumption and a proportion to sell to pay for the next year's costs. The benefits would be spread according to contribution with the farm labourers earning the equivalent of a salary for their fulltime work.

All this may sound like an easy ideal model, but there were days of discussion about the 'what ifs'. What would happen if the first crop failed? How much money did the farm workers need for subsistence in the first year? What if some migrants refused to participate?

There were very positive discussions about building on the different skills and experiences of the three groups. The farm labourers made a speech about how they appreciated Mogopa's experience of being independent and in control of a whole enterprise; they on the other hand knew about advanced farming methods, but only on a production level.

A serious problem was that a sector of the Machavie group wanted the community representation system to be on the model of a chief and council – and the chief to be the Machavie chief. The other groups and a section of the Machavie people rejected this model out of hand; their own experience of chiefs had been too devastating. It was clear that the Machavie chief and a group of followers would split off.

Notwithstanding this difficulty the process was very inspiring. The farm-workers who saw the move as the chance of a lifetime, blossomed from being tentative and suspicious to being positive and pragmatic in all their proposals. For the Mogopa and Machavie people it held out a promise of ending their present suffering, even though it was not the land which they regarded as home.

And so the final arrangements for the move and for the first season's ploughing were made. Just as these were completed the government announced that it had expropriated the farm.

Reports were received that the local Lutheran minister and a delegation of white farmers had complained to Pretoria, and Pretoria had responded just before transfer of the land was to be registered in the deeds office. The expropriation illustrates the system of land tenure in apartheid South Africa: racial control through the state.

Part III: Land Struggles in the 1980s – Changing Parameters

The struggle for land in the 1980s has seen some advances, but it is by no means won, or nearly won. Millions of people still have the threat of removal, eviction or incorporation hanging over their heads. Valiant local struggles are still in the balance. Now, in October 1989, a group of people are camped at Mogopa, surrounded by police and waiting for the results of the state's application for a legal eviction order. Scores of people at Braklaagte are badly injured following an attack by the Bophuthatswana police on their village after its incorporation earlier this year, and the people of Potsdam, moved unlawfully into the Ciskei, have marched over the border and into South Africa for the third time. Men have deserted the village of Leeuwfontein because of constant police raids. (These are ostensibly searches for the people who killed Bophuthatswana police at an anti-incorporation meeting in July 1989.)

The struggle for land remains primarily a defensive one against further dispossession by the state. Struggles to secure more land exist, but are extremely vulnerable. The odds against rural people are great.

Yet the outlook is not entirely bleak. The 1980s have seen developments and openings which provide opportunities and possibilities that did not exist before.

Land struggles obviously take place in the context of wider political developments. The early 1980s was a relatively open period. Mass-based organizations such as the unions and the United Democratic Front mobilized popular support and initiated various campaigns to challenge the state.

The state responded by trying to legitimize its position and stabilize the situation through various reforms. It distanced itself from the more crass ideological aspects of apartheid. The principle that blacks could be in the common area of South Africa only as temporary servants and employees was jettisoned. The pass laws were repealed and the Restoration of South African Citizenship Act introduced. It had become clear that certain bantustan leaders would never opt for independence. This realization combined with concessions in the pass laws and citizenship provisions means that the internal logic of the bantustan policy has been dealt a severe blow. All the ground rules for the state have changed, and this has made concessions more possible than in the 1960s.

Not only the political climate has changed. There have also been basic shifts in the economic priorities which informed much of the history of removal and eviction. These open up an entirely new set of pressures and possibilities.

Put simply, the situation has changed from one of labour shortage to one in which unemployment is so severe that it is creating problems of political instability.

The purpose of the Land Act and the legislation restricting labour tenancy was to proletarianize black people. The insistence that blacks were fitted only to be servants of white masters was intrinsic to this purpose. Now the pendulum has swung in the opposite direction. Capital and the state are touting 'small businesses' and the informal sector as possible solutions to unemployment.

Accordingly it is no longer inconsistent for blacks to farm land deserted by whites. Indeed, the Development Bank has stressed the importance of small-scale black farmers and even hinted at the abolition of the Land Act. There is growing disenchantment with the inefficiency of heavily subsidized large-scale white farmers and the state is no longer committed to propping up unprofitable agriculture.

The present period of opportunities, contradictions and pressures has led to some anomalies. In one small area of the western Transvaal are three rural communities which are well-known for their resistance to forced removal. All three are 'black spots'. One of these, Mathopestad, was reprieved by Minister Gerrit Viljoen in late 1988. Although surrounded by white farms, its position as a farming community is secured.

Another, Mogopa, was forcibly removed in 1984. Since then the people have made various attempts to get back their land. In spite of an Appellate Division decision holding that the removal was unlawful, the government, represented by Minister Viljoen, refuses to allow them to return. Those who have gone back in defiance are threatened with eviction. They have been offered alternative land on the borders of Bophuthatswana as compensation for Mogopa. A cabinet undertaking has been given that, should they accept such land, it would always remain part of South Africa and never be incorporated into Bophuthatswana.

In the same year as this promise was made to the Mogopa people, Minister Viljoen met with the Braklaagte committee. They had requested a meeting to put their vehement objections to the threatened incorporation of their land into Bophuthatswana. Notwithstanding these, Viljoen signed an order incorporating their land into Bophuthatswana.

The Mathopes are allowed to farm land surrounded by whites, the Bakwena ba Mogopa are not. The Bakwena ba Mogopa are saved from incorporation into Bophuthatswana by a cabinet undertaking. The Braklaagte community is not. Instead they are catapulted into the heart of the 'prickly pear', as Mangope has called his 'country'.

The situation is confusing and depressing but also presents opportunities for exposing the contradictions in state policy and using concessions as precedents.

Conclusion: Grassroots Resistance – a Reality on which to Build

The combination of determined local resistance, legal support and publicity can be a very strong one. The inhumanity of the removals policy and the unlawful actions of local officials who are confident of absolute power over black people provide opportunities that can be maximized by rural communities.

A community threatened with removal or incorporation should identify issues that can be won at the local level. On the one hand this steers legal challenge away from explicitly racial law and provides more prospects of victory. On the other hand it strengthens the position of the rural community in relation to the local balance of power. This has significant results; increased confidence leads to increased participation. If the state receives reports that a community is strong, organized and militant it may abandon its attempt to move the community in order to avoid using violence and the concomitant publicity this would attract.

When removals are challenged primarily in the Supreme Court the major actors become the lawyers from either side.[32] The outcome of the struggle then depends not on community strength, but on the cunning, intelligence and hard work of their lawyers. This is not to say that victories in the Appellate Division do not redress the balance of power. They are major challenges to state policy and power, and as such advance the objective position of rural people. But it is only battles which are fought, experienced and won at a community level that expose both the contradictions and possibilities for organization inherent in rural society.

Again and again, state threats have had a unifying and politicizing effect on previously segmented or apathetic communities. Local resistance to a common threat has often led to rapid learning, to role changes and to new political alliances. As such it has provided opportunities for progressive transformation that are generally rare in traditional society. If land issues are addressed primarily at a national level or in the Supreme Court this local transformation does not take place and victories often serve further to entrench the position of the established leadership.

However, rural society, like all society, is not necessarily egalitarian and democratic. Sometimes the heroic battles that rural people have fought have created romantic visions of a group of valiant peasants fighting for a just and free future.

The reality is often different. For example, one of the reasons Soweto businessmen fought the Driefontein removal was because they wanted to set up shops and bar-lounges on their plots. Some of the strongest people resisting removal at kwaNgema are people who are the masters of labour tenants themselves. The more secure the land, the more profitable the production of their free labourers. Often the labour tenants who take militant stands in court are patriarchs whose income depends on the extraction of labour from their wives and children.

In local struggles it has been necessary that all the different groups and sections of society form alliances to fight the common enemy. Thus tenants and landlords have united, men and women, young and old, chiefs and comrades, migrants and tribal elders. These alliances have often led to new roles and status for previously disadvantaged groups. In Mogopa, for example, women were not originally allowed to attend village meetings but during the crisis women began to attend meetings and then to speak, albeit, at first, on their knees. Then they spoke standing up. Soon they became leaders. Nobody quibbled, women were arguing with the police, rebuilding roads and taking great risks to reoccupy land.

Sadly, once victory has been achieved there are often attempts by former leaders to reassert control over the groups who were their allies during the crisis. But the women, tenants and the young are unwilling to relinquish their new roles and status.

The matter of internal division and conflicts of interest is a complex one. Many of the institutions and traditions of rural society are conservative and hierarchical and will not be easily changed. There are serious divisions in black rural society and different sides have opposing interests.

In addition to local struggles, other forms of challenge and intervention are important in the assertion of the rights of rural communities. The Freedom Charter's ideological challenge to the present constitution, protests against the Land Act, debates about land reform, legal challenges to state power and action in the courts are just some of the critical aspects of a challenge to the status quo. Those involved in the land question must work towards supporting rural people in the development of principles and priorities on which to build a unified land policy.

Any land strategy or policy in South Africa will be viable and progressive only if it is built on the traditions of the land struggles that have been fought in South Africa. For this to happen rural people must have a voice in government and particularly in policy-making for the rural areas. To say this is to state the obvious but even now rural issues are neglected by political organizations and there is a glaring lack of rural leaders in national political structures.[33] The existing urban focus of the Mass Democratic Movement and the trade unions and the general ignorance about the realities of rural life is part of the problem. But part also rests with the rural communities themselves.

Rural leaders may be excellent within the parameters of rural life, but are often disadvantaged in wider forums. They do not have the same experience, exposure and education as urban people. Thus eloquent, democratic and militant rural leaders will often sit quietly in national meetings so that they can observe, gauge and understand the forces operating around them.

In order to redress the existing urban bias, it is not sufficient that some rural leaders be invited to participate in national political forums. Urban people, political leaders and policy-makers will have to educate themselves about the realities of rural life and the history of rural struggle. They will have to consult rural community leaders on their own terms.

The land issue is not an empty page that requires someone to come and write on it. Every piece of land in South Africa has a history and people who lay claim to it. An appropriate land strategy must be based on a proper understanding of the traditions, beliefs and dreams that have inspired people to fight the battles they have fought. Only a policy that grows out of these traditions and incorporates the dreams and necessities of people will win popular support. Without popular support, no policy can succeed.

Notes

1 The Zulu word 'Umhlaba' has a much wider meaning than the English 'land'. It also means the soil, and is closer to the English concept 'earth'.

2 These were the opening remarks by Petros Nkosi at a meeting to discuss the formation of a regional committee representing seventeen different rural committees in the south-eastern Transvaal in July 1989.

3 This Bill became Act 104 of 1988 and amended the Prevention of Illegal Squatting Act 52 of 1951.

4 Black Land Act 27 of 1913.

5 Quoted in Human Awareness Programme *Land in South Africa.*

6 R T Caluza quoted in L Callinicos *Working Life 1886-1940* (Johannesburg: Ravan 1987) 18.

7 L Platzky & C Walker for the Surplus People Project *The Surplus People: Forced Removals in South Africa* (Johannesburg: Raven 1985) 10.

8 This process is described in *The Myth of Voluntary Removals* (Transvaal Rural Action Committee 1984). See in this volume Haysom at 103 and Marcus at 20.

9 See for example C Desmond *The Discarded People: An Account of African Resettlement in South Africa* (Harmondsworth: Penguin 1971); *The Surplus People* (note 7 above) and material referred to in the bibliography in this volume at 235.

10 See Plasket in this volume at 214.

11 Act 38 of 1927. See Marcus in this volume at 18 for a discussion of the history and scope of section 5.

12 From the minutes of a meeting held in Pretoria on 30 May 1983. The biblical story tells of Ahab, King of Sumaria, who demanded that Naboth give him his vineyard. Naboth refused, saying that he would not give away the inheritance of his fathers. When Ahab told this to his wife, Jezebel, she arranged for Naboth to be murdered. Ahab then took possession of the vineyard, for which he was cursed by God (I *Kings* ch 21).

13 Gerrit Viljoen, press statement 1 February 1985 cited in *The Surplus People* (note 7 above) at xxviii.

14 See 1987/88 *Race Relations Survey* 1.

15 Plasket discusses this policy at 210 in this volume.

16 The Moutse case is reported as *Mathebe v Die Regering van die Republiek van Suid Afrika* 1988 (3) SA 667 (A). The Botshabelo case is *Lefuo v Staatspresident 1989* (3) SA 924 (O).

17 Act 21 of 1971, see Plasket at 215 in this volume.

18 Act 2 of 1980, see Plasket at 217 in this volume.

19 Commission of Inquiry into the constitutional and political future of Moutse and the appropriate method to determine and amend the boundaries of the self-governing territories (the Rumpff Commission) appointed in *GG* 11360 of 24 June 1988 Proc R104.

20 C Simkins *Four Essays on the Past, Present and Possible Future of the Distribution of the Black Population of South Africa* (Cape Town: SALDRU 1983) 123 cited in H Bradford 'Reformulating Resettlement: A Review of The Surplus People' (1988) 14 *Social Dynamics* 67 at 71.

21 *The Surplus People* (note 7 above at 10) estimates 1,1 million. A Baldwin *Uprooting a Nation: The Study of 3 million Evictions in South Africa* (London: Africa Publications Trust 1974) estimates that over 1 300 000 farm dwellers were moved between 1960 and 1974.

22 The legal and physical restrictions that have been imposed on black farmers and tenants are described in *Toehold on the Land* (Transvaal Rural Action Committee 1988). This publication discusses labour tenancy in its historical context. See also Hathorn & Hutchinson in this volume at 194.

23 These figures are reproduced in *The Surplus People* (note 7 above) at 10. See also The Surplus People Project *Forced Removals in South Africa* (Cape Town 1983) particularly vol I pp 1-30.

24 F Wilson & M Ramphele *Uprooting Poverty* (Cape Town: David Philip 1989) 24.

25 For descriptions see *Toehold on the Land* note 21 above. Two recent examples of prosecutions following the death of farm labourers by farmers were the Vorster case and Venter and Fouche. Vorster was convicted of culpable homicide and sentenced to five years' imprisonment suspended for a period and an effective fine of R3 000. In addition he was ordered to pay the deceased's widow R130 per month for five years. He had tied the deceased, Eric Sambo, to a tree and whipped him over a two day period for allegedly killing a dog with a tractor (*Sunday Tribune* 13 November 1988; *The Argus* 26 January 1989). This case led to attempts to impeach the presiding judge, Mr Justice J J Strydom (*The Argus* 27 January 1989, *The Star* 26 January 1989). Venter and Fouche were convicted on two charges of assault and were each sentenced to a fine of R1 200 or four months' imprisonment with a further six months' imprisonment suspended for five years. They had assaulted a farm labourer who later died of a brain haemorrhage (*The Argus* 20 April 1989, *Sunday Tribune* 23 April 1989).

26 *Makala Zikalala v Groenewald* 1922 NLR 150 at 152-3.

27 See *The Surplus People* (note 7) 128ff.

28 The following section describes the tension caused by land hunger in the black spots.

29 The amendments were introduced in Act 104 of 1988.

30 *South African Indicator* vol 4 no 4.

31 For a description of the statutory concepts of scheduled and released land see Robertson in this volume at 127ff.

32 See also Haysom in this volume at 113ff.

33 See also Haysom at 115ff.

GEOFF BUDLENDER

Urban Land Issues in the 1980s: The View from Weiler's Farm

The 1980s present a confusing picture in relation to urban forced removals. The pass laws are repealed: but many suspect that the government's policy of 'orderly urbanization' will be a new form of influx control. A number of urban townships are reprieved from the threat of forced removal: but Langa/Kabah is removed, and others remain under active threat. Harsh amendments to the Prevention of Illegal Squatting Act are enacted: but 'informal housing' is now apparently part of the government's urbanization strategy.

What does it all mean? Is there any coherence to state policy on urban removals, or are we simply seeing a series of ad hoc responses to different situations and pressures?[1] In answering these questions, two issues need to be considered. First, in what circumstances will the state consider it necessary to remove forcibly an urban community, and secondly, once that decision has been made, what mechanisms are used to effect such a removal?

The key to answering the first question lies in an analysis of the purpose and effect of the abolition of influx control. The first section of the paper is concerned with this. The second part is concerned with the manner in which forced removals may be effected in the 1980s. This requires an assessment of the role of local authorities.

In order to provide an illustration of the full complexity of the situation, the questions will be answered against the backdrop of the story of one threatened community, Weiler's Farm, some 30 kilometres south of Johannesburg, where many of the current issues are being played out.

If one looks at the issues through the prism of this community, current state policies and strategies are refracted into recognizable forms. Many of the nuances reveal themselves, contradictions become apparent, and the opportunities for threatened communities to defend themselves become clearer. It is therefore through this prism – Weiler's Farm – that I wish to attempt to analyse the current situation in and around the cities.

The Weiler's Farm story

The relevant part of the Weiler's Farm story starts in 1974,[2] when farm land in Grasmere was expropriated in order to provide for new 'coloured' and Indian township development south of Johannesburg. The farmowners moved on, but the farmworkers and their families – many of whom had lived and worked in the area for generations – had nowhere else to go. Also in Grasmere, but not expropriated, was a farm owned by two elderly brothers, the Weilers. They carried on only limited farming activity, and they allowed people who needed accommodation to stay on the farm, as long as they paid rent. The numbers grew. Despite repeated police raids and arrests from May 1981, it was estimated that by 1983 there were 300 people living on the farm.

In mid-1985 the Weiler brothers – now in their eighties – finally lost control of the situation. They abandoned the farm and went to live in Johannesburg. By this time, there were probably about 1 500 people living on the farm. With their departure the community grew even faster. An official survey in September 1987 counted 12 997 people.[3]

At the end of 1987, the area was declared an emergency squatting camp in terms of section 6 of the Prevention of Illegal Squatting Act,[4] and regulations were made for the area.[5] The government has refused to accept the permanency of the settlement, and insists that the community must move. Two alternatives have been offered to residents: land in a new informal settlement, established in terms of section 6A of the Act, some eight or nine kilometres further south at Orange Farm; or land in a formal extension of the Evaton township, some 20 kilometres south of Weiler's Farm. Although the government says that the community cannot remain at Weiler's Farm, it also says that it does not want a forced removal: the residents will be 'persuaded' to move.[6] Against this background I now turn to look at the first of the issues with which this paper is concerned, the abolition of influx control.

The Abolition of Influx Control

The crumbling of the grand apartheid dream

As is well known, government policy in the 1970s was that, in due course, all of the 'homelands' would become independent. Once that happened, there would be no more African citizens of South Africa. All Africans would find their political home, and exercise their political rights, in the 'homelands'. In this sense, their residence in South Africa was temporary.[7]

Fundamental policy imperatives flowed from this: the consolidation of the 'homelands'; the removal of 'black spots'; the prohibition on African ownership of land in the cities; and the pass laws, which had an organic connection with the 'homeland' policy. As the Director-General of the Department of Co-operation and Development crisply put it: 'You can't practise independence in a vacuum, if all your people are gone.'[8]

At some point, this policy changed, and the government finally abandoned the dream of grand apartheid as a complete solution to the problems of political power in South Africa. We can debate when that happened, and why – but that it happened is indisputable.[9] I would suggest that a number of the major 'reforms' of the mid-1980s really flowed from this change: the new attitude to 'black spot' removals; the acceptance of African freehold ownership in the cities; the restoration of South African citizenship to some of those who had been denationalized; and, at least in part, a rethink on the pass laws. On the last point, the connection was explicitly made in the *White Paper on Urbanization*:

> The Government has since accepted the permanence of Black people in the RSA .... The Government therefore states emphatically that influx control can no longer serve any constitutional objective.[10]

The Abolition of Influx Control Act and orderly urbanization

From the early 1980s, the authorities became alarmed by the growing settlement at Weiler's Farm. Their response was simple: prosecute the residents under the pass laws, and persuade or compel them to 'return' to the 'homelands'.

From 11 May 1981 to 11 May 1985 there were 23 pass raids at Weiler's Farm, and 686 arrests were made.[11] When one considers that towards the end of this period – during April 1984 – there were only about 350 people living in the area,[12] the scale of the arrests becomes clearer.

The official insistence that the residents go to the 'homelands' is very clearly indicated by the fact that the official survey of April 1984 classified the residents by 'homeland', with two families being classified as 'Oranje-Vaal Ontwikkelingsraad'. The homeland 'solution' is further indicated by the fact that during June and July 1984, representatives of QwaQwa and Transkei were taken to the farm to speak to the residents. It was reported to senior officials that after 'negotiation', the residents had agreed to 'return' to the 'homelands'.[13]

From this perspective, what changes have there been during the second part of the 1980s?

Early in 1986, following a report from the President's Council,[14] the government published its *White Paper on Urbanization*, which announced that influx control would be abolished. The *White Paper* was followed by the Abolition of Influx Control Act,[15] which repealed all of the laws traditionally regarded as forming part of the pass law system.

In announcing the abolition of influx control, the government said that it would follow a policy of 'orderly urbanization'.[16] The Minister of Constitutional Development and Planning stated that 'urbanization must be regulated in terms of ordinary and universal laws on housing, squatting, health, slums, township establishment and so forth'.[17]

This new policy, taken together with the failure to reverse more than a limited part of the denationalization of TBVC citizens,[18] led to a good deal of scepticism about whether influx control would really be abolished. The scepticism was hardly surprising. When the previous Minister had announced the 'Koornhof Bills', which would have sharpened and intensified influx control,[19] he cast himself in the role of Wilberforce the liberator, breaking the bondage of the pass laws. If, as John Kane-Berman once pointed out,[20] 'New deal for urban blacks' was the staple banner headline for some newspapers during the 1970s, 'New deal on pass laws' was beginning to look like the 1980s equivalent, with about the same degree of truth.

Thus Michael Robertson, in an article entitled '"Orderly Urbanization": the New Influx Control', suggested

> If any conclusions can be drawn at this early stage, it would seem that the state's new urbanization strategy... heralds relatively insignificant changes from past apartheid policies .... [T]he repeal of influx control merely shifts the focus to other exclusionary laws which purport to be, but in effect cannot be, non-racial.[21]

He was far from alone in this view, although some others were more cautious.[22]

Those of us who were sceptical about the consequences of the Abolition of Influx Control Act raised three main questions which would, it was thought, determine whether the state would really give up control of influx into the cities. Those issues were citizenship, the allocation of urban land for African housing, and the use of other control measures, in particular, the Prevention of Illegal Squatting Act.

Citizenship

As a result of the constitutional independence of the Transkei, Bophuthatswana, Venda and Ciskei (TBVC), some eight or nine million South Africans were deprived of their South African citizenship. By the operation of statute, they became aliens in South African law.[23] The potential consequences of this are drastic. No alien may enter or remain in South Africa unless he or she has a permanent or temporary residence permit.[24] It is a serious criminal offence to accommodate or employ an alien without the necessary permission.[25] According to the official survey in April 1984, a significant proportion of the Weiler's Farm community was potentially subject to this form of influx control through the Aliens Act: just over 50 per cent of the residents were described as being from one of the constitutionally independent territories.

Until 1986, the Aliens Act was of little immediate practical relevance to influx control, for two reasons. The first is that on the constitutional independence of each of the TBVC territories, the Minister of Home Affairs administratively[26] exempted all of the citizens of the territory from the need to obtain temporary residence permits to reside in South Africa.[27] TBVC citizens thus did not need any permission in terms of the Aliens Act to be in the Republic of South Africa: the real control was exercised through pass laws.

The second reason is that each of the four statutes conferring 'independence' on the TBVC territories[28] contained an identical provision which was believed to protect the rights of those TBVC citizens who were resident in South Africa on the date of 'independence'. It was widely thought that these provisions preserved the right of permanent residence in South Africa for millions of people.[29]

The validity of the concern about a new influx control through the Aliens Act became apparent immediately after the repeal of the pass laws.

During July 1986 the Department of Home Affairs produced a pamphlet which was 'intended as a guide to employers of alien Blacks'. The pamphlet pointed out that with the repeal of the Blacks (Urban Areas) Consolidation Act[30] and the Black Labour Act[31]

> the employment of alien Blacks is now governed by the provisions of the Aliens Act .... An alien is a person who is not a South African citizen. With certain exceptions citizens of Transkei, Bophuthatswana, Venda and Ciskei are aliens.

It set out the procedure to be followed by an employer who wished 'to recruit foreign black labour'. Such an employer –

> should in the first instance obtain a 'No objection to recruiting' recommendation from the nearest Divisional Inspector of the Department of Manpower. Thereafter he should approach the nearest office of the Department of Home Affairs which will consider the request to recruit a specified number of workers from a specific country.
>
> Before leaving his country of origin for South Africa a recruited worker must be in possession of a valid travel document, a written contract of employment which must provide for his return to his country of origin at the employer's expense and a full set of fingerprints .... In the case of workers from Transkei, Bophuthatswana, Venda or Ciskei who will not neccessarily enter South Africa through a port of entry, employers should ensure that after arrival they call on the nearest Regional or District office of the Department of Home Affairs to produce their documents and have their passports or travel documents endorsed ....
>
> No foreign Black may be taken into employment without the prior approval of the Department of Home Affairs, in the form of a work permit authorizing employment by a specific employer for a specified period. Change of employer without prior official approval is not permitted.

Any similarity with the migrant labour system is not entirely coincidental.

The pamphlet closed with the comforting reassurance that these provisions apply to all aliens, 'and not to Blacks only', and with a warning about the 'heavy penalties' for non-compliance.

This was clearly not an aberration. A circular letter to employers from the Director-General, Home Affairs, dated 30 September 1986, repeated and further explained this advice. It also referred to a recent announcement by the Minister of Manpower that there were an estimated 1,3 million foreigners working in the country illegally, and to an appeal by the Minister of Home Affairs to employers to assist his Department to resolve the illegal employment of aliens in South Africa.

The significance of citizenship as a possible means of influx control has now been further increased by the decision of the Appellate Division in the *Tshwete* case.[32] The effect of the majority judgment is that whatever the savings provisions in the independence-conferring statutes may mean – and it is not clear that they have any meaning at all – they do *not* preserve a right of permanent residence in South Africa. As a result, the legality of the residence of TBVC citizens in South Africa now hangs on a very slender thread, namely the Aliens Act exemptions.[33] These exemptions are fragile indeed, as they can be withdrawn or amended at any time by administrative action. There have been individual instances of the withdrawal of exemptions in the case of people regarded as undesirable. Tshwete is an example of this, as are the two National Union of Mineworkers officials who were 'deported' to the Transkei during 1986.[34]

Despite the Minister's dire warnings and the experience of individuals such as Tshwete, to the best of my knowledge there has been no attempt to bring a new migrant labour system into operation. There are a number of possible explanations: large employer organizations complained vigorously; there was a good deal of doubt about the legal validity of the requirements, as the Aliens Act exemptions probably have the effect that TBVC citizens do not need any permission to work in South Africa; and in any event, the system was simply unworkable. Particularly with the recent enactment of the Restoration of South African Citizenship Act, it became very difficult to know who were aliens, who were South African citizens, and who were aliens entitled to South African citizenship.

Neither at Weiler's Farm, nor anywhere else, has TBVC citizenship been regarded as an impediment to the right to reside or work in the area concerned. We may thus conclude that while the risk remains, and there is a need for continued vigilance, citizenship is not presently being used to produce a new system of influx control.

Land and housing

If there is not any evidence of citizenship being used as a means of limiting the number of people in the urban areas, what about land and housing? To what extent has that been an issue at Weiler's Farm?

For at least 25 years, the allocation of land and the provision of housing funds were used as an instrument of influx control.[35] By maintaining residential segregation and deliberately restricting the amount of urban land and housing available to Africans, the government sought to reinforce the legal mechanisms of influx control. Clearly one of the tests of the government's real purpose in its orderly urbanization strategy would be the extent to which it allocated further land for housing in the urban areas. Communities such as Weiler's Farm constituted a major test case in this regard.

In 1986, in a speech delivered on his behalf, the Deputy Director-General of the Department of Constitutional Development and Planning stated that four solutions would be applied in dealing with what he called the 'main problem' of the acquisition of more land: unoccupied land within existing (black) towns would be identified and made available for housing; 'bufferstrips' would be looked at and, where appropriate, used for residential areas; new land adjacent to existing towns would be identified; and new towns away from existing towns would be identified.[36]

New development areas[37] – that is, areas set aside for African ownership and occupation – are now frequently announced in the *Government Gazette*. In the Pretoria-Witwatersrand-Vereeniging (PWV) area, much of the new land has been in the third category, i.e. land adjacent to existing towns. The amount of land made available is significant, but it is nowhere near the amount actually needed.

As far as Weiler's Farm is concerned, both a consortium of planners appointed by the Minister of Constitutional Development and Planning, and the Transvaal Provincial Administration (TPA) recommended that it be developed as a permanent residential area. This was also the community's proposal. It would have meant allocation of land in the fourth category, i.e. a new area away from existing towns. The government rejected this. The major reason seems to have been a high degree of sensitivity to the views of white voters in the area.

This is far from an unusual result. In many areas the views of white voters in the vicinity seem to have played a decisive role in the determination of policy. Thus the proposed development at 'Norweto' (Diepsloot) to the north of Johannesburg has been considerably scaled down, and the area will be developed as a middle-class township.

The result is that where land has been developed in the fourth category, it has generally been well away from the city centres and white residential areas. Orange Farm, Motherwell (Port Elizabeth) and Khayelitsha (Cape Town) are examples of this.

However, whatever its limitations, additional land in the PWV area has been acquired by the government, and has been offered to the Weiler's Farm residents. There has not been an attempt to use the shortage of land to compel them to leave the urban areas. Similar land has also been offered to other 'squatters' in the Johannesburg area.

What conclusions can one draw? I would suggest five: that the government has made available substantial amounts of additional land for housing; that it is not nearly enough; that the votes of white people in the area are often a decisive factor; that new areas are generally situated some distance from the city centre and white residential areas; and that there is not really any evidence of a deliberate policy of restricting the land made available in order to keep down the number of people in the urban areas.

Prevention of 'squatting' and other control measures

When the Abolition of Influx Control Act was introduced, many commentators noted that at the same time as it repealed the old pass laws, it significantly increased the penalties for contraventions of the Prevention of

Illegal Squatting Act.[38] Not unreasonably, many suspected that the Act would become a major means of limiting the number of people in the urban areas. The subsequent enactment of the Prevention of Illegal Squatting Amendment Act[39] has strengthened this suspicion.

In my opinion, this is a mistaken view. The 1988 Act has to be seen in its context: from the government's point of view, a social crisis in the cities. One of the effects of the pass laws was that the government could turn a blind eye to the vast shortage of housing in the cities. Many of the people who did not have proper accommodation were 'illegally' in the cities. As far as the planners were concerned, they were not there at all – obviously no provision would be made for them. This unrecognized group of people was enormous: many took the view that in order to know the real African population of the major cities, one ought to take the official (legal) figure and at least double it.[40] With the repeal of the pass laws, the state of the shortage of land and housing finally came into the open as the people concerned no longer needed to pretend that they were not there. Where vacant land was available – as at Weiler's Farm – people were now able to move out of their overcrowded situations (for example in township backyards) and provide their own homes. This, together with the departure of the Weilers, is the reason for the very rapid growth of the settlement from 1 500 in mid-1985 to about 13 000 in September 1987.

The government's response to this crisis of a loss of control was entirely typical. It further penalized the conduct which was troubling it, it assumed vast administrative powers, and it attempted to exclude judicial control of official actions. The analogy with the state of emergency is obvious: the Prevention of Illegal Squatting Amendment Act is to the housing crisis what the emergency regulations are to the political crisis.

The 1988 amending Act is a dreadful piece of legislation but it is not designed to reduce or limit the number of people in the urban areas. Rather, it is an instrument of control – a means of ensuring that whenever it considers it necessary, the government has the power to shift groups of people around without interference from the courts.

Summary: the abolition of influx control and orderly urbanization

In my view, there is no evidence that the new policy of orderly urbanization has been a form of influx control in disguise. Certainly, that has not been the experience of the Weiler's Farm community. The new policy is to control – through the allocation of land, through the use of the Prevention of Illegal Squatting Act, through other measures. It reflects an attempt to control the shape and structure of the metropolitan areas, rather than an attempt to limit the number of African people living in them. Doug Hindson's conclusion on the President's Council report is apposite:

> [C]ritics who probe no further than the report's parentage underestimate its departure from traditional apartheid. The report does not propose traditional influx control in disguise. It reflects a strategic shift in urbanization policy.[41]

This is of course not just an interesting academic distinction. It has real practical consequences. A mis-analysis of the policy can lead to fundamental errors, for example in assisting a threatened 'squatter' community to make strategic decisions about how it will respond to pressures from government.

What I have said so far provides (I hope) a context for understanding shifts in policy on forced removals, and planning a response to them.

The first point that emerges is that the 'homeland' imperative is no longer a major factor in urban removals. Again, Weiler's Farm illustrates the point: while the government wants to move the community, there is no suggestion whatsoever that they should be moved to the 'homelands'.

Oukasie (Brits) very clearly illuminates this issue. Previously, the dominant context of the removal was the 'homeland' policy. In 1971 part of the Oukasie community was moved to Mothutlung, which was later incorporated into Bophuthatswana. Subsequently, the rest of the community was told that it would have to move to Lethlabile, which was also scheduled for incorporation into Bophuthatswana.[42] During 1985, however, it was announced[43] that Lethlabile would no longer be incorporated (and in 1988 legislation was enacted to give effect to this decision[44]) – but that the Oukasie community would nevertheless have to move.

It is clear that the 'homeland' policy is no longer any part of the reason for the threatened Oukasie removal. The official reason is the unsatisfactory conditions at Oukasie. The real reason is that 'white' Brits has extended to the very borders of Oukasie, which is now said to hinder the further development of the town. White voters do not want Oukasie there, therefore it must be removed.

This combination of group areas thinking and sensitivity to white voters is surely the key to the major removals carried out or threatened during the past few years: think of Kabah (Langa), Lawaaikamp, Port Nolloth, and now Weiler's Farm. The shift in policy emphasis raises two major issues and opportunities.

First, it seems that decisions will be made on the basis of an ad hoc weighing of the different political and other costs, rather than on the basis of any fundamental ideological position. To the extent that the costs of removal are increased and outweigh the (white) political costs of reprieve, removals are unlikely to take place.

Secondly, it seems that an area's status as formal township or 'illegal squatter' community is likely to be much less significant than in the past. Thus, Oukasie must go despite its status as a formal township; conversely, if Weiler's Farm had been adjacent to an existing 'black town', the community might well have been allowed to remain there, even though they were 'illegal squatters'.

This analysis of the circumstances in which urban forced removals are likely to occur leads me to the second concern of the paper: the mechanics of such removals. This is the subject of the following sections.

Methods of Removal

Methods of removal vary tremendously, and could be the subject of a separate paper. Here I can make only some very summary remarks on the main legal mechanisms.

The legal mechanism used in the Kabah case was a Supreme Court application by the local authority, in which all of the residents were joined as respondents. The court granted an order for removal.[45] The basis of the judgment is not entirely clear. It was not a true vindicatory action, as the applicant was not the owner of the land in question. Was it a sort of quasi-vindicatory action which vests in local authorities? The judgment does not tell us, and we shall have to wait and see. There are certainly likely to be further judgments on the issue as there is reason to believe that this is a method favoured by central government.

Another mechanism is the use of the summary demolition procedures in the Prevention of Illegal Squatting Act,[46] which confer the widest powers on provincial government, local government and owners. Those wishing to use this method face two problems.[47]

First, while this is a very convenient means of 'mopping up' small settlements which spring up from time to time, it is not that easy with large and established communities, as widespread publicity is likely. Each removal has to be specially and publicly justified in the light of current state policy that there will be no more forced removals. And one cannot always carry out the removal swiftly before there is 'interference' from the courts.

The second difficulty with this method is that it is not certain that the 1988 amendments to the Act achieved one of the intended results, namely to prevent the courts protecting 'squatters' whose homes are threatened with unlawful demolition. This is partly because in the process of requiring that the applicant first show bad faith on the part of the spoliator, the legislation removed the often onerous requirement of showing a right or title to the land. More fundamentally, and as is hinted at in the *Vena* case,[48] it is not at all clear that unlawful demolitions are actions 'under' the section,[49] and therefore protected by the ouster clause. In addition, it is worth noting that the courts seem to be taking an increasingly sympathetic attitude towards people caught in the trap of the Act.[50]

A third method of achieving removals will obviously be the administrative removal procedures under section 5 of the Prevention of Illegal Squatting Act. Thus far I have seen it used only in very limited circumstances but it will be difficult to deal with the wide discretion given to magistrates to order removal. It seems that the section will have to be construed in the context of the Act, and it will have to be argued that the powers granted to the magistrate may be used only to further the general policy and purposes of the Act.[51]

Again, Weiler's Farm provides us with some lessons. Although all of these methods were available to the authorities, and although the authorities were determined that the community should be removed, none of them has – as yet – been used. There is a clear preference for other methods, including negotiation – although that is often a very euphemistic description for a process that involves sitting around a table and giving instructions. However, the expressed preference for agreed solutions does offer some space and opportunities.

The problem of local authorities

The official preference for 'negotiated' removals raises the problem of local authorities and participation in official structures. Again, Weiler's Farm has lessons for us.

Initially the community elected an informal committee to represent it. To a limited degree this committee was recognized by the TPA. When the area was declared an emergency camp, the regulations made provision for the election of a committee. The committee would have no executive powers, but would only represent the residents in dealings with officials.

The question of participation immediately posed itself, and the usual questions were debated. Ultimately it was decided to participate. Part of the reason for this was that all the 'formal' committee would be required to do was what the informal committee was already doing. It would have no duty to carry out policy or decisions not made by the community.

The committee has achieved a good deal, but its position has increasingly come under attack, because it is seen by some as the agent of the TPA rather than the agent of the community. This perception has been fostered by some astonishingly clumsy and inept behaviour by officials.

Now the community and the committee face a new problem of participation. At the new area which has been designated for them, provision is to be made for a committee with wider powers than the existing committee, but less power (and fewer duties) than a black local authority. If the residents move, the question of participation will again arise. Where, if anywhere, are they to draw the line?

The same question has arisen at Koster, a western Transvaal town under threat of removal. The official town committee supported the removal, which was opposed by the residents' association. In October 1988 the residents' association decided to participate in the municipal election, and swept the boards. Now the official authority in the area – the town committee – is opposed to the removal. There can be no doubt that this will make the removal more difficult to achieve. What the other results of participation will be, one can only speculate.

This question will grow in importance as more and more powers are delegated to the black local authorities. It was easy to decide not to participate in the Urban Bantu Councils of the 1970s – in 1976 the students derided them as the 'Useless Boys Clubs' for good reason. Now, I suspect, the issue has become much more complex.

This raises crisply the question of the administration of township housing.

The administration of township housing

With the enactment of the Conversion of Certain Rights to Leasehold Act,[52] the powers of local authorities have increased considerably – and so, one can confidently predict, will allegations of corruption, and litigation about the limits of the councils' powers.

The Act (which came into effect on 1 January 1989)[53] repealed the old township regulations[54] in their entirety. That is the good news. The problem is that those regulations provided certain limited but important security for the holders of residential permits, the people who 'rented' council houses. For example, their tenancy could not be terminated except on specified grounds;[55] and on the death of the permit holder, the family often had a legal right to preference in the allocation of the house.[56] None of these rights is saved in the Act: the holders of residential permits have simply become tenants of the council.[57] The Act is silent on the grounds on which the lease may be cancelled by the council, and on what notice.

It requires little imagination and even less experience to anticipate that some councillors will seize on the opportunities created by this 'deregulation'. Given the heavy demand for houses, there will be a strong temptation to cancel a tenancy and sell the house to a prospective buyer. The opportunities for corruption will increase dramatically, and so, I suggest, will the corruption itself. It will be necessary to attempt again to persuade the courts that there is an implied condition in a local authority lease that it will not be cancelled except on reasonable grounds; or alternatively, that a local authority may not act unreasonably or arbitrarily, in exercising 'commercial' as well as 'administrative' functions.[58]

Disputes over rent and service charges have been a recurring theme of the 1980s. The massive rent boycott of the middle of the decade continues in some areas. Although the boycott is probably strongest in the Pretoria-Witwatersrand-Vereeniging area, the policy issues which it raises are of relevance almost everywhere – both in the cities and in the platteland dorps. I cannot hope to deal adequately here with the causes of, possible solutions to, and likely outcomes of the boycott. The issues are superbly described and analysed in the recent report by Planact for the Soweto Delegation.[59] All I can do is summarize some of the findings on issues which are of particular relevance.

The report concludes that despite the extremely poor quality of the services, most Sowetans cannot afford the current service charges. For this and other reasons, Soweto has an enormous deficit, currently not less than R700 million, of which about R200 million is attributable to arrear rents and service charges. At the core of the financial problem is the 'apartheid city': unlike white residents of Johannesburg, Soweto residents do not have their rates subsidized by the income generated from the city's commercial, mining and industrial base. Any lasting solution will have to address this issue.

The report highlights another possible outcome of the crisis. If a successful attempt is made to enforce payment of service charges, the inevitable result will be to force the poorest sections of the community out of the townships. They will become the new 'squatters'. If this happens we will see a major new form of removal: economic removals. They will be very difficult to resist other than through community organization, precisely because they are individualized.

Meanwhile, argument continues to rage over the reasonableness of rents and service charges. At least in the older townships, the interest on and redemption of the initial capital cost of the land and houses must have been paid many times over. Ordinarily, this would of course be irrelevant. Tenants never acquire a right to ownership of the land they occupy, no matter how much rent they have paid over the years. However, community leaders have argued that because Africans were prevented by law from buying land in the cities, and were compelled to be tenants of the local authorities, their position is different. Now that ownership is legally possible, they should be given the ownership which they would have acquired had they been legally able to do so.

The argument is morally and logically compelling. I suspect that, in principle, many senior policy-makers would not be unhappy to see this happen. It would tie in with the policy of promoting home ownership. The cost would be limited, as in the older townships house rentals are only a small part of the overall charge. In any event, if people are paying nothing at the moment, and this could be part of a deal whereby they agree to start paying service charges, the local authorities would end up receiving more than they are receiving now. Finally, the recent decision of the Appellate Division in the *Mngomezulu* case[60] has the result that a significant proportion of existing house rents are probably unlawful, and has immeasurably complicated the prospect of recovering rents everywhere.

The stage seems set for a comprehensive negotiated solution, and this is what the Soweto Delegation in particular is trying to achieve. However, there is widespread suspicion that the Joint Management Committee (JMC) is attempting to undermine and obstruct these negotiations, presumably because of the political profile and affiliations of the members of the Delegation.[61]

This raises the important question of the role of the security management system in major urban policy decisions. The role of the 'security forces' at Weiler's Farm could be the topic of an entire paper. Here I will make only two points. First, security forces have displayed astonishing arrogance and appear unaccountable. For example, both police and South African Defence Force representatives have simply refused to come to meetings between the TPA and the committee to discuss complaints about official conduct. Secondly, it seems clear that major decisions about 'squatters' and land allocation in the PWV have been processed through the JMC system. This is by no means unique. It is widely believed that the decision to remove Langa/Kabah, after a negotiated solution had apparently been arrived at, had its origins in the security management systems.[62] Paul Hendler has recorded a similar role played by the security forces in Tembisa and the Vaal.[63]

As we enter the next decade, one of the most intriguing questions is whether the post-P W Botha era will see some reduction of the policy role of the security apparatus. I have little doubt that if this does happen, it will have a deep impact on urban land issues, and mainly for the better.

Some Conclusions

Where does all this leave us? What lessons can we draw as the 1980s come to a close? I would suggest five major lessons from this necessarily selective overview.

First, it is necessary that community groups, community workers and lawyers closely analyse and understand the changing state strategies, drawing on the basis of their experience on the ground. Properly understood, the abolition of the pass laws represented a major popular victory achieved after decades of struggle and at great cost and sacrifice. To portray it (as some did) as a cunning victory for the state is disparaging of those who fought the pass laws for so long, and suggests that the state is so powerful that limited but significant victories are not possible. It can also lead to errors of judgment in determining strategic responses to the changing urban environment.

Secondly, the crumbling of the grand apartheid dream has opened up spaces and opportunities. The more pragmatic – and often ad hoc – approach of those in power makes negotiated solutions to practical problems more feasible than has been the case in the past; that is if 'security' considerations are not permitted to dominate, as they often have. In many cases, the decision will depend at least in part on a weighing of the political costs of the different alternatives, rather than on measuring the alternatives against fixed ideological criteria.

Thirdly, these changes make the question of community organization a central issue. Increasingly, this will be something which lawyers ignore at their peril. Our professional training and experience ill-equip us for the roles we have to play, and we all need to give much more attention to how to deal with the problems which arise in representing communities as opposed to individuals.[64]

Fourth, the courts have shown an increasing willingness to consider the claims of those affected by 'race' or 'apartheid' legislation.[65] This naturally opens up possibilities for the defence of communities under threat.

Finally, and despite what I have said about a growing pragmatism on the part of the state, the fundamental obstacle remains the basic political structures which determine urban land issues. Again, Weiler's Farm tells the story. There can be little doubt that the reason for the government's insistence on moving the community has been its concern about the response of (white) voters in the area to the existence of Weiler's Farm. Similarly, there can be little doubt that if the 13 000 residents of Weiler's Farm had the parliamentary franchise the policy decision would have been very different.

Notes

1 This issue is also discussed by Sutcliffe, Todes & Walker in this volume at 86.

2 This history is derived from J Adler, M Beetge & S Sher 'The "New" Illegality: Squatters with Urban Rights but No Houses' (1984) 2 no 2 *Indicator SA Urban Monitor* 8; J Adler, M Beetge & S Sher 'Efflux in the Grip of Influx Controls: The Informal Settlement of Grasmere' (1985) 3 no 1 *Indicator SA Urban Monitor* 6; an unpublished manuscript by Mark Phillips; and my own notes and observations over the several years during which I have represented the Weiler's Farm community.

3 Department of National Health and Population Development *Verslag oor 'n Sosio-Ekonomiese opname te Weilersfarm* (September 1987) 1.

4 Act 52 of 1951.

5 Board Notice 85 of 1987, *GG* 11084 of 31 December 1987.

6 See the Deputy Minister's statement in response to a question in Parliament: *House of Assembly Debates* 4 August 1987 col 463: '[F]orced removals are contrary to Government policy; the squatters will therefore have to be persuaded to move to the new site.'

7 *White Paper on Urbanization* 1986 para 5.1.1.

8 Quoted in H Zille *Political power and poverty: An Examination of the Role and Effect of Influx Control in South Africa* Carnegie Conference Paper no 83 (1984) 38.

9 See, for example, the State President's speeches in *House of Assembly Debates* 25 January 1985 col 14 and 19 April 1985 col 3805.

10 Para 5.1.2.

11 Letter dated 23 May 1985 from Chief Director, Orange-Vaal Development Board, to Chief Commissioner, Bloemfontein.

12 Ibid. In considering the size of Weiler's Farm during this period, one should also take into account that, according to the letter referred to in note 10, an additional 49 families (250 people?), who had been found to qualify to live in the area under the pass law, were resettled in Evaton. The total number of people who lived at Weiler's Farm during the period was therefore about 600 rather than the 350 found there at a particular time. One presumes that few, if any, of the arrests were of people who qualified to live in the area, and thus the intensity of police action is better reflected by the comparison of the figure of 350 inhabitants against 686 arrests which is used in the text.

13 Unsurprisingly, nothing came of this.

14 *Report of the Committee for Constitutional Affairs of the President's Council on an Urbanization Strategy for the Republic of South Africa* PC 3/85.

15 Act 68 of 1986.

16 White Paper on Urbanization passim. The policy was also described as 'positive' and 'planned' urbanization, but it was the word 'orderly' which caught public attention.

17 *House of Assembly Debates* 9 June 1986 col 7662.

18 According to the Minister of Home Affairs, it was estimated that the Restoration of South African Citizenship Act 73 of 1986 would affect 1 751 400 TBVC citizens: *House of Assembly Debates* 23 June 1986 col 9375. This was somewhere between 20 percent and 25 percent of those who had been denationalized.

19 Black Community Development Bill B112/82; and the Orderly Movement and Settlement of Black Persons Bill B113/82.

20 J Kane-Berman *Soweto: Black Revolt, White Reaction* (Johannesburg: Ravan Press 1978) 231.

21 In A Rycroft (ed) *Race and the Law in South Africa* (Cape Town: Juta 1987) 107 at 116.

22 H Schoombee & D Davis 'Abolishing Influx Control – Fundamental or Cosmetic Change?' (1986) 2 *South African Journal on Human Rights* 208; and see my 'Influx Control in the Western Cape: From Pass Laws to Passports?' (1986) 11 (8) *South African Labour Bulletin* 34-41.

23 See the definition of 'alien' in s 1 of the Aliens Act 1 of 1937: 'an alien is a person who is not a South African citizen'.

24 Section 2 Aliens Act. This prohibition is subject to certain qualifications which are not relevant here.

25 Section 5 *ter* Aliens Act.

26 Acting in terms of his powers under s 7 *bis* of the Aliens Act.

27 Simultaneously, acting in terms of his powers under s 40(2)(a) of the Admission of Persons to the Republic Regulation Act 59 of 1972, he also exempted them from the need to have visas in order to enter the Republic of South Africa.

28 Status of the Transkei Act 100 of 1976; Status of Bophuthatswana Act 89 of 1977; Status of Venda Act 107 of 1979; Status of Ciskei Act 110 of 1981.

29 This is how the provision in the Status of Bophuthatswana Act was interpreted in *Ex Parte Moseneke* 1979 (4) SA 884 (T).

30 Act 25 of 1945.

31 Act 67 of 1964.

32 *Tshwete v Minister of Home Affairs* 1988 (4) SA 586 (A).

33 In *Tshwete's* case, the lawfulness of his residence was saved by the provisions of s 12(1)(a) of the Aliens Act. However, since the amendment of the definition of 'domicile' by s 1(a) of the Matters Concerning Admission to and Residence in the Republic Amendment Act 53 of 1986, this source of a right of permanent residence is no longer available. For a full discussion see my paper 'On Citizenship and Residence Rights: Taking Words Seriously' (1989) 5 *South African Journal on Human Rights* 37.

34 *The Star* 12 December 1986.

35 A Chaskalson & S Duncan *Influx Control: The Pass Laws* Carnegie Conference Paper No 81 (1984) 12.

36 H P Fourie *How the Government's Urbanization Strategy Will Work* (Roneo) delivered at a meeting of the Cape Town Chamber of Commerce, 21 August 1986, 3-4.

37 In terms of s 33(3) of the Black Communities Development Act 4 of 1984.

38 See for example Robertson cited above note 21.

39 Act 104 of 1988.

40 A useful list of the varying estimates of the population of Soweto is given in Planact *The Soweto Rent Boycott* (1989) 20.

41 D Hindson *Pass Controls and the Urban African Proletariat in South Africa* (Johannesburg: Ravan Press 1987) 94.

42 Borders of Particular States Extension Act 2 of 1980, Schedule 2 para (b)(i).

43 By the Minister of Constitutional Development and Planning; see the record in *Mahlaela v De Beer NO* 1986 (4) SA 782 (T) at 788.

44 The Excision of Released Areas Act 54 of 1988 makes provision for the development of Letlhabile as a town within the Republic of South Africa. Strangely, however, Letlhabile has still not been removed from the Schedule to the Borders of Particular States Extension Act, even though that Act was also amended during 1988 (by the Borders of Particular States Extension Amendment Act 59 of 1988).

45 *KwaNobuhle Town Council v Andries* 1988 (2) SA 796 (SEC).

46 Section 3B.

47 See also O'Regan in this volume at 174-6.

48 *George Municipality v Vena* 1989 (2) SA 263 (A) at 266E.

49 Compare *Minister of Law and Order v Hurley* 1986 (3) SA 568 (A).

50 Here I have in mind cases such as *Vena*, both in the Appellate Division and the Court a quo (*Vena v George Municipality* 1987 (4) SA 29 (C)), *Ntshwaqela v Chairman, Western Cape Regional Services Council* 1988 (3) SA 218 (C) (upheld on appeal, unreported), *Munisipaliteit van Port Nolloth v Xhalisa* CPD Case no 8580/88, unreported, and *S v Lotu* 1989 (2) SA 279 (T).

51 In the same way as the power of incorporation in s 1(2) of the National States Constitution Act 21 of 1971 was interpreted and limited in *Mathebe v Regering van die Republiek van Suid-Afrika* 1988 (3) SA 667 (A).

52 Act 81 of 1988.

53 GN 226, *GG* 11648 of 30 December 1988.

54 GN R1036 of 14 June 1968, as amended.

55 Regulation 7(4)(a), Chapter 2.

56 Regulation 17(2), Chapter 2.

57 Section 6(1)(a).

58 Compare *Scholtz v Cape Divisional Council* 1987 (1) SA 68 (C).

59 Planact cited above note 40.

60 *Mngomezulu v Soweto City Council* 1989 (2) SA 331 (A).

61 Planact cited above note 40 6-7, 30-1.

62 M Swilling *'Because your yard is too big': Squatter Struggles, the Local State and Dual Power in Uitenhage, 1985-1986* (1988) 31.

63 P Hendler *Urban Policy and Housing* (Johannesburg: South African Institute of Race Relations 1988) 14, 33, 38.

64 See Claassens in this volume at 61 and Haysom at 115ff.

65 This is not the occasion for an extended discussion of this issue. The paradox of the apparently differing approaches to 'race' and 'security' cases is tangentially raised in my 'Lawlessness in South Africa' (1988) 4 *South African Journal on Human Rights* 139, and is also referred to in D Davis & H Corder 'A Long March: Administrative Law in the Appellate Division' (1988) 4 *South African Journal on Human Rights* 281.

MICHAEL SUTCLIFFE, ALISON TODES AND NORAH WALKER[1]

Managing the Cities: An Examination of State Urbanization Policies Since 1986

Introduction

The 1986 *White Paper on Urbanization*[2] marked a substantial shift in the state's approach to urbanization. The most significant feature of this shift was that the state, for the first time in many decades, recognized that African urbanization was inevitable and in some respects desirable. Its previous policy of containing and deflecting urbanization by way of coercive influx control measures was, therefore, to be replaced with a strategy of planned 'orderly urbanization'. In its implementation, this strategy has sometimes been perceived as ad hoc and as indicative of the absence of a coherent state policy towards urbanization.

The purpose of this paper is to make sense of the state's current approach to urbanization. More particularly we attempt to assess the extent to which an urbanization policy exists and, secondly, to examine how it is manifested on the ground. We argue that although the *White Paper* and its various associated policies (for example the restructured policies on local government and housing) embody the central elements of an urbanization policy they appear ad hoc on the ground. One of the primary reasons for this is that the policies allow for regional variations and bring into play a greater number of significant agents than was previously the case. Further, state action has shifted from attempting to control all aspects of urbanization to managing the spatial form of urbanization and its political consequences. In contrast to earlier interpretations of the *White Paper* and, to a degree, to statements contained within it, we argue that there appears to be a shift away from considering urbanization policy as a form of influx control. To some extent then, state policy has moved beyond the provisions of the *White*

Paper. This does not, however, mean that state policy accords with popular demands. While there have been significant concessions in terms of access to urban areas, access to land, housing, services and facilities remains problematic for most Africans, and is increasingly so for the poor.

In attempting to understand state urbanization policy, we have drawn together current evidence on the main patterns and processes of urbanization in the metropolitan areas, and of the actions of the state and other important agents at this level.

In what follows, we outline the main forces which led to the current urbanization policy, the central features of that policy and its application in practice. Finally we analyse what this means for Africans wishing to live in urban areas.

Part I: Historical Context

The relative political quiescence of the 1960s is important in tracing the immediate context of urbanization policy in the 1980s, for it made it possible for the state to restructure the pattern of urbanization, and to establish what were to become the building blocks of state reform in the 1980s. During this period state urban policy was primarily directed towards displacing African urbanization to the bantustans. Not only were Africans removed from white farms to the bantustans but some millions of Africans were displaced through the destruction of shanty towns, forced removals to bantustans and the gerrymandering of bantustan borders. At the same time, few houses were provided for Africans living in white areas.

The resulting spatial organization has persisted. On the one hand, a considerable proportion of the increasing population of the bantustans (from 4,7 million in 1960 to 11,3 million in 1980) occurred in formal and informal ('fringe') settlements adjacent to, or within striking distance of, white metropolitan and urban areas.[3] On the other hand, there emerged a pattern of 'rings' of African settlement surrounding white metropolitan areas, some up to 250 kilometres away[4] containing commuters and irregular workers in metropolitan areas. These settlements contain fewer daily commuters and permanent workers as the distance from the metropolitan areas increases.

State policy to contain urbanization in white urban areas included parallel measures such as industrial decentralization and the development of commercial agriculture. Such schemes, it was hoped, would create employment opportunities in bantustan areas and non-metropolitan white urban areas close to the bantustans. While these schemes did not create many jobs they contributed to the production of an uneven spatial surface through the creation of low-wage and low-skilled employment in these areas.[5]

The policies of containing African urbanization in white areas, while partially successful, could not ignore the fact that the African urban population was increasing. These policies simply curbed the rate at which the African urban population grew in non-bantustan areas. For example, Spies and Biggs[6] indicate that the percentage growth rates for various census periods from 1936 to 1980 ranged as follows: 4,0 to 6,6 to 4,5 to 3,9 to 3,2 per cent per annum. By 1980, however, African urbanization could no longer be controlled. Migration to urban areas and the natural increase of African populations had the combined effect of increasing the growth rate from 3,2 per cent per annum before 1980 to approximately 5,5 per cent per annum in the post-1980 period, a scale almost unprecedented in South Africa's history. This led demographic experts to suggest that, for example, the Pretoria-Witwatersrand-Vereeniging (PWV) population would by the year 2020 reach the current population level of Yokohama-Tokyo (presently the largest metropolitan complex in the world). By 1985-6 most experts were suggesting that the rate of African migration to urban areas was of the order of 6,2 per cent per annum and would continue at this level at least until the year 2000.[7]

Estimates and predictions of high urbanization rates seemed to be supported by the rapid development of squatter settlements in the early 1980s, particularly Crossroads in the Cape. The resistance of squatters to removal to bantustan areas, and the high rates of urbanization, were formative in the state's acceptance of the *White Paper* in 1986. By the mid-1980s it was clear that the state could no longer control African urbanization. But changes in state policy towards urbanization depended on more than high rates of urbanization alone.

Changes within state policy towards urbanization can be seen as a response to the broader political and economic crises facing the state in the 1970s and 80s, and to the shift in the political orientation of the state towards business since the late 1970s. These pressures and changed conditions have underpinned a process of 'reform' which has altered the basis of state urban policy.

A number of analysts of the South African state[8] have suggested that state reform can be understood in terms of two phases: an earlier period beginning in 1979 in which the state attempted to implement a series of limited reforms associated with the Riekert[9] and Wiehahn[10] Commissions, and a later phase characterized by an emphasis on deregulation, privatization and orderly urbanization.[11]

The earlier period focussed on creating division and differentiation amongst the African population along social and spatial lines. The Riekert

Commission in particular, attempted to divide the African population into 'urban outsiders' with permanent rights to live in urban areas, and 'rural outsiders' who would have even less access to urban areas than before. This strategy involved granting concessions on property rights and labour mobility to 'insiders', while 'outsiders' would be kept out through a reinforcement of policies of industrial decentralization and homeland development.

These reforms were also associated with concessions to workers and trade unions (in terms of the Wiehahn Report), and with the beginnings of a process of restructuring both the central and the local state. The principles of 'own' and 'general' affairs provided a basis for incorporating 'coloured' and Indian groups into a 'tricameral' parliament. While ethnically defined groups would have their own structures, there would be joint decision-making powers. Africans became a 'general affair', but their political aspirations were to be accommodated in bantustans or in Black Local Authorities (BLAs)[12] in urban areas.

These policies emerged in a context in which the state was beginning to restructure its role. The reform process has involved the state withdrawing from a generalized and direct role in the economy, particularly in relation to the provision of social and infrastructural services. While state expenditure on these services has not necessarily declined, the state has increasingly attempted to place greater emphasis on regional and local government, and on the role of the private sector and the market. It has been argued that a greater role for the market would provide an important force for differentiation as well as removing the 'heat' from the state politically and economically.[13]

However, while the policies of privatization and devolution of authority to local and regional government were present in the early 1980s, they have only really come to the fore since 1986.

By the mid-1980s it was apparent that the reforms associated with the Riekert Commission, in particular controls on urbanization, were unworkable. Not only had it become practically impossible to regulate urbanization, but there were pressures from both capital and popular organizations for more fundamental change. The reforms of the early 1980s generated new contradictions as BLAs faced fiscal crises and as privatization brought declining real incomes and living conditions in urban areas to the fore. An increasing number of political challenges to the state deepened the crisis. Mass-based (particularly urban) struggles rejected Botha's reforms. At the same time the growing strength of the unions, together with the increasing effectiveness of the African National Congress through its Political Military

Councils, forced the state to abandon some of its earlier policy directions. Most important from our perspective was the dropping of the Riekert insider-outsider divide, and the acceptance of Africans as citizens of South Africa and as residents in urban areas. It is worth noting that business, particularly through the Urban Foundation, played a key role in lobbying for the lifting of influx control. For business, influx control no longer served any economic purpose, was excessively costly, and added to political instability.

The 1986 *White Paper on Urbanization* was one of the key documents of the new phase of reform. It formally scrapped influx control and laid a far stronger foundation for the policies of devolution, deregulation and privatization which had emerged in the earlier period. Policies of deregulation and privatization were given expression in the Black Communities Development Act of 1984 (as amended in late 1986)[14] and associated subsequent legislation as well as in housing policy and a number of other areas.

Significantly, the policies of deregulation and privatization, at least in relation to housing, have come to be seen as important elements of a renewed growth path focussed on 'inward industrialization'.[15] It is argued that housing is an important area where the 'black market' can be tapped. From this perspective, state policy must strive to remove the obstacles to private sector involvement in housing. This emphasis is clearly reflected in the Black Communities Development Act of 1984 as amended.

Further, since 1986, the state has begun a process of 'bottom up' constitutional reform placing the resurrected BLAs on a new footing either through state subsidy or through their incorporation into a system of Regional Services Councils (RSCs). These authorities and the restructured Provincial Administrations have come to play an increasingly important role in the urbanization process.

The period since 1986 also saw the establishment of the National Security Management System (NSMS) and a greater role for repressive and non-administrative forms of intervention in urban development. A number of analysts have argued that the NSMS championed a strategy of 'winning the hearts and minds' of the people through socio-economic reforms and improvements.[16] However, as we show later, this particular strategy has been used in only a limited number of highly visible cases, whereas more repressive forms of NSMS intervention in fact occurred on a far more generalized basis.

Part II: The White Paper on Urbanization

The *White Paper on Urbanization* laid the basis for a new approach to urbanization, reflecting the conditions of the mid-1980s. It represented a major reversal of the past policy of containing and deflecting urbanization, and instead set out to develop a broad framework for managing urbanization. It drew together and reflected many of the policy strands which had already been established in the early 1980s: the principle of 'spatial balance' and industrial decentralization, the emphasis on privatization, the devolution of authority to lower tiers of government, constitutional restructuring and the principle of 'own affairs', and the development and incorporation of a black petty bourgeoisie. The particular contribution of the *White Paper* was to set out a strategy of planned 'orderly urbanization'.

The *White Paper* defines 'orderly urbanization' as

> the freedom of movement of all citizens and also refers to the operation of economic and social forces and continent obligations. It means further that the process of urbanization must be ordered, planned and directed by predominantly indirect forms of control, such as incentive and restrictive measures, as well as by direct measures comprising legislation and ordinances.[17]

So while the *White Paper* accepted the principle of freedom of movement, and the necessity or even the desirability of urbanization, it emphasized that this process should be 'ordered'. At the time its critics[18] suggested that while orderly urbanization was a major departure from previous policies, the emphasis was still on controlling the form of urbanization. Whereas in the past the emphasis was on keeping Africans in the homelands, the *White Paper* attempted to channel migration to the urban periphery, particularly to decentralization and deconcentration points. The mechanisms through which this was to occur included a variety of direct and indirect controls.

The most important way in which direct measures are defined in the *White Paper* is in relation to 'approved accommodation'. The controls include measures to contain illegal squatting and the development of slums, and also allow the state to determine where and how development occurs through land-use planning and the allocation of land.

Indirect controls, on the other hand, refer essentially to market forces – exaggerated or distorted by policies to increase the cost of living in metropolitan areas and to encourage industrial development outside metropolitan core areas. Measures of this sort cited in the *White Paper* include spatially differentiated Regional Services Council (RSC) taxes, full cost recovery for housing and other services, and provision for a differentiation of service levels between areas.

The *White Paper*, however, also refers to 'incentive' measures. These essentially relate to the development of land and creation of employment through the policy of industrial decentralization. In effect, critics argued, the *White Paper* depends upon and reinforces the pattern of spatially uneven development which had been created in the past.[19] This interpretation is certainly consistent with a number of statements in the *White Paper*, and, importantly, with the definition of 'orderly urbanization' itself. However, the *White Paper* is a rather vague and even contradictory document: it allows for a wide range of interpretations. While making extensive reference to the regional development policy, for example, it also emphasizes development in and around metropolitan areas, at times even arguing for a more compact form of urban development.[20] Since the publication of the *White Paper*, as we argue in later sections, implementation of the policy has tended to follow the latter rather than the former path, although it is quite possible that the 'uneven spatial surface' is exerting an influence on actual patterns of urbanization.

While the spatial form anticipated by the *White Paper* is perhaps open to interpretation, other elements are more clearly defined. The most important elements are:

- the principle of group areas and 'own' local government;
- deregulation and acceptance of service standards of varying levels, allowing for a differentiation of areas according to income;
- the principle of privatization, particularly in relation to housing; and
- an insistence that urbanization should be ordered at least in the sense that unplanned and uncontrolled squatting are to be avoided.

Part III: Policy in Practice

Since the tabling of the *White Paper*, the form and nature of African urbanization, especially in the major metropolitan areas, has altered. Whilst some of these changes obviously emerge as a result of the *White Paper* itself, not all are immediately apparent from that document. Perhaps the most important features of urbanization policy in practice are that a wider set of forces is being allowed to shape urbanization, and that the state has restructured the way it intervenes in the urbanization process.

Forces influencing urbanization

Whereas in the past the nature and form of urbanization was dictated by the central state, current policy is characterized by the relative withdrawal of the central state from such a visible and direct role in the process. A more complex set of agents – developers, local organization and the more peripheral organs of the state operating within the broad principles laid out in the *White Paper* – are having an important influence over precisely where and how urbanization occurs. There is less co-ordination between these different agents. When this is coupled with the uncertainties and confusions caused by the unfolding of the reform process, differential applications and/or interpretations of state policy, local struggles, and regional variations in the availability of land and cost of development, it is not surprising that the state's approach to urbanization on the ground appears ad hoc.

For our purposes, important actors have emerged out of two aspects of the current reform strategy: the restructuring of government and the policy of privatization.

(i) Restructuring of government

The restructuring of government since 1983 has established what might be termed a set of peripheral organs of the state: the tricameral Parliament and the reconstituted local and regional governments, all of which influence urbanization in specific ways.

Since 1983, the housing departments of the Houses of Representatives and Delegates (and more particularly the former) have emerged as important agents in struggles for land and housing in urban areas and have often been the force behind the removal of African squatters. This is a logical outcome of the tricameral parliamentary system and its lack of popular legitimacy. There are considerable pressures on these Houses to provide land and housing, particularly as this is virtually the only way of securing legitimacy for the tricameral system and votes for the ruling parties. And it has been possible for them to do so through their control over their respective budgets and their access to the channels of resource allocation. Although the Houses of Delegates and Representatives have on occasion intervened directly in the development of housing, superceding local authorities or building outside their boundaries, they prefer to play a more indirect role by, for example, providing private developers with bridging finance.

The devolution of authority to the second (provincial) tier and third (RSC and local) tier of government has also influenced the way in which urbanization occurs. Devolution (however constrained) does provide the potential for a more varied set of outcomes, and for greater regional and local variations than has been the case in the past. This is recognized and accepted in the *White Paper*. Nonetheless, the actions of authorities at lower levels will also be determined and constrained by their subordinate position with respect to the national state and their specific powers, duties and areas of jurisdiction. The actions of local and provincial governments are, therefore, bound to reflect these tensions.

In the past few years, the Provincial Administrations have come to play an increasingly important role in relation to management of urbanization. Responsibility for planning for urbanization and black settlement now falls under the restructured physical planning sections of the Provincial Administrations. These departments are a combination of older physical planning departments, responsible primarily for regional and local planning essentially outside African areas, and the old development boards, with their particular histories. Ultimately, it is, however, envisaged that the functions of the development boards will be assumed by the BLAs. The Provincial Administrations are now more firmly under the control of the central state, and subject to its direction. Furthermore, Joint Management Committees (JMCs) appear to have played a central role at this and local levels. The different histories and influences exerted by the four Provincial Administrations have affected and will continue to affect the way these bodies implement state policy. Regional variations will also play their part.

RSCs have been set up in a number of areas inter alia to co-ordinate the supra-local provision of services and the provision of housing for squatters. In earlier government reports it was suggested that RSCs would become the major source of finance for these purposes. While for the most part they have been willing to take on this task, the finance they have been able to raise has generally been too limited. In some instances their finances have been further restricted as they have had to take over deficits from local authorities. For example, the western Cape RSC took over the deficits of the Divisional Council of the Cape. RSCs have also on occasion been forced to assume financial responsibility for development projects initiated by central government. It appears, for example, that the state is trying to shift the responsibility for the upgrading of African townships onto the RSCs. This is evidenced by the reduction of provincial community service budgets and bridging finance allocations and by the reduction of money allocated to upgrading by the Department of Constitutional Development Planning.[21]

Although the RSCs have now been able to raise loans from alternative sources, and have budgeted for infrastructural development and upgrading in a number of areas, many projects have yet to get off the ground.[22]

It was intended that BLAs would take on the task of developing and managing their areas and in so doing assume roles similar to those of white local authorities. In spite of the state's attempts to devolve certain functions and powers down to the BLAs, their role is being undermined by their limited resources, poor management skills and lack of political credibility. They have been unable to run their areas on a cost recovery basis, let alone improve services.

BLAs have distorted and hindered private sector developments. Developers complain that their ineptitude and inefficiency is pushing up costs and slowing the rate of development. It would appear that corruption is also playing a role in this process.[23] Furthermore, BLAs have tended to insist on a fairly high standard of services and have resisted low cost developments. Ironically their actions seem to be informed at least in part by fear of criticism from popular organizations which have long demanded better housing conditions.

The net outcome of the restructuring of government is that the peripheral organs of the state have had to assume greater responsibility for meeting the needs of urban Africans and are now an important set of agents shaping urban development. The effect of the restructuring of government has also been to confuse lines of authority, levels of responsibility and, particularly in the short term, to hinder the process of development.

(ii) Privatization and its effects

A second set of agents, equally diverse and complex, has emerged in response to the dynamics of privatization. The application of this principle has clearly influenced the way in which urbanization is accommodated. To begin with, privatization has further facilitated the state's withdrawal from the direct provision of services, and to some extent from the financing of housing. This has not meant that the state has withdrawn completely from the housing terrain, only that the emphasis has shifted to more market-based forms of housing provision. In the second place, privatization has increased the involvement of private developers, financial institutions, non-profit utility companies, individuals (via their own savings and sweat equity) and, to a lesser extent, employers, in the provision of housing and services.

Privatization has influenced African urbanization in a variety of ways. First, it has directly contributed to various types of urban forced removals. 'Squatters' are being forced to move by developers to make way for new housing schemes which, in some cases, are for the black middle-class. A case in point occurred in Durban in 1988 at Emzomusha where approximately 4 000 Africans had settled on land designated for 'coloured' housing. A housing developer then violently evicted these residents in order to build middle-class housing for 'coloureds'. Another case is presently unfolding in the Ematshaheni area near Pietermaritzburg where low-income Africans living in the area are being removed to make way for the developent of middle-class African housing. Further, privatization has increased the potential for the poorest to be pushed out to the urban periphery. This is because the few remaining well-located portions of undeveloped land in the African group area are being allocated to private developers for formal up-market housing.

Secondly, privatization means that only certain social classes, usually the wealthiest and/or those with access to housing subsidies, are catered for. This is partially because low-income black housing is considered risky and unprofitable.[24] There are high administrative costs associated with small loans,[25] and the majority of urban residents cannot afford the products the developers have on offer. In 1987 approximately 40 per cent of the money spent on housing went to houses costing more than R40 000 and only 15 per cent was invested in housing costing less than R15 000.[26] This means that 40 per cent of the money was spent on meeting the needs of just 10 per cent of the urban black population whilst only 15 per cent of it went towards meeting the needs of 57 per cent of these people.[27]

Other contradictions emerge. While some people might have access to a housing subsidy, the housing shortage limits the degree to which this facility is used. Although the production of houses for Africans living outside the bantustans has increased from 2 500 houses in 1986 to 3 600 houses in 1988,[28] the impact of this rate of production on the national housing backlog, estimated by the Urban Foundation to be about 80 000 units,[29] is negligible.

Thirdly, because developers are assuming increasing control over the housing delivery process, the problems people experience when trying to get access to land and housing have changed. Not only, as mentioned above, are private developers becoming a force for removals and providing housing which is beyond the economic reach of large numbers of people, but there is also substantial evidence that the scale of corruption over land deals has increased markedly since the advent of privatized housing delivery. The James Commission[30] provides evidence of this, as does the host of investigations into corruption and allegations about land-holding in African areas which has occupied the Durban courts for the past year.[31]

In overview, the restructuring of government and the adoption of the policy of privatization has meant that the urbanization process is being shaped by a wider range of actors than was previously the case and, moreover, it has led to increasing poverty. Whilst the emergence and actions of these actors are by and large consistent with the principles outlined in the *White Paper*, the impression on the ground is that urbanization is occurring in an ad hoc manner and in the absence of a policy framework.

State action

State action has not been limited to a confined, reactive role focussed around privatization and the devolution of certain functions to lower tiers of government. In fact, we believe the state's major role has been to attempt to *manage* the urbanization process spatially, socially, economically and politically. This emphasis on management derives, we believe, from the recognition by the state that urbanization is here to stay and that its role is to direct that process. This view, we might add, contrasts to some degree with the initial interpretation of the *White Paper* which suggested that the state was simply replacing an influx control system based on pass laws with new forms of influx control based on the Prevention of Illegal Squatting Act, the Trespass Act, and limits on access to land and housing.[32]

There are a number of developments which suggest that the state is not really interested in restricting and resisting the location of Africans within metropolitan regions but is more concerned with managing how and where Africans live within cities. While such 'evidence' is only indicative at present, when examined collectively it does suggest a change in government thinking since 1986.

Firstly, there appear to be some shifts in state policy at the supra-urban level. The state's spatial management strategies have traditionally been cast within the context of balanced regional development, the diversion of urbanization away from metropolitan areas and the creation of an uneven spatial surface. Although the state has continued to implement its industrial decentralization policies, there are signs that it is moving away from any emphasis on, or role in, managing the distribution of the population and is concentrating instead on a few select areas. In addition, there are also indications that the revised industrial development proposals will place substantial emphasis on, and provide positive developmental support for, metropolitan areas.

Secondly, it appears that, over the past two years, the state has been relatively unconcerned with influx control. Pass arrests which totalled 262 904 in 1983, ended in 1986 as a result of the abolition of influx control. One would expect that if squatting, vagrancy and other, similar legislation was intended to replace the pass laws as a means of influx control, then an equivalent number of violations of this legislation would have been recorded. In addition, one would expect an increase in the rate of the forced removal of informal settlements to ensure that the overall urbanization rate does not increase significantly. Not only have there been relatively few such arrests, but forced removals have generally not occurred in order to restrict the influx of Africans to the cities. Only a handful of people have been repatriated to the homelands since 1986: only 157 Africans in 1986[33] as opposed to 5 614 in 1985.[34] Most groups threatened with removal have been offered alternative, albeit inferior, land within the city area. A case in point is the Weiler's Farm squatter community which has been offered land in Orange Farm and Wildebeesfontein. This land is 7-10 kilometres from its existing location.

This information suggests that the state has used the Trespass Act and the Prevention of Illegal Squatting Act to establish control over squatters and manipulate how and where they live in the urban areas rather than to exclude them. Recent amendments to the Prevention of Illegal Squatting Act indicate that the state is intending to increase its powers in this field rather than reduce them.[35]

The squatters who have been particularly vulnerable to removal are those who are living on land earmarked for the development of up-market housing. Eviction notices have been served on squatters: (i) living in a group area other than their own, for example, in Luganda (near Durban) and Uitkyk (near Cape Town); and (ii) living in their own group area, for example, Ematshaheni (near Pietermaritzburg) and the Mshengu squatter camp in Mofolo (Soweto). Squatters whose presence in a particular area becomes a political issue are also vulnerable. Examples are Weiler's Farm in the PWV area where the presence of squatters became an important issue in the local white elections and Langa, Uitenhage, where the highly politically organized community was considered a threat by local whites.

Thirdly, in the post-1986 period, the state has allocated more land for African housing within metropolitan areas than for many years before. Estimates suggest that over 30 000 hectares of land have been (or are about to be) made available for African housing.[36] As this land is in metropolitan areas, it supports the view that the state is more concerned with management than influx control.

Finally, one might speculate that the state is unconcerned about African influx because it is not a major component of African urbanization in many areas any more. There do appear to be indications, for example, that the population growth rates in the African urban (formal and informal) areas are not as high as once estimated. While in 1985 average national urban growth rates of 6 per cent and 7 per cent per annum were estimated for the African population as a whole, recent work suggests these rates are more likely to be between 3 per cent and 4 per cent per annum. Simkins notes, for example, a figure of 3,95 per cent per annum for the PWV broken into natural increase (2,75 per cent) and migration (1,2 per cent).[37]

Using the Durban Functional Region as a case in point, it should also be noted that high estimated growth rates were partly the result of methodological problems. It was assumed, for example, that the rate of growth in structures (shacks) during the early 1980s in Durban exactly mirrored the rate of growth in Durban's population. However, it appears there was something of a reduction in household occupancy rates. For example, surveys of household size and structure in the formal settlements indicate the following reductions: in Kwamashu from 9 persons per household (pph) in 1985 to 5 pph in 1988; in Umlazi from 9 pph in 1985 to 4,6 pph in 1988; and in Lamontville from 12 pph in 1985 to 8 pph in 1988.[38] Work in the PWV area and in Cape Town also suggests that most shack development is due to demand from already urbanized people.[39]

The view that the larger portion of urban growth is not attributable to in-migration is further supported by a wide range of surveys done in the informal settlements in the PWV area, Cape Town and Durban. Surveys conducted by the Black Sash Transvaal region in 1988 in Weiler's Farm, Vlakfontein, Daveyton, Johannesburg and Wilgespruit indicate that between 75 per cent and 97 per cent of the residents had lived in the PWV area for more than five years. A Centre for Policy Studies study of informal settlements in the PWV indicates that 45 per cent of those interviewed had lived in their present informal house for over five years. Additional research in the settlements of Fred Clarke, Dlamini and Tladi found no respondents who came from outside the PWV area.[40] In Durban a wide range of surveys indicates that in the informal settlements no more than one-third of household heads were born in rural areas.[41]

The conclusion we are drawn to is that what appears to be relatively limited immigration to urban areas cannot be linked to influx control. The physical growth of shack areas is rather the result of factors such as the reduced density of African areas within the metropolitan functional regions, natural increase and changing household composition.

Urban management strategies

State urban management strategies since 1986 have tended to focus on controlling where and how African people live in cities. While the anti-urbanization policy of the pre-1986 period and even the state's decentralization policy is waning, state urban management strategies reflect the dominant current elements of the spatial and institutional consolidation of racial segregation, the social and spatial stratification of the African urban population, and attempts to control that population politically through selective delivery of housing and facilities or alternatively through local institutional structures.

(a) Extension and consolidation of separate African areas

The first strategy is based on increasing the capacity of the urban areas to accommodate Africans in a manner that facilitates control and promotes the development of BLAs. To this end the state has, as mentioned previously, opened up approximately 30 000 hectares of land for Africans since 1986. In December 1987 approximately 38 per cent of the land that had been set aside was situated in the PWV area.[42] Very little land has been opened up in, for example, the Durban and Cape metropolitan areas. In the case of Durban possible reasons are the proximity of kwaZulu and the difficulties associated with finding suitable land. The establishment of Khayelitsha in the early 1980s possibly explains why land is not now being opened up at a more rapid rate in the western Cape.

Two distinct approaches to the release of land are identifiable. The first is the establishment of new self-contained towns. As the following statement made by the Deputy Minister of Constitutional Development and Planning shows, Khayelitsha – although established before 1986 – has served as a model for this pattern of land release:

> Khayelitsha is an excellent example of the sincerity of the government to solve the squatting problem and address the urbanization needs of all South Africans on a reasonable basis.[43]

Others might more appropriately refer to Khayelitsha as a controlled squatter camp. With the exception of Port Elizabeth, this strategy has proved difficult to apply in other parts of the country largely because of the problems encountered in finding large tracts of suitably located land. Attempts to apply this strategy in the PWV area by developing Norweto were strongly opposed by local white residents.

A more common approach to the opening up of land has been the extension and consolidation of the existing African areas. Examples of this are the land near Bapsfontein north of Daveyton/Benoni, Brown's Farm in the Cape and the expansion of Chesterville in Durban. The opening up of 13 000 hectares of land adjacent to Soweto falls into both categories. Here, attempts have also been made to improve the rate base of the area by including industrial land in the proposed African township.

Whilst the amount of land being made available is nowhere near the amount required to overcome the shortage of land for Africans, the scale on which it is happening exceeds that of years prior to 1985.

(b) Location of land on the urban periphery

A further feature of the land made available to Africans is that much of it is located on the urban periphery, distant from most urban amenities and places of work. A less significant amount of land has been made available in the better located buffer strips which have traditionally separated 'African' residential areas from those of other race groups. The buffer strips have by and large been allocated to middle-class housing. Reasons for this range from security considerations (middle-class people are considered to be less of a political threat to neighbouring areas) to practicalities such as the fact that buffer strips are easier for private developers to develop as services are available. As no free settlement areas (FSAs) have been proclaimed yet, it is difficult to assess how extensively they will be used. It is, however, anticipated that in the proclamation of FSAs the emphasis will be on responding to de facto changes in the racial composition of residential areas and not on opening up a large number of residential areas to 'multi-racial' occupation.

(c) Social engineering: gentrification and the creation of class divisions

Current urban management strategy is marked by attempts to create social differentiation. This is consistent with a political strategy, which emerged in the late 1970s, of building a black middle class sympathetic to free-market principles.[44] Privatization, cost recovery and the application of different standards of development to cater for different income groups, form the basis of this strategy.

Examples of how this strategy has been implemented are Spruit View ('South Africa's first garden suburb') and Khayelitsha.[45]

Spruit View, which is located 18 kilometres away from Johannesburg's CBD, is not attached to any of the existing black townships and is designed to accommodate people who can afford houses in the R80 000 to R150 000 bracket. Khayelitsha, on the other hand, (on the outskirts of the Cape Town metropolitan areas) represents little more than controlled squatting.

Critics of the *White Paper*[46] have argued that it lays the foundation for the gentrification of the existing townships. It is, however, difficult to evaluate whether a marked social stratification has resulted from the sale of council houses and the upgrading of existing townships. If anything, factors such as the slow response to the sale of state-owned housing, the ongoing rent boycotts (in Soweto and elsewhere) which prevent raising service charges to cost recovery levels, and the high incidence of backyard shacks prevent the development of rigidly defined social strata within African townships. A recent study in the PWV metropolitan area suggests that for every one house there are approximately two backyard shacks.[47] Clearly, only once substantial inroads are made into that backlog in formal housing will such social strata develop. Similarly, while the intention may be to locate only the poorest groups in peripheral areas, in practice middle-income housing is also being developed on the periphery due to the absence of alternative land. It is nevertheless true that all new housing construction has been for relatively high-income groups.

(d) Political management

The fourth dimension of state action is more explicitly political. It is based on the recognition that the poor material conditions under which many township residents live is a source of political instability and it therefore has the twin objectives of 'winning the hearts and minds' of the residents and of undermining the ability of 'revolutionary elements' to mobilize around housing issues.

One of the mechanisms used to achieve these objectives has been the direct allocation of central government funds to specific projects. These allocations appear to be guided by the JMCs and have given priority to the upgrading of areas which are politically the most volatile, which have high public profiles and in which resistance has to be crushed. The most important examples are Alexandra and Mamelodi in the PWV area, Crossroads in the Cape and Inanda in Durban. In most cases the state's approach to upgrading has been multi-faceted. In Alexandra, for example, the upgrading process has been accompanied by the repression of local political organizations, ideological interventions aimed at legitimizing the state's reform programme, and the reorganization of its local urban management structures.[48]

Secondly, as urban political management requires a vehicle through which it can be implemented, increasing use is made of patronage networks designed to bolster and co-opt community leaders and groups. These networks develop when local warlords are given the power to control and allocate resources. In the Crossroads squatter camp this strategy assisted in dividing the community and also enabled the state to re-establish control over the area[49] and win support for its local government proposals. It is, however, unlikely that this strategy will always work in favour of the state, and it cannot be universally applied. A case in point is the Inanda squatter camp where the power of the local warlord does not depend solely on the power of the state. Nevertheless, it is highly likely that the state adopts this strategy out of force of circumstance rather than out of choice and that the JMCs play a central role in its adoption.

Finally, the establishment of controlled squatting areas is an explicitly political attempt to ensure that the 'problem' posed by squatters does not spread. Here, the state is attempting to control the location and form of informal settlements so that squatters do not spread themselves in unmanageable pockets throughout the urban areas.

Concluding comments

What, then, do these changes mean for Africans, particularly poor Africans, wishing to settle in the cities of 'white South Africa'? In brief, we would suggest that the following are just some of the implications of the arguments developed above. First, African people are now relatively free to move to and from the cities. If they earn reasonable salaries and/or qualify for housing subsidies, they may be able to buy housing built by private developers and utility companies. Because of the shortage of land and housing, their access to a house or developed site is, however, not guaranteed. Moreover, they are likely to have little choice over where they can buy in the city and will probably be forced to live on the periphery.

Secondly, if they have been living in formal urban housing and are poor, they may in the longer term be forced out by rising rates and charges for services, or by the sale of houses (if they are lessees). Much will depend on local struggles and the concessions which they manage to gain from the state both centrally and locally.

Thirdly, if they have been living in informal areas for sometime they may be able to win the right to have their area upgraded or they may be removed to a more peripheral location to make way for middle-class housing. Forced removals generally occur in areas where specific and immediate development (usually inspired by the private sector) is to take place or where the presence of squatters is a political issue.

Finally, if people do not fall into the above categories, i.e. are not well established in cities, their access to accommodation will be influenced by their social networks and by the availability of rented accommodation in backyards (shacks, garages etc) and in informal settlements. These people may have access to the city through 'controlled squatting' (for example Orange Farm), or through existing or newly emerging illegal informal settlements. As part of the latter they will have to struggle for the right to remain on the land, or may have to give their support to local warlords who are at least covertly accepted by the state.

In the coming years, the struggles in urban areas are likely to focus increasingly on the city and the way in which its resources are distributed, managed and controlled.

Notes

1 We acknowledge Clive Forster's participation in the early stages of this paper.

2 Government of South Africa *White Paper on Urbanization* (Pretoria 1986). See also Budlender in this volume at 69ff.

3 C Simkins 'Urbanization in South Africa: Some notes on its Desirability, Form and Short Term Future', paper presented to the Institute of Management and Development Studies workshop on core and periphery in Southern Africa. UNITRA, Umtata (1983) 13.

4 See A Mabin 'Material and Political Factors in South African urbanization, with some illustrations from Transvaal', paper presented at University of Natal, Durban (1986) 7.

5 D Dewar, A Todes & V Watson 'The South African State and Urbanization Policy: Crisis and Response' (1985) 9 *Habitat International* 188.

6 PH Spies & FP Biggs 'Issues in the socio-economic environment of South Africa' in *Urban-rural Interactions in South Africa* (Unit for Futures Research, University of Stellenbosch 1983) 65.

7 See for example J Grobbelaar 'Projections and Analyses of the South African Population for the Period 1980-2015' (unpublished paper, Unit for Futures Research, University of Stellenbosch 1988); WP Mostert & L van Tonder *Projections of the South African Population 1985-2035* Report S-158 (Pretoria: HSRC 1987).

8 For example see D Hindson *Pass Controls and the Urban African Proletariat* (Johannesburg: Ravan Press 1987); M Morris & V Padayachee 'State reform policy in South Africa' 1988 *Transformation* 7; and M Swilling & M Phillips 'Reform, Security and White Power: Rethinking State Strategies in the 1980s', paper presented at the Annual Conference of the Association of Sociology of Southern Africa, University of Durban-Westville (1988).

9 *Report of the Commission of Inquiry into Legislation affecting the Utilization of Manpower (excluding legislation adminstered by the Departments of Labour and Mines)* (Riekert Commission) *RP 32-1979*.

10 *Report of the Commission of Enquiry into Labour Legislation* (Wiehahn Commission) RP 47-1979.

11 Morris & Padayachee above note 8 at 9.

12 In terms of the Black Local Authorities Act 102 of 1982.

13 See S Greenberg 'Ideological Struggles within the South African State', paper presented to the conference on Economic Development and Racial Domination, University of the Western Cape, Cape Town (1984).

14 Black Communities Development Act 4 of 1984 as amended by Acts 52 of 1985; 90 of 1985; 34 of 1986; 74 of 1986 and 75 of 1986 as well as Regulations 1897 and 1898 *GG*10431 12 September 1986 and 2451 *GG*9990 1 November 1985.

15 J Lombard 'Channelling Housing Finance for Development – the South African Scenario and Priorities for the Future', paper presented to the Conference on International Future Trends in the Financing of Housing CSIR (Pretoria 1988).

16 See, for example, Swilling & Phillips above note 8.

17 Note 2 above, at 71.

18 For example see W Cobbett 'Orderly Urbanization' (1986) 11 (8) *South African Labour Bulletin* 77 and V Watson 'SA Urbanization Policy' (1986) 11 (8) *South African Labour Bulletin* 106.

19 Ibid.

20 For example see s 6.15.7.

21 *South African Institute of Race Relations: Social and Economic Update* no 5 (1988) 46.

22 *South African Institute of Race Relations: Social and Economic Update* no 6 (1988) 44.

23 *South African Institute of Race Relations: Social and Economic Update* no 3 (1987) 34.

24 RS Tucker 'The Building Societies', paper presented to the Conference on Innovations and Future Trends in the Financing of Housing, CSIR (Pretoria 1988).

25 Ibid.

26 *South African Institute of Race Relations: Social and Economic Update* no 6 (1988) 28.

27 *Weekly Mail* 10 March, 1989.

28 *South African Institute of Race Relations: Social and Economic Update* no 5 (1988) 33 and No 6 (1988) 35-36.

29 South African Institute of Race Relations: Social and Economic Update no 6 (1988) 28.

30 The Commission was appointed by the State President on 24 June 1988 (*GG* 11380) and tabled its report on 10 March 1989.

31 See for example 'Ex Mayor in R50 000 Probe' *Sunday Tribune* 2 June 1989; 'Top Inkatha Man in Row over Land' *Sunday Tribune* 26 February 1989; 'Ndebele Dispute Land Proclamation' *Sunday Tribune* 26 February 1989; and 'Umlazi Man's Claim Against Ulundi Leads to Probe of Allocations' *Sunday Tribune* 12 March 1989.

32 Cobbett above note 18; Watson above note 18.

33 1987/88 *Race Relations Survey* 461.

34 1986 *Race Relations Survey* 335.

35 See O'Regan in this volume at 162ff.

36 Black Sash (Transvaal region) 'Nearly an A-Z of Homelessness on the Witwatersrand' unpublished paper (1989).

37 Simkins cited in Black Sash above note 36.

38 MO Sutcliffe 'Household Characteristics' in Tongaat-Hulett Properties Ltd. *The Durban Functional Region Planning for the 21st Century* Report 1 The Current Situation (1989) Appendix 4, p 3.

39 Black Sash above note 36.

40 All cited in Black Sash above note 36.

41 Sutcliffe above note 38.

42 South African Institute of Race Relations: Social and Economic Update no 4 (1988) 38.

43 *Natal Witness* 29 September 1988.

44 See J Searll 'The Sale of State Houses' in G Bloch & D Kaplan (eds) *South African Research Papers* Department of Economic History, University of Cape Town (1984).

45 *Financial Mail* 7 August 1987.

46 D Hindson 'Alternative Urbanisation strategies in South Africa: a critical evaluation', paper presented to the University of York Conference on the Southern African Economy after Apartheid (1986) 11.

47 Centre for Policy Research, cited in Black Sash above note 36.

48 K Jochelson 'People's Power and State Reform in Alexandra' (1988) *Work in Progress* 14.

49 J Cole *Crossroads, the Politics of Reform and Repression 1976-1986* (Johannesburg: Ravan Press 1987) 122-38.

NICHOLAS HAYSOM

Rural Land Struggles: Practising Law Democratically

The eastern Cape historian, Jeff Peires, recently researched the law practice of a former prominent attorney in the Seymour district of the eastern Cape.[1] He concluded that in the first half of this century lawyers contributed significantly to the dispossession and removal of 'coloured' and African communities in the district. Armed with contractual devices and an enthusiasm for sharp practice, they were central agents in 'separating' black people from their land and their resources. Interviews with former residents of these communities elicited the response ''n agent is mos 'n skelm ding'[2] and '[die lawyer] was die jakkals wat die skape gevang het'.[3]

While contractual artifice is no longer a principal device for effecting the dispossession of black communities, the law remains a 'skelm ding' for South Africa's rural population. For them it is a capricious phenomenon. It is elusive when its protection is sought, but threatening and hostile when manifest, taking either the form of the deputy sheriff or the South African police.

The exclusion of blacks from the political process in South Africa has meant that they have no say in the making of the racist and repressive laws which govern their lives. Similarly, black South Africans have no control over the executive bureaucracies (the police, departmental officials and black commissioners) which rule over them in their name. This radical absence of political accountability affects perceptions of the law that black people have. Rural black South Africans are further distanced from legal institutions because the law is obscure and remote. Before the poor can exploit what limited rights the law accords them, they must acquire the services of someone who can decode the law's mysteries.

However opaque and biased the law may be, this paper argues that lawyers have a vital role to play in rural struggles. Their most immediate task is to impose legal controls on state practices in an area where the pervasive character of legislation is that it empowers state officials and landowners to act outside legal supervision. This task must be performed with the sober realization that simply increasing the accessibility of the courts will not, of itself, alter the political and economic deprivations that rural communities suffer. As Geoffrey Budlender points out,[4] no number of lawyers can bring justice where the laws are unjust. He cites Kentridge:

> Even if every accused person or litigant had a lawyer, and even if every judge were a Centlivres or a Schreiner, the courts could not alter the fundamental realities of South African life. Only a radical political change could do that.[5]

In response to the challenge which the South African legal system poses to lawyers wishing to assist rural communities, lawyers must define their task within the framework of community 'empowerment'. Such an approach goes beyond the 'access to justice' approach to delivering legal services to disadvantaged communities. It envisages a role for lawyers in which their contribution is to facilitate a process in which the communities act and speak for themselves. In examining the problem of practising law democratically, the second part of this paper will argue that empowering rural communities through legal support involves a critical understanding of the limits of traditional lawyering.

The Limits and the Potential of Legal Intervention

The history of the Mogopa

One effective illustration of the potential and the limitations of legal assistance to rural communities is the struggle of the Mogopa tribe for the right to remain on their ancestral lands.[6]

The Mogopa tribe purchased two farms in the fertile Ventersdorp district in the western Transvaal (some 200 kilometres from Johannesburg) in 1913 and 1931 respectively.[7] (See map on p 15.) They prospered on these farms, building schools, churches, medical clinics, shops, reservoirs and producing an agricultural surplus, until the 1980s. In 1982 the tribe deposed their government-appointed headman on account of his corruption. They discovered, to their consternation, that the government would not endorse their choice of a new headman. In 1983 the local black commissioner informed the tribe that he would never remove Mr Jacob More from his position as headman and that More had agreed to the 'voluntary' removal of the tribe to a farm in the dry Marico district hundreds of kilometres away. The tribe emphatically expressed their rejection of any proposed removal and denied that More had any mandate to negotiate on their behalf.

Jacob More duly left with a minority of the tribe for the Groot Marico district. The remaining members of the tribe were subjected to a variety of pressures to compel them to join More at his resettlement camp 'voluntarily'.

The tribe's fresh water pumps were removed, depriving them of access to fresh water. The tribe's schools were closed and then demolished. Public transport to and from the nearby town was discontinued. Payment of pensions was refused and pensioners were referred to the local authority in the Marico district. Similarly, contract labour permits and applications for reference books were refused and applicants referred to the Marico district. In this way Mogopa residents were prevented from obtaining employment in the urban areas. The community's four churches and the medical clinic were bulldozed, as were houses of some of the absent migrant residents. This campaign of harassment by the authorities was intended to engineer a 'voluntary removal'.

However, the Mogopa tribe persisted with its refusal to move and set about rebuilding their community facilities.

In the face of the failure of the campaign of harassment, the 'velvet glove' was removed. On 16 November 1983 the tribe received notice in terms of section 5(1)(b) of the Black Administration Act[8] that they were to move from the area within ten days and never to return. The tribe sought an interdict staying the execution of the order on the grounds that the Act allowed an objecting tribe to demand parliamentary approval of an intended forced removal. The interdict was refused as was leave to appeal. The tribe then petitioned the Chief Justice for leave to appeal and requested the government not to execute the order until they had exhausted their legal remedies. Without notice on 16 February 1984, the Mogopa farms were cordoned off by the South African police and the inhabitants were forcibly loaded onto trucks and taken to the land of their former headman in the Marico district. Many of the tribesmen were compelled to sell their cattle to neighbouring white farmers at knock-down prices. The tribe did not remain in the resettlement camp but left and sought refuge in the Bethanie district.

Having been granted leave to appeal the tribe now placed their hopes in the Appellate Division of the Supreme Court. To their astonishment, in 1985 the government introduced clause 9 of the Laws on Co-operation and Development Amendment Bill.[9] This provision sought to rectify the defect in the forced removal. It was an extraordinary provision having *only* retrospective effect. After local and international opposition the provision was withdrawn.

In 1985 the Appellate Division upheld the tribe's objection to the removal order and declared the order invalid.[10] This turned out to be an empty victory. Without notice to the tribe, the government had already expropriated the Mogopa lands in terms of the Expropriation Act of 1975.[11] The tribe was now entitled to return to their farms in terms of the Black Administration Act but, if they did, would face charges in terms of the Trespass Act[12] for being on property owned by the government.

From 1986 to the present the tribe has attempted to negotiate with the government for land in compensation for Mogopa.[13] In 1987 they raised funds from church groupings to buy a mission station farm, Holgat, upon which to settle. Only days before the conclusion of the deal, Holgat too was expropriated by the government which claimed that it required the land for 'public purposes'. In late 1987, the tribe, weakened by disease and demoralized by their persecution by the host Bethanie community, resolved to march back to their ancestral lands even if it meant risking the final disintegration of the tribe. The government intervened and offered to reopen negotiations and to temporarily resettle the community at Onderstepoort pending the resolution of further negotiations. Towards the end of 1988, 60 or so tribal elders occupied the Mogopa lands in order to maintain the traditional graveyard. In March 1989 the government brought a Supreme Court interdict seeking the urgent ejectment of these members of the tribe. In October 1989, the community defended the ejectment action on the ground that the land belonged to them. They argued that the expropriation was invalid because the Minister of Co-operation and Development acted as the effective expropriator, the expropriatee, and, simultaneously, as the trustee of the interests of the tribe. They lost on a technical point and the matter is now on appeal.

It is cold comfort to the Mogopa tribe that their campaign focussed such international attention and opposition on the policy of forced removals that the government has now publicly declared that there will be no further forced removals and that the 'forced removals' clause of the Black Administration Act[14] has been repealed.

Law and strategy

Three observations may be made at this point. Firstly, although legal victories have placed the tribe in a more favourable bargaining position, they have not guaranteed the rights of the tribe. The government and the tribe have employed a variety of legal and extra-legal strategies to further their objectives. The tribe's fate has depended to a significant extent on their capacity to survive as a group, to maintain cohesion, purpose and morale. If the community had disintegrated in this six-year legal battle, there would be no prospect of eventually returning to the land. Legal strategies, even successful ones, which undercut community cohesion may work against the long-term survival of the community. On the other hand, legal strategies may be important for non-legal (political) reasons. Such strategies may provide both the time and a platform for community organization and broader political campaigns. Legal challenges may also contest the parameters of legitimate resistance, or, by engaging the government on the legal terrain, expose state practices.

Secondly, because the government has sought to rely on provisions which are designed to evade legal control, legal efforts on behalf of the tribe have been primarily directed at introducing legal and political accountability. This strategy has led the state to engage with groups and organizations it otherwise refused to recognize or to negotiate with.[15]

Finally, the law is used to enforce rights or gains which have been won by the community previously. In rural areas, rights which are not enforced are quickly abused.

In the following section, state avoidance of legal accountability is described. The last part of the paper deals with the first issue raised above: that of the interaction of legal action and community interests in rural struggles or practising law democratically.

Escaping legal accountability: 'minimum interference' and 'privatized repression'

Current state strategies for enforcing its policies are nowhere clearer than in recent legislation including the latest emergency regulations. A distinct bifurcation has taken place within the structure of South African law. Those laws that deal with non-contentious areas of social policy (including the ordinary criminal law) retain a 'legal' character.[16] Those that deal with security issues display a martial law or despotic character in which judicial review, legal supervision of official conduct and the elements of natural justice are routinely excluded. This aspect of state strategy can be called the policy of minimum legal interference. It confers upon the state the power to act in a flexible and arbitrary fashion, without public exposure or delay and represents the move from rule through law to social management. The emergency regulations and applied security legislation are the clearest examples of such a policy of official lawlessness.[17]

Statutorily enacted evasion of legal interference runs side-by-side with a second strategy for evading legal responsibility – the privatization of repression. This involves a delegation of repressive powers, or the re-allocation of the power or duty to enforce apartheid policies to private agencies, such as vigilantes.[18] The state has persistently failed to prosecute vigilantes or to protect anti-apartheid activists and community organizations which have been the principal victims of this violence.

Both original legislation affecting rural black people and recently enacted amendments to it reveal these two characteristics: the policy of minimum interference and the privatization of repression. It is instructive to review the principal features of this law in three key areas: land law, farm labour and the institution of chiefs.

(i) Land and the law

The grid of legislation that sets out South Africa's racial geography is hostile to the assertion of rights by black inhabitants of the land.[19] Original legislation and subsequent amendments have removed the right to receive notice or make representations in regard to a variety of measures which may affect the right to occupy land or closely related rights to citizenship.[20] Such laws have often restricted the scope of legal redress, for example by limiting the right to launch urgent interdicts to prevent unlawful action. Recent legislative amendments have contained similar provisions: The Alteration of Boundaries of Self Governing Territories Bill[21] sought to reverse and evade recent court rulings which have prevented the cession of Moutse and Botshabelo to homeland governments.[22] The 1988 amendments to the Prohibition of Illegal Squatting Act[23] expressly seek to limit the jurisdiction of courts.[24] At the same time the amendments not only seek to empower private agencies to evict tenants or squatters, but sharpen further the incentive to enforce apartheid privately by increasing the penalties on those landowners who do not evict black squatters.[25]

(ii) Farm labour

The conscious and deliberate omission of any protective legislation for farm labourers has ensured that the relationship between South Africa's approximately one million farm labourers and their employers has been regulated primarily through the common-law contract of employment. Operating on the fiction that the individual labourer and the employer have reached 'agreement' on the terms of their contract, the courts are unable to inspect the feudal content of the contract.[26] The dependency of the farm labourer ensures that the working conditions of farmworkers remain abysmal. No legislation protects them from dangerous working conditions, exploitative terms of remuneration, and the absence of proper housing or welfare provision for them or their families.

The farmer's disciplinary powers are extensive, particularly the power to dismiss and evict. In the rural setting the farmer is also the landlord. Eviction can have catastrophic consequences for the labourer's family.[27] It is a testament to the dependent social and economic position of farm labourers that farmers frequently physically assault their labourers.[28]

Although the state has not seen fit to extend the Labour Relations Act[29] and other protective legislation to farm labourers, it has supplemented the farmer's disciplinary powers with drastic statutory powers: the Trespass Act,[30] the Prevention of Illegal Squatting Act,[31] and provincial pound ordinances.[32] Farmers have the power to fire, evict and sell up the cattle of their labourers or labour tenants. Save for the limited right to 'notice', labourers have barely any rights with which to contest the actions of their employers.

(iii) Chiefs

By guaranteeing the wide traditional powers of chiefs and headmen, supplementing these with statutory powers, and by making chiefs accountable to no one except the state,[33] the government has introduced its most widespread and effective form of rural control. It is upon the chief that the most impoverished of South Africa's citizens are dependent for land and a variety of permits. Lawyers have struggled unsuccessfully for decades to introduce an element of accountability into the relationship between the chief and his subject and to impose limits on the powers of the chiefs. Their failure to do so effectively has been in part because the courts have adopted an atavistic 'Shaka Zulu' interpretation of the despotic powers of traditional chiefs.[34] Chiefs have become prime agents in engineering government policy, particularly in regard to removals.

Practising Law Democratically

Decoding the law

Generally, lawyers are unwilling to devote the resources, time and specialization required to deal with legal problems in the rural areas. The difficulty of overturning existing practices, language difficulties, the barrenness and inscrutability of the law and the remoteness of the areas, maintain an urban concentration of legal resources, and inhibit lawyers from 'venturing into the interior'. Besides, professionals are removed from the problems and needs of the rural poor and see the work as unglamorous.

One alternative, the legal education of these communities, is hampered by the esoteric language and procedures that lawyers have developed and which serve to entrench a monopoly over their skills. Yet the first requirement of democratic legal practice is a commitment to reciprocal education:

teaching and learning from the rural poor. This transforms individual expertise into collective knowledge, and, as Selznick suggests, civic assertiveness and competence:

> Students of the poor have stressed a persistent dependency – the difficulty, for example, of breaking the cycle of unemployment, underemployment, failure, and public assistance. It is argued that nothing so promotes that dependency as a sense of helplessness, of being at the mercy of another man's arbitrary will. Therefore a great aim of legal assistance is to enlarge the *sense* of competence, which can only be achieved by experience which demonstrates that self-assertion works, that rights can be vindicated, that the world of power and authority is something less than opaque, that the individual need not perceive himself as a manipulated object.
>
> Some forms of advocacy can exacerbate that dependency, if the law remains for the client a vehicle of mystification, if no educational experience is encouraged, if the lawyer neatly separates the client from his own problems, leaving him no less helpless and confused than he was before.
>
> But advocacy can have a direct psychic benefit, and contribute to genuine learning, if it helps the client to understand his situation, enlarge his alternatives, and – perhaps above all – stiffen his spine in the face of official authority and private power.[35]

Selznick's comments are even more pertinent in South Africa. The preceding Cook's Tour through the principal features of the laws and powers governing rural struggles indicates the difficulties communities face in finding legal toeholds from which to enforce any rights they may have. In more ways than one the difficulty is severely compounded by the inscrutability of the law. From the Mogopa case we can observe that the range of legal areas in which the tribe has had to contest government actions includes property law, welfare legislation, constitutional law, customary law, the law of trusts, administrative law, criminal law and the law of expropriation. This feature is not peculiar to the Mogopa struggle but applies to many rural struggles.

Special mention must be made of homeland legislation. The process of constitutional devolution of powers to the bantustans requires that an attorney practising in the Transvaal, for example, maintain updated legislation in respect of South Africa and six of the homelands. Furthermore, some South African legislation is applicable in the homelands, but this legislation is the South African legislation as it was either when the homeland government achieved self-governing status, or as it was when the homeland became 'independent'.[36] The attorney is required to know the date each of the homelands reached the three stages of constitutional development, what legislation was applicable in South Africa at that date, and finally, whether legislation has been enacted by the homeland since it became 'self-governing' or 'independent'. This information is not available in the ordinary collection of updated South African legislation. Only one firm of attorneys in Johannesburg maintains a complete collection of homeland legislation. Many university libraries do not. How, one must ask, can a rural community be expected to know what legislation is applicable to it?

Empowering or undermining rural communities

Legal action does not of itself necessarily assist a community. Indeed there are numerous ways in which lawyering can undermine a rural struggle. It is in reconciling the advantages of legal assistance with the importance of retaining community organization that the lawyer must find an appropriate role.

Lawyers can and often do disempower a community. They introduce time limits, divisions, and priorities, in line with a legal strategy. The tempo and pace of community-based strategies must fall into line with them. Furthermore legal strategies may produce new and potentially destructive divisions into a community. Thus a legal strategy may distinguish between those with South African citizenship and those without. It may divide those with rights to be on the land from those who are squatters. It may separate the claimant and his or her claims from a collective strategy. Legal strategies favour those in a community who have remedies.

Less visibly a legal strategy may introduce an elitism into the community. This danger is particularly great where rural communities are concerned as the law involved is so complex. Law is not inherently democratic. When lawyers as the experts are not actually prescribing to the community they take their lead from an elite group of literate or sophisticated leaders which may not enjoy the confidence of the community. They may consult with community leaders only to discover later that this group does not represent the aspirations of the community nor has it consulted fully with the community.

Finally, the lawyer may activate a process in which the community divests itself of responsibility for its own cause and comes to rely on the lawyer and the legal remedy for their salvation. Here the legal initiative replaces all others ('legal substitutionalism'). More than one lawyer has returned to a community which was expected to passively await the outcome of a court case only to find that the community has disintegrated. The consequences may be worse when the case has been lost and the community is compelled to turn to other resources.

Commenting on the role of lawyers in developing countries Abel remarks:

> The legal representation of similarly situated individuals, even when it takes the form of a 'class' action, tends to substitute for, rather than foster organization. The inescapable conclusions, however reluctant we may be to draw them, are that the clientele of legal aid does not lend itself to organization, and that the offer of legal assistance actually may undermine collective action.[37]

Working with rural communities requires a commitment to practicing law democratically – to work *with* people and not *for* them. It does not require lawyers to be social workers or community organizers – that may extend the dangers of legal intervention.

> Professional people generally have a tendency to 'take over' because they are 'experts'. While the 'experts' may succeed in solving the client's immediate problem the simultaneous result may be to reinforce the client's position of powerlessness and dependence. Lawyers are particularly prey to this tendency, but they share it with other professions.[38]

The Driefontein Legal Clinic Committee in the eastern Transvaal provides a model of practising law democratically.[39] The clinic was set up at the request of the community which was seeking practical projects to act as a catalyst for community organization and restore community confidence following the assassination of its charismatic leader, Saul Mkhize. The committee of the Driefontein community participated in the institution and development of the clinic. It also participated in the running of the clinic. Members assisted in taking statements and in explaining the potential legal remedies that were available to the claimant. Through this involvement members of the community came to understand the collective nature of the individual claims. For example, the refusal to pay a particular woman her pension was part of the victimization of the entire community in order to induce it to move to the resettlement area. Secondly, the community learnt about the potential and the limits of the legal process. The community or the committee was involved in discussing appropriate strategies in regard to each complaint. In this way both legal and non-legal options were considered. The community could decide, for example, to challenge refusal to pay pensions by way of litigation before the Supreme Court, or by confronting the relevant official in the area and putting him on terms directly. Either way the community participated in the process and was in a position to learn from both victories and defeats. Most importantly, however, the relationship between the lawyer and the community was different. The lawyer was no longer the moral entrepreneur appropriating causes and victories. The victories, even those won through legal means, belonged to the community and served to bolster their confidence in dealing with the bureaucracy and in solving community problems. This is a particularly important feature where communities may be confused and lack confidence in dealing with officialdom, and whose confidence is further eroded by the notion that only a lawyer, the decoder, can do so on their behalf. In addition, participation in collective action and increasing knowledge of one's legal rights can, according to Dias and Paul

> replace feelings of alienation, resignation and dependency with a new awareness of one's dignity and rights – a crucial condition for self-reliance. Similarly, this knowledge can stimulate collective action aimed either at realizing rights to an equitable allocation of state resources or at remedying abuses of power.[40]

This picture of the Driefontein Clinic is somewhat idealized. It glosses over the frustrations of dealing with the minutiae of rural oppression. It does illustrate, however, not only the importance of democratic lawyering, but also that the role of the lawyer may be important in attending to a community organization, assisting in drafting a constitution, advising on a contract or negotiating with the landlord for office premises (precisely the services that a corporation demands of its corporate lawyer). These functions may be as important in sustaining a community's ability to deal with a hostile world as a test case. This should not be interpreted as meaning that test cases are not important. The broader significance and reach of a test case makes it particularly significant. Furthermore, the Appellate Division appears receptive to creative challenges to government policy in rural areas.

I have argued that the lawyer's role is to introduce legal accountability into the law which deals with the lives of rural people. There are other reasons why lawyers should involve themselves in rural struggles, not least the rewards of working with people who exhibit so much courage, dignity, humour and gratitude. One important reason for lawyers to involve themselves with rural struggles, and to do so democratically, is that the process enables the community to learn about the principles of natural justice, about the importance of protecting their rights and the rights of others, and about the necessity of due process and a just judiciary. Lawyering with, rather than on behalf of, rural communities, and involving these communities in a process of education and discussion will not only assist in preparing such participants to struggle for their rights within the existing institutions but will also politicize them to resist the undemocratic values which underpin such institutions. Indeed, such lawyering may assist to shape a future democratic order. It is not only in colonial societies that the rural poor find themselves disadvantaged or ignored in favour of urban elites. The experience elsewhere in the world, including Africa, reveals that for the rural poor, social and political assertiveness is as important after the removal of an oppressive regime as before. The 'empowerment' paradigm recognizes this.

Sensitive participation by lawyers in rural struggles can contribute to a process of empowerment and perhaps counter the belief that the role of law is to bolster those in power and to exploit those without it.

Notes

1 J Peires 'The Legend of Fenner-Solomon' in B Bozzoli (ed) *Class, Community and Conflict* (Johannesburg: Ravan 1987) 65.

2 Ibid at 89.

3 Ibid at 65.

4 G Budlender 'On Practising Law' in H Corder (ed) *Law and Social Practice* (Cape Town: Juta 1988) 321. Budlender also refers to Paul Raines' comments in regard to Chile: 'the question of access to justice is only relevant when people have claims to make within the system ... for many of the poor, the problem of access to justice is simply not relevant, since they have no claim and are outside the institutional system, however accessible the system may be.'

5 S Kentridge *Law and Lawyers in Changing Society* The First Ernie Wentzel Memorial Lecture, unpublished paper (1987) 19.

6 The history of the Mogopa tribe is set out in the court records in *More v Minister of Co-operation and Development* 1986 (2) SA 765 (A) and *Minister of the Department of Agriculture and Water Supply v Daniel Molefe* TPD 2 May 1989 Case No 2077/89, unreported. See also Marcus at 20ff.

7 As a device to provide for perpetual ownership of the land, and to prevent individual chiefs from selling their farms, the tribe registered their land in 1932 in the name of the Minister of Native Affairs to be held in trust for them.

8 Section 5(1)(b) of the Black Administration Act 38 of 1927 which empowered the State President to order any black, black tribe or group of blacks to move from one area to another area. See Marcus at 18 in this volume.

9 Bill 89/85 (GA).

10 See *More v Minister of Co-operation and Development* note 6 above.

11 Act 63 of 1975.

12 Act 8 of 1959. See Keightley at 180-93 in this volume.

13 See Claassens at 55ff in this volume for an account of some of these negotiations.

14 Section 1 of the Abolition of Influx Control Act 68 of 1986.

15 Examples of rural communities with whose leaders the government has entered negotiations after, or in prospect of, litigation include the Mogopa tribe, the Mathopestad community, the Braklaagte community, the Driefontein community and the kwaNgema community.

16 See G Budlender 'Law and Lawlessness in South Africa' (1988) 4 *South African Journal on Human Rights* 139.

17 The notable features of the emergency regulations are: the granting of a wide discretion to arrest suspects and detain them without trial and without furnishing reasons for the detention (regs 3(1) and 3(3) R97 *GG* 11340 10 June 1988); the exclusion of the right of access to legal counsel (reg 3(7)(a) Proclamation R97 *GG* 11340 10 June 1988; and see *Omar v Minister of Law and Order* 1987 (3) SA 859 (A)); the prohibition on the Supreme Court from 'pronouncing upon the validity' of emergency regulations or setting aside the actions of security officials (s 5(b) of the Public Safety Act 3 of 1953); an indemnity to state officials from the consequences of unlawful actions (reg 15 Proclamation R97 *GG* 11340 10 June 1988); the grant of wide powers to local Commissioners of Police enabling them to rule by edict in the areas under their jurisdiction (reg 10 read together with the definition of 'commissioner' contained in reg 1(1) of Proclamation R97 *GG* 11340 of 10 June 1988); routinely conferring discretion on state officials in a subjective form (see regs 3,7 and 8 of Proclamation R97 *GG* 11340 of 10 June 1988) and the prohibition on the media from reporting either on conditions of detention or on the actions of the South African Police or the South African Defence Force in 'unrest' situations (Proc R99 *GG* 11342 of 10 June 1988, 'the Media Regulations').

18 N Haysom *Mabangalala The Rise of Right Wing Vigilantes in South Africa* (Johannesburg: Centre for Applied Legal Studies 1986); *Now Everyone is Afraid* (London: Catholic Institute of International Relations 1988).

19 See Robertson at 122ff in this volume.

20 See Armstrong & Haysom *Population Relocation: Social Engineering on a Vast Scale* Carnegie Paper no 86 (1986); see also Plasket in this volume at 214.

21 The Alteration of Boundaries of Self Governing Territories Bill 76 /89 (GA). This Bill, which has now lapsed, also sought to give the State President discretion to incorporate any part of South Africa into a 'homeland' without reference to any specific purpose.

22 *Mathebe v Government of the Republic of South Africa* 1988 (3) SA 667 (A); *Lefuo v Staatspresident van die Republiek van Suid-Afrika* 1989 (3) SA 924 (O).

23 The Prevention of Illegal Squatting Amendment Act 104 of 1988; see O'Regan in this volume at 162ff.

24 Section 3B(4)(a) of the Prevention of Illegal Squatting Act makes it more difficult for a person wishing to restrain the unlawful demolition of his house

by placing an onus upon him to show that the demolition is also male fide. In addition cl 10 of the Group Areas Amendment Bill 124/88 (GA) sought to remove from the courts the discretion to order eviction after conviction in terms of the Act (see *S v Govender* 1986 (3) SA 969 (T)). This Bill has been withdrawn.

25 See ss 5 and 7 of Act 104 of 1988.

26 See N Haysom & C Thompson 'Labouring Under the Law: South Africa's Farm Workers' (1986) 7 *Industrial Law Journal* 218; see also Hathorn & Hutchison at 194 ff in this volume.

27 *Farm Labour Report: Submission to the Manpower Commission on Farm Labour* (Johannesburg: Farm Labour Project 1982).

28 'Human Rights Index' (1989) 5 *South African Journal on Human Rights* 103.

29 Section 2(2) of the Labour Relations Act 28 of 1956.

30 Act 8 of 1959; see Keightley at 180-193 in this volume.

31 Act 52 of 1951.

32 See for example, Transvaal Pound Ordinance AN 2/29 as amended.

33 See s 2 of the Black Administration Act 38 of 1927; see also *Buthelezi v Minister of Bantu Administration and Development* 1961 (4) SA 835 (A) which stresses the absolute power of the State President to appoint chiefs. See also Unterhalter in this volume at 222-6.

34 See *Mokhatle v Union Government* 1926 AD 71 at 82.

35 P Selznick 'Social Advocacy and the Legal Profession in the United States' in D MacCormick (ed) *Lawyers in their Social Setting* (Edinburgh: W Green & Son 1976) 72-3.

36 The National States Constitution Act 21 of 1971 specifies that 'homelands' with self-governing status shall have legislative authority over certain matters listed in the schedule, but that legislation from the South African central government applies in other matters. See also A Whiteside & N Haysom 'A Separate Development: Labour Legislation in the Homelands' (1984) 5 *Industrial Law Journal* 251.

37 R Abel 'Law without Politics: Legal Aid under Advanced Capitalism' (1985) 32 *UCLA Law Review* 474 at 496-7 cited in G Budlender, above note 4, at 329.

38 Budlender at 329.

39 For other accounts of the Driefontein clinic see Claassens in this volume at 32ff and Lucie E White 1988 *Wisconsin Law Review* 699.

40 See C Dias & J Paul: 'Educating for Alternative Development: Sharing Knowledge about Law' in *Developing Resources with Third World's Poor* (TWLS 1985) cited by P Rutsch *Empowering the Disadvantaged* unpublished paper (1989) 19. See also P Selznick above note 35.

rt two: The Legal Context

A Man and his Land, Braklaagte
(Gill de Vlieg, Afrapix)

MICHAEL ROBERTSON

Dividing the Land: An Introduction to Apartheid Land Law

This chapter aims to provide an overview of apartheid land law in the late 1980s. I shall seek mainly to explain where the different laws apply, and how they interrelate. A historical introduction to some of the central legislative ancestries is provided elsewhere in this book[1] and readers would benefit from those insights before tackling this chapter.

In attempting to decipher the complex of racially-orientated land laws, I perceive three major streams of white parliamentary activity. They emerged most clearly after 1950 but their predecessors date to 1923 and before. The three streams are:

- The law, originating in concerns of sanitation in the 1880s, which commands the group areas system.
- Laws concerned with the great rural divide between white and African, formally entrenched in 1913 and culminating in today's 'national states' with their peculiar constitutional significance.
- Laws aimed at controlling the entry to and residence of Africans in the white-controlled urban areas. The first Natives (Urban Areas) Act[2] has an approximate descendant in a law of 1984.[3] Controls and restrictions have been loosened along the way in a number of important respects[4] but the policy to develop discrete African urban and peri-urban enclaves persists.

For the sake of completeness one should add a fourth category, a host of removal laws, sometimes inseparable from the ones above, which have all sought directly and indirectly to give effect to the grand apartheid scheme. Not as much in evidence as five or ten years ago, these permitted the brutal process of moving hundreds of thousands of people against their will.

This chapter will not deal directly with modern removal measures but one notes that some of the laws (identified by pioneering researchers in the 1970s) which were used by the state to uproot millions have subsequently been repealed. This is evident from a glance at the relevant pages of the first volume of the Report of the Surplus People Project.[5] For example, section 5(1)(b) of the Black Administration Act[6] was repealed in 1986.[7] This was a wicked law, permitting the summary removal of tribes or communities from one place to another, and none of its victims could have rued its passing. What is not widely known is that this very section has resurfaced, not through Cape Town's general affairs process, but at Ulundi's ethnic equivalent. The words 'State President' have been substituted by 'Minister' but the power remains unaltered. This appears, on the face of it, to be a singularly retrogressive move and it remains to be seen how the authorities there intend using it.[8] In passing one could note, too, the recent use by kwaZulu's Chief Minister of the other part of that section: 5(1)(a). This permits the State President to define, alter and adjust tribal boundaries. In a notice issued last year[9] the Chief Minister, purporting to rely upon these extraordinary presidential powers, contrived to excise certain farms from the control of a tribal authority. It might appear to the cynic that some of the worst of Pretoria's legacy lives on in its surrogates.

Two of the three legislative currents identified above have manifested modern subdivisions. The present family tree reveals, for the purpose of illustration, six distinct geographical offspring. A seventh (g) is not fully a member of the family.

1. Group areas	(a) modern group areas systems, with prospects for a little official mixing.
2. The black-white rural divide	(b) black (African) reserve areas outside the bantustans. (c) bantustans which are not 'independent' (national states). (d) bantustans which are 'independent' (TBVC countries).
3. Black enclaves in white-controlled, (mainly) urban areas	(e) established black townships in white cities and towns. (f) new black townships outside the bantustans.
	(g) informal settlements; some legalized, others not.

Each of these categories, (a) to (g), will be explained in more detail.

(a) Group areas land

The first Group Areas Act proper was passed in 1950.[10] The current statute dates back to 1966.[11] This is a complex piece of legislation, most often understood more in its social impact than its insidious technicality. It seeks to differentiate between people who are perceived somehow to manifest variances of humanity. These are deemed to be sufficiently significant to warrant the provision of separate – and unequal[12] – living spaces. Nowadays the Act concentrates its prescriptions in areas outside the work place.[13]

One of the most disturbing, if not notorious, judicial pronouncements regarding the purpose of the Group Areas Act was made in 1961 when a judge of the Appellate Division declared, without comment, that the Act was a 'colossal social experiment' and it was not for the court to decide whether it had any merit.[14] (Whether the judge correctly acquiesced in this regard raises pertinent questions about the role of the judiciary.) But the Act has been hugely costly in social terms. Although it cannot last, its legacy will be felt long after its demise.

It seems to me that the core features of the Act can be summarized in response to the following four questions:

1. Where does the Act apply?

Everywhere, except in ('scheduled' and 'released') black areas, black urban townships (see below), national parks, and other less significant areas.[15] It is not an altogether inaccurate simplification to say that the Group Areas Act applies wherever Africans are not permitted to own or to occupy land. This amounts to about 85 per cent of the country.

2. To whom does the Act apply?

The Act contemplates three major groups: white, African (referred to in the Act as 'black') and 'coloured'. It also permits the declaration of certain sub-groups by proclamation.[16] The classificatory criteria are both notorious and complex. They differ from those laid down in the Population Registration Act[17] with the result that a person may be classified differently under each Act.

Although the legislation anticipates group areas for Africans, in fact none have ever been declared, presumably because African land needs have been thought to have been sufficiently catered for in some of the other legislation outlined in this chapter. In concept, African group areas would not be different from African townships in urban areas (formalized under different legislation)[18] or perhaps even the rural tracts which are now largely contained within the bantustans.

The failed Group Areas Amendment Bill of 1988 was resisted because it aimed to tighten the enforcement sections of the Act.[19] The Bill also proposed to turn developing or future African enclaves (as contemplated in the Black Communities Development Act)[20] into African group areas. Had this particular provision been passed the legal situation might at least have been slightly simplified.

Group areas land is doubly restrictive against Africans in so far as ownership and occupation is concerned. This is because the Act's implementation has excluded all Africans and because the 1913 Land Act[21] forbids Africans from holding any rights to land outside those set aside for them.[22] This restriction was superceded (not repealed) by the introduction of group areas controls under the first Act of 1950. A section of that law provided that the 1913 restriction no longer applied wherever the Group Areas Act had force.[23] (I mention this because, by my understanding, in the unlikely event the Group Areas Act were to be repealed, this disqualification against Africans in the 1913 Act would 're-activate' these areas. It follows that the latter law's restrictions on Africans in white areas would also need to be repealed.)

3. *What are group areas?*

These are carefully described areas which are set aside by the State President for members of a specified group only, either to own, to occupy, or both.[24]

It is sometimes not appreciated that group areas proper constitute a proportionately small amount of the land to which the Act applies. When the first Group Areas Act came into operation in 1950 it permitted the state to declare all the areas to which it applied 'controlled areas'. From these, actual group areas have been proclaimed from time to time and the process continues.[25] The effect of the 'controlled area' designation was the immediate introduction of racial controls on ownership and occupation: the occupier had to be of the same racial group as the owner of the property.[26] In effect this has meant, particularly in white-owned rural areas, that it has been unnecessary to invoke the machinery of the Act any further.

By the end of 1987 there were 1 321 group areas for white, 'coloured' and Indian people, covering a total of 902 852 hectares.[27] This represents less than one percent of the area to which the Act applies.[28]

The Act also permits the declaration of at least another six types of area (such as 'specified' and 'defined' areas). Unlike group areas themselves, these remain part of the controlled area. Their significance, and dismal technicality, would not seem to command attention here.

Two recent developments do require mention. First, the State President may declare that the Act's restrictive and punitive provisions do not apply in central business districts. These are the so-called 'free trading areas'[29] which have been and continue to be established in urban areas countrywide.[30] Second, 1988 saw the passing of the Free Settlement Areas Act[31] which allows the appointment of a board (which has been appointed[32]) to advise the State President on the declaration of residential areas in which racial restrictions should not apply.[33] These are the impending 'free settlement' areas.

4. How does the Act work?

At the core of the legislation lurks a creature called a 'disqualified person'. Chameleon-like, it varies in hue according to the type of area concerned. For illustration, where a group area has been declared for ownership and occupation of group x, a disqualified person is one who is not of group x. This device extends also to things other than those human. A 'disqualified company' is otherwise a proper company which, by dint of its control being exercised by beings of a wrong colour, is prohibited from owning land in a right area.[34]

The Act permits the authorities unusually wide powers to enforce its provisions.[35] In many ways the most effective policing is achieved with the assistance of the various Deeds Registries where any attempt to register ownership in the name of a disqualified person would be thwarted. Purchasers must depose to an affidavit declaring their racial group.

Some of the harsher aspects of the Act's enforcement were blunted in the 1982 *Govender* judgment.[36] Here the court spoilt things for the state by requiring the prosecutor to place before the court information to permit a proper decision on whether eviction of the group areas transgressor is appropriate. This information includes evidence of 'the personal hardship which such an order may cause and the availability of alternative accommodation'.[37] The amendments proposed in 1989, subsequently withdrawn, aimed to deal with this 'problem'.[38]

(b) Black areas outside the bantustans[39]

The Land Act of 1913, abetted by a 1936 law,[40] resulted in the creation of African reserve areas, a process more fully described in the next section. These areas were gradually acquired in ownership by the South African Development Trust whose function was (and is) to maintain them for the benefit and well-being of their black occupants.[41] The executive arm responsible for these functions used to be the Department of Native Affairs, now called the Department of Development Aid.

Most reserves have been turned into self-governing and even 'independent' states. Trust areas – the bits which remain under the direct control of the white government and which amount to above 2,57 million hectares[42] – seem predominantly to be rural in nature, but there are some urban pockets. Durban's Inanda, Newtown and kwaDabeka fall into this category, while Umlazi and kwaMashu did before being incorporated into kwaZulu at the end of 1986.[43]

Townships which remain under the control of Development Aid attracted a special set of housing and administration regulations.[44] These were the '293' regulations of 1962 which, in 1988, were largely replaced by various proclamations,[45] which had the cumulative effect of putting tenure on a firmer footing. This was in line with the state's stated policy of recognizing the permanence of black urban dwellers.

Officially, Trust towns are expected to become 'associated' with a bantustan whose ethnic character fits with that of the town[47] (hence the lot of Umlazi and kwaMashu, amongst many others). In some instances the 'inter-ethnic'[48] complexion of a town makes it unsuitable for this attachment. What then? One state solution is to excise it from the Trust area and to place it into what I identified earlier as the third category. This happened recently to the Transvaal Trust towns of Soshanguve and Lethlabile which, by Act of Parliament,[49] suddenly found themselves reclassified as 'section 33' areas.[50] (See p 131, on the development of new black towns.)

Other powers to dabble with the composition of the released areas are granted to the Minister of Development Aid under the 1936 Act.[51] For example, in July 1989, certain released land in Natal's Estcourt district was excised through this process.[52] Where land, prior to excision, belongs to the Trust, on transfer it immediately becomes state-owned land. Conversely, state land incorporated into the released area is thereby vested in the Trust.[53]

In the rural Trust areas the allocation of land to individuals takes place under a 1969 proclamation.[54]

The significance of the 1913 law appears to be diminishing as more Trust land is transferred to homeland governments whose own administrations gain control over the use and disposal of the property. In white-dominated South Africa the real controls are exercised through the Group Areas Act. But in respect of the remaining Trust cum Development Aid lands, the 1913 provisions remain significant.

(c) The 'non-independent' bantustans

Under this sub-heading and the next, I attempt to outline the fate of the bulk of the black lands identified in 1913,[55] added to since 1936,[56] and more recently consolidated into what the legislation refers to as 'national' and 'independent' states.

Critics of apartheid have had no difficulty identifying the process of internal decolonization as one of the main struts of government policy for about 30 years. Bantustans began as a vain yet sometimes brutal attempt to place people in ethnic, geographic compartments with the transfer of political (but not economic) power to local elites who were more often than not passed off as real leaders. It has been suggested that the homelands dream was still being taken seriously as late as 1987.[57] Whether this was true of the latter half of 1989[58] is difficult to judge because of the relative paucity of government policy on many major issues. What does seem clear is that the remaining self-governing territories are not disposed towards accepting the 'independence' of the four TBVC countries.[59] Yet, given the plethora of powers which the self-governing homelands have accepted, there is not a great deal to distinguish them from the TBVC countries, other than the lack of local armies, diplomats, casinos and farcical border-posts.[60]

The Development Trust and Land Act of 1936[61] identified certain lands to be 'released' for African occupation, thereby expanding the reserves defined ('scheduled') in 1913. (The segregation restriction contained in the latter Act [62] applied with equal force to those released areas.) The acquisition of released lands by the South African Development Trust was not to exceed a stipulated quota in each province.

This needs some explaining. Although a certain proportion of the 1936 released lands was then already state-owned, a large percentage was also in private ownership. The Trust's task was to take title of the state's land in released areas (and in the 1913 'scheduled' areas, for that matter) and gradually to purchase the private lands identified for release. This process has continued for over 50 years. Its pace, presumably, has been determined largely by the amount of money made available to the Trust by the state each year.

By the end of 1987 about 5,5 million hectares had been acquired for bantustan consolidation at a cost, since 1936, of 1,27 billion rand.[63] Figures for 1986 show that released lands, purchased by the Trust, variously increased the sizes of the bantustans. Transkei, although not benefiting from any land in 1986, remained the largest with 4,28 million hectares. Bophuthatswana (4,18 million hectares) and kwaZulu (3,18 million) were the next biggest.[64] The 'quotas' which set the upper limits of how much land might be acquired under the 1936 Act were exceeded by 1987 by about 10 per cent, with the result that the ten bantustans now constitute about 13,8 per cent of South Africa's surface.[65]

The state's ability to fiddle with the fences of the national states, and therefore with the lives of all those affected by acts of incorporation, apparently knows no bounds. Powers granted under the National States Constitution Act[66] were recently found by the courts to be insufficient to effect the purported incorporation of Botshabelo into QwaQwa and Moutse into kwaNdebele.[67] Not to be outdone, the awesome artillery of the Alteration of Boundaries of Self-Governing Territories Bill was then introduced.[68] If passed, this bill would have negated the courts' findings and, except in the case of Moutse (presently under judicial inquiry), validated the invalid proclamations.[69] As for future land shifts, the State President would have been free to do what he deemed expedient after consultation with his own Minister and the 'cabinet' of the territory affected – but not with the inhabitants concerned.[70] Fortunately, the Bill has lapsed.

The self-governing territories (or national states) have already received title of the land in their jurisdictions, and legislative authority in land affairs. This happened when prior to December 1986 the State President used his considerable powers[71] to extend schedule 1 of the National States Constitution Act to include numerous items such as '31Z', which specifies land affairs. The Act itself provides that as from the date of self-governing status the legislative body concerned inherits the capacity to make laws within the schedule's categories.[72] In the case of the six self-governing territories (Lebowa, Gazankulu, QwaQwa, kwaNdebele, kwaZulu and kaNgwane) item 31Z was brought into operation by decree on 31 December 1986.[73] By no coincidence, a separate set of six proclamations effective from the same date (31 December) transferred from the government of the Republic to the six governments concerned, all the land situated in their jurisdictions, the ownership or control of which had until then been vested in the government, a provincial administration or the Trust.[74]

This massive transfer in six directions was accomplished at the strike of a pen by means of powers vested in the President and provided in three separate Acts. In a third simultaneous manoeuvre the Minister of Education and Development Aid used his powers to transfer administrative and other functions relating to '293' townships (see above) to the various governments concerned (thereby giving effect to item 28 of the schedule 1). In the case of kwaZulu this notice included the townships of Umlazi, kwaMashu, Mpumalanga and Mpophomeni.[75]

Therefore, taking kwaZulu for illustration, from 1 January 1987 the legislative authority at Ulundi acquired sovereignty in land affairs. The Zulu government also received the relevant South African legislation, 'frozen' at that point. From then on, Ulundi was free to repeal, amend or replace all the existing land legislation it inherited. In 1988 kwaZulu's Department of the Interior published the kwaZulu Land Bill.[76] Its proposals amount to a consolidation of existing legislation, the preservation of certain rights and the removal of some restrictions, but without altering the existing powers and functions of tribal authorities, chiefs or headmen. Of interest is the schedule of laws which will be repealed, either in part or entirely. These include the Black Land Act of 1913, the Development Trust and Land Act of 1936, parts of the '293' regulations governing land tenure in towns and the whole of the rural areas land regulations of 1969.

(d) TBVC countries

The TBVC countries all acquired the power to legislate over land matters at a certain point of their constitutional histories. The South African state also transferred to them its ownership rights, located mainly with the South African Development Trust. Since then each of these countries has passed its own land laws.

In the case of the Transkei the transfer of the authority in land matters was authorized by the Transkei Constitution Act of 1963.[77] The first local changes were made in 1968[78] and later through the repeal of the Group Areas Act there in 1976.[79]

In Bophuthatswana, which was granted 'independence' in 1977,[80] the Land Control Act of 1979[81] made a number of changes, including the repeal of the 1913 and 1936 Acts. More land has been granted to Bophuthatswana through the Bophuthatswana Border Extension Act.[82] The reverse process has also applied by means of Bophuthatswana's own Border Adjustment Act[83] with the subsequent re-acceptance of this land by the South African authorities.[84]

A general measure designed to facilitate Pretoria in the easy transfer of sovereignty in land matters is the Borders of Particular States Extension Act of 1980,[85] amended again recently.[86] The 'particular states' to which the Act applies are the TBVC countries and it grants the State President the power to proclaim that, as from a certain date, land defined in the schedule shall be transferred to the 'sovereign and independent state' concerned.[87] A comparison between the areas described in this Act's schedule and those listed in the schedules of the 1913 and 1936 Land Acts suggest that much, but not all[88] of the newly identified land was never included as potential black areas in the earlier legislation,[89] and was therefore not part of the massive transfers at or about various dates of 'independence'. By means of the 1980 Act, certain transfers have already been effected. For example, some farms in the districts of Stutterheim and East London were incorporated into Ciskei by proclamation in 1989.[90] The fate of land in the

Rustenburg district which became part of Bophuthatswana in February 1989 was similar.[91]

(e) Black townships in white-controlled urban areas

Townships in this category have a different legislative history from those which were established on Trust land. The Natives (Urban Areas) Act of 1923,[92] replaced by a consolidating measure in 1945,[93] permitted the establishment by local authorities and others of formal black townships and institutions such as men's hostels. Until the 1970s official state policy was not to recognize the permanence of black urban dwellers. The laws under which these often deprived enclosures were managed, and which dictated the quality of tenure,[94] were consistent with the generally antagonistic attitude towards a permanent black urban workforce. When this policy began to change it was merely a matter of time before the laws themselves would require alteration.

The new enactment has recently emerged, styled the Conversion of Certain Rights to Leasehold Act,[95] and it permits the relatively easy conversion of existing rights under the outmoded regulations into rights of leasehold for a period of 99 years. In so doing lessors are placed on the same footing as those granted leasehold in new townships[96] (see next section) and this opens the door for further conversion to common-law ownership under certain circumstances.[97] Unlike the Trust townships, these are controlled by the Department of Constitutional Development and Planning whose powers and responsibilities have been delegated to Administrators in each province.

(f) Development of new urban townships for blacks

The Black Communities Development Act[98] is, in effect, a group areas act for Africans outside the bantustans. In its own language, its main purpose is 'to provide for the purposeful development of black communities outside the national states'. In other words it allows for controlled development of new African townships upon land currently governed by the Group Areas Act. Together with its regulations[99] this Act presents a picture which is hardly user-friendly, even to a lawyer. But for the purpose of this overview, it would seem sufficient to point out that it is essentially a law which enables the identification and designation of land ('section 33 areas') and, thereafter, the development of black townships.[100] As a result of amendments two years after its enactment, tenure granted to residents of these new suburbs includes both 99-year leasehold and ownership, again reflecting the shift in government policy alluded to above.

(g) Other settlements

This, the final category which was identified earlier, is included for the sake of completeness. Aspects of informal settlements of various kinds are the subject of other chapters. But in the context of this piece it is necessary to point out that some informal settlements can acquire special legal recognition different from any of the statutory regimes mentioned above.

Prior to the 1988 amendments, the Squatting Act[101] made provision for the declaration of 'emergency camps' and those that were declared[102] before the amendments have been preserved.[103] The Act now contemplates 'transit' areas which involve the establishment by local authorities of temporary settlements for homeless people.[104] The Act also makes provision for the designation, by an Administrator, of land for the development of residential areas.[105] This may require the expropriation of land and the declaration that certain laws (including the Group Areas and Slums Act) will not apply to the areas so designated.[106]

There may be other provisions in other laws which seek to regularize unplanned settlements. For example, a recent amendment to the 1913 Act permits the State President to make regulations to prevent overcrowding of land in black ('scheduled' and 'released') rural areas.[107]

Conclusion

To the extent that apartheid involves a preoccupation with racial categories, developments in South Africa's land laws in the last decade reveal little or no deviation from the predominant white mentality. The three major avenues of racist law-making in land affairs have, I suggest, not changed in any fundamental respect. There are new categories, new terms, new methods and even perhaps new expectations, but universally notorious geographical and residential apartheid is as much in evidence in 1989 as it was in the 1950s and 1960s. Only the rhetoric has changed (propaganda tends to steer clear of the word 'apartheid'). It remains to be seen whether the state as presently constituted is capable of breaking with the obsessions which translate into a vast patchwork of racially defined lands. Many doubt it is.

Notes

1 See Bundy in this volume at 3ff and Marcus at 14ff.

2 Act 21 of 1923.

3 Black Communities Development Act 4 of 1984.

4 Such as the dropping of formal influx control: Abolition of Influx Control Act 68 of 1986.

5 Surplus People Project *Forced Removals in South Africa* vol I (Cape Town 1983) 86-95.

6 Act 38 of 1927.

7 Section 1 Act 68 of 1986. Other major laws repealed include the Blacks (Urban Areas) Consolidation Act 25 of 1945.

8 KwaZulu Black Administration Amendment Act of 1988.

9 KwaZulu GN 391 of 1988 in kwaZulu *GG* of 15 July 1988, affecting the farms Stedham and Welgevonden.

10 Act 41 of 1950. See Dodson in this volume at 137 for further discussion of the Group Areas Act.

11 Act 36 of 1966.

12 *Minister of the Interior v Lockhat* 1961 (2) SA 587 (A).

13 Following the introduction of free trading areas (s 19) in 1984 many central business districts have been deregulated.

14 *Lockhat* at 602.

15 Definition of 'controlled areas' in s 1(1) and s 23(6)(c).

16 Section 12.

17 Act 30 of 1950.

18 Black Communities Development Act 4 of 1984, and see below.

19 Clause 17(2) of B124/88 (GA).

20 Section 33 Act 4 of 1984.

21 Black Land Act 27 of 1913.

22 Section 1.

23 Section 38(6) Act 41 of 1950.

24 Section 23 Act 36 of 1966.

25 For example, in May 1989 group areas were proclaimed at Koekenaap, George, Idasvallei, Goodwood and Cloetesville for various 'groups': Procs 67, 68, 69, 70 and 71 of 26 May 1989, GN 11883.

26 Section 20 Act 36 of 1966.

27 1987/8 *Race Relations Survey* 491.

28 Based on deduction made from figures in *Race Relations Survey* ibid, 877.

29 Section 19.

30 For example, at Lichtenburg in May 1989: Proc 66 of 26 May 1989, GN 11883.

31 Act 102 of 1988 brought into operation on 1 March 1989 by Proc 12 of 24 February 1989, *GG* no 11724.

32 Proc 12 of 24 February 1989, *GG* no 11724.

33 Section 7 Act 102 of 1988.

34 Definition of 'disqualified company' in s 1(1) Act 36 of 1966.

35 Sections 38-46.

36 *S v Govender* 1986 (3) SA 969 (T). Inexplicably this judgment was reported only in 1986.

37 At 971.

38 Clause 10 Group Areas Amendment Bill 124/88 (GA).

39 This section deals with reserves for Africans. There is legislation governing the 23 reserves which exist for 'coloured' people, the Rural Areas Act 9 of 1987(HR).

40 Act 27 of 1913 and Act 18 of 1936 respectively.

41 Section 4.

42 1987/8 *Race Relations Survey* 878.

43 GN 864 of 24 December 1986, *GG* 10559.

44 Proc R293 of 16 November 1962, *GG* 373.

45 Procs R29, R30, R404 and R405 of 9 March 1988, *GG* No 11166. The remainder of R293 was repealed by Proc R95 of 23 June 1989, *GG* 11965.

46 See, for example, 'Statement by Minister of Education and Development Aid' on repeal of Proc R293 of 1962, issued by Ministry of Education and Development Aid on 9 March 1988; and *Financial Mail* 6 January 1989 at 26; and Memorandum to Conversion of Certain Rights to Leasehold Bill 70/88 (GA).

47 Memorandum to Excision of Released Areas Bill 62/88 (GA).

48 Memorandum ibid.

49 Excision of Released Areas Act 54 of 1988.

50 Section 33 areas are 'development areas' under Act 4 of 1984.

51 Sections 2(2) and 2(2)(a) Development Trust and Land Act 18 of 1936.

52 Proc R130 of 21 July 1989, *GG* 12015.

53 Section 2 Development Trust and Land Act 18 of 1936 as recently amended by s 1 Act 31 of 1989.

54 Proc R188 of 1969 as amended.

55 The 'scheduled' areas under Act 27 of 1913.

56 The 'released' areas under Act 18 of 1936.

57 1987/8 *Race Relations Survey* 850.

58 See for example H Corder & C Murray 'Homelands Incorporation: the Courts Overruled' (1989) 21 *De Rebus* 529.

59 These are Transkei, Bophuthatswana, Venda and Ciskei.

60 The powers handed to the self-governing states are extensive; see s 3 and schedule 1 of the National States Constitution Act 21 of 1971.

61 Act 18 of 1936.

62 Section 1 Act 27 of 1913.

63 *Natal Mercury* 22 April 1988. Other figures, based on *Hansard*, put the areas at 6,7 million hectares: 1987/8 *Race Relations Survey* 877.

64 1987/8 *Race Relations Survey* 877.

65 Ibid 877 and 878.

66 Section 1(2).

67 Proc R169 of 2 December 1987, *GG* 11051 affecting the incorporation of Botshabelo; and Proc R227 of 31 December 1985, *GG* 10053 affecting the incorporation of Moutse. The cases were *Lefuo v Staatspresident van die Republiek van Suid Afrika* 1989 (3) SA 924 (O) (dealing with Botshabelo) and *Mathebe v Regering van die RSA* 1988 (3) SA 667 (A) (dealing with Moutse).

68 Bill 76-89 (GA).

69 Clause 3.

70 Clause 2; and see Corder & Murray above note 58 at 529.

71 Section 37A Act 21 of 1971.

72 Section 3 Act 21 of 1971.

73 GN R2751 of 31 December 1986, *GG* 10570.

74 Procs R228, R229, R230, R231, R232 and R233 of 24 December 1986, *GG* 10560.

75 GN 864 of 24 December 1986, *GG* 10559.

76 KwaZulu GN 835 of 1988.

77 Section 59 and item 9 of First Schedule, Act 48 of 1963.

78 Act 4 of 1968 (Transkei).

79 Act 15 of 1976 (Transkei); and see A Beck 'Land Tenure and Social Justice: An Outline of the Situation in Transkei' in C Cross & R Haines (eds) *Towards Freehold? Options for Land and Development in South Africa's Black Rural Areas* (Cape Town: Juta 1988) 276 at 280.

80 Status of Bophuthatswana Act 89 of 1977.

81 Act 39 of 1979 (Bophuthatswana).

82 Act 8 of 1978.

83 Act 25 of 1985 (Bophuthatswana).

84 Incorporation of Certain Land in the Republic of South Africa Act 42 of 1989.

85 Act 2 of 1980.

86 Borders of Particular States Extension Amendment Act 59 of 1988, which amended the Act's schedule.

87 Section 1.

88 For example, in relation to land potentially for the benefit of Transkei certain farms in the Maclear district ('Anstey' and 'Stretton') appear in the schedule of both the 1936 and 1980 Acts. It would seem therefore that these lands did not, at the date of land transfer on 'independence', form part of the area described as Transkei (see s 2 Transkei Constitution Act 48 of 1963); nor may they have been acquired by the state or the SADT by the relevant date. Note that the 1980 legislation anticipates that some of the land identified in its schedule will already have been acquired by the SADT: see s 2 Act 2 of 1980.

89 The 1913 and 1936 Acts; for example, land in the Queenstown district which is identified in the 1980 Act is not mentioned in the earlier laws.

90 Proc 15 of 3 March 1989.

91 Proc 4 of 3 February 1989. See also Proc R98 of 30 June 1989, transferring various land to Bophuthatswana.

92 Act 21 of 1923.

93 Blacks (Urban Areas) Consolidation Act 25 of 1945.

94 GN 1036 of 1968.

95 Act 81 of 1988, brought into operation on 1 January 1989; Proc 226 of 30 December 1988.

96 Section 4; new townships are possible under Act 4 of 1984.

97 Section 57A Act 4 of 1984.

98 Act 4 of 1984.

99 GN R2451 of 1 November 1985, GNs R1897 and R1899 of 12 September 1986 and GN 1002 of 25 May 1988.

100 Sections 33-40.

101 Section 6 of the Prevention of Illegal Squatting Act 52 of 1951, see O'Regan in this volume at 176-7.

102 For example relating to Brits in BN 26 of 26 April 1988, *GG* No 11272.

103 Section 11(6).

104 Section 6(3).

105 Section 6A.

106 Section 6A(4).

107 Section 1 Development Aid Laws Amendment Act 53 of 1988, amending s 9 Black Land Act 27 of 1913. Similar powers are granted to local authorities under s 32 Slums Act 76 of 1979.

ALAN DODSON

The Group Areas Act: Changing Patterns of Enforcement

The location and importance of the Group Areas Act 36 of 1966 ('the Act') in the overall mesh of apartheid land law is described in an earlier chapter.[1] What will be examined here are certain of the provisions of the Act relating to its enforcement.

It might be asked whether such an investigation is necessary in the light of the current policy surrounding the Act. The controversial Group Areas Bill[2] which sought to facilitate enforcement, has been dropped by the government and the number of prosecutions under the Act has declined dramatically, prosecuting authorities conceding that enforcement is often virtually impossible.[3]

Nevertheless, the following considerations justify this exercise. First, a widespread form of low intensity enforcement persists in the form of police investigations. These are carried out in terms of provisions of the Act which seriously impinge upon fundamental rights. Secondly, reassertions of official determination to protect group interests and rights suggest that more vigorous enforcement is a real threat, particularly once more 'free settlement areas' have been established.[4] Thirdly, enforcement by agencies other than the police remains possible in terms of the existing provisions. Two manifestations of this are increased evictions by landlords under the Act, with or without pressure from the authorities, and proposed 'notification points'. Fourthly, an examination of enforcement mechanisms in the Act is of jurisprudential interest. The prevalence of executive discretion throughout the Act and the response of the courts in adjudicating its exercise has had a widespread effect on the development (or underdevelopment) of administrative law.[5] In this chapter, enforcement will be considered

Meeting of Labour Tenants, eastern Transvaal
(Cedric Nunn, Afrapix)

separately in terms of police enforcement, judicial enforcement and private enforcement.

Part I: Low Intensity Police Enforcement

While there are at present few prosecutions under the Act, an ever-increasing number of complaints is being investigated by the police. Thus in 1987 there were two convictions under the Act and 1243 complaints investigated. The figures for 1988 were 10 and 1641 respectively.[6] Groups monitoring the enforcement of the Act report persistent visits by the police to houses of suspected offenders and the associated disruption of lives, to the extent that investigations on their own constitute a form of enforcement. Often visits will be followed by a warning from a police officer requiring the occupants of premises to vacate or face prosecution.

Section 43 of the Act, read with section 46, accords the South African Police exceptionally wide powers of investigation, which seriously infringe rights of privacy and property and the right to remain silent. Thus a police officer investigating an offence under the Act (or any other law affecting landownership or occupation) is allowed by section 43, without any warrant:

(a) to enter any premises at any time of day or night and 'make such examination and enquiry as may be necessary' (section 43(1)(a));

(b) to require documentary or other evidence to be produced 'then and there' (section 43(1)(b));

(c) to seize or copy such documents or other evidence and require explanations of entries in documents (section 43(1)(c));

(d) to interrogate any person on the premises 'either alone, or in the presence of any other person, as he thinks fit' (section 43(1)(d));

(e) to require any potential witness to appear before him for the purposes of interrogation (section 43(1)(e)).

To add insult to injury, any person in such premises is required to assist the police officer by providing the officer with whatever 'facilities' are required in order to exercise these powers, on pain of committing an offence (section 43(4) read with section 46(1)(c)). Similarly, it is an offence to hinder a police officer in the exercise of these powers, to make a false statement to an officer or to refuse or fail to provide a full and satisfactory reply to any questions (section 43(1) read with section 46(1)(g), (h) and (i)).

The question arises whether the provisions in section 43(1)(d) for solitary interrogation at the discretion of the police officer would allow him or her to exclude legal representation. Our law allows interference with this right only where such interference is provided for in the statute expressly or by necessary implication.[7] While our courts have, of late, not hesitated to read in such a necessary implication,[8] it is submitted that this is clearly not the case here. Support for this contention may be derived from section 43(3) (discussed below) which provides that people interrogated in terms of section 43(1)(d) or (e) retain 'all privileges to which a person giving evidence before a *court of law* is entitled'. It is unlikely that residents will be aware of these privileges or that they will successfully be able to insist upon them, in the face of pressure by the police. I would argue that in framing the legislation the legislature could not have envisaged that residents would be aware of these privileges, nor could it have expected that they would be able to claim such a privilege without the advice and assistance of a legal representative. Interpreting the section so as to permit the exclusion of legal representation thus gives rise to an unreasonable result which could not have been intended by Parliament. The retention of privileges provides an important qualification to the powers of interrogation. Perhaps the most important privileges in this context would be the privilege against self-incrimination and marital privilege. The wide range of offences and other types of administrative penalty provided for in the Act would mean that most people interrogated would be at risk of incrimination and could, by claiming these privileges, maintain their right to silence.

An important issue is whether persons being interrogated are entitled to refuse to provide their addresses on enquiry where the reply is incriminating. If the police officer regards himself or herself as conducting an enquiry solely under the Act, the privilege clause would apply. On the other hand, section 41 of the Criminal Procedure Act 51 of 1977 confers wide powers on peace officers to require suspects and potential witnesses of any offence to provide their name and address. It would thus be important to establish from the police officer under which legislation he or she purported to act. In any event it is submitted that it could never have been the intention of Parliament in framing section 41 to force a witness to risk self-incrimination and that, having regard to the purpose of the section, it would not be unlawful either to refuse to provide an address or, instead of refusing, to provide a work address. The latter option would be completely acceptable as our courts prefer a wide definition of the concept of an 'address', meaning essentially a place where the person concerned may be contacted.[9]

A final observation is that the new inspectors under a scheme recently announced by the government which aims at 'sensitive' enforcement, will not have any claim to the powers in section 43 as they are officials employed by the Department of Local Government and Housing.[10]

Part II: Judicial Enforcement

The main method of enforcement contained in the Act is criminal prosecution. This is illustrated by the fact that the only provision for eviction of offenders is that contained in section 46(2) which allows a magistrate to order the eviction of a person upon conviction for illegal occupation under the Act. Prosecutions are at present rare. Many ascribe this to the 1982 decision of the Transvaal Provincial Division in *S v Govender*[11] where Goldstone J held, inter alia, that personal circumstances, which may include the availability of alternative accommodation, must first be considered before a magistrate exercises his discretion to grant an ejectment order (the case is discussed in more detail below).

The present position may soon change. It has been predicted that the new inspectors will facilitate ejectment orders by identifying alternative accommodation.[12] Other reasons have already been suggested in this chapter.

Section 26 of the Act, which, read with section 46, provides for the prosecution of 'disqualified persons' illegally occupying a group area (and persons allowing such occupation), is the key provision. An examination of the section is informative as it links up with a number of other pivotal provisions of the Act. The complexity of the links provide room for creative defences.

The charge

In order to secure a conviction under section 26, the state must prove:

(a) the existence of a proclamation by the State President in terms of section 23(1)(a) that the area concerned is an area for *occupation* by a particular group only (a proclamation in terms of section 23(1)(b) relating to *ownership* only would not be sufficient);

(b) that the premises concerned fall within the proclaimed group area;

(c) that the accused person occupies or occupied (or allows or allowed the occupation of) the premises concerned;

(d) that the accused person is a disqualified person in that he or she is not of the same group as that for which the area has been proclaimed;

(e) that proper notice has been given in terms of sub-sections 23(2) or 23(3), if the accused was in lawful occupation of those premises immediately prior to the proclamation of the group area;

(f) unlawfulness;

(g) mens rea on the part of the accused.

These elements will be dealt with separately, together with possible special defences relating to unlawfulness and mens rea.

Proclamation of a group area

The Act does not in itself create group areas but sets up the machinery for doing so. The proclamation of a group area is ultimately effected by the State President in terms of section 23(1). This he may not do unless the responsible minister has first considered a written report made by the Group Areas Board (section 32). The preparation of such a report must be preceded by the publication of a notice (in a specified manner) identifying not only the matter being investigated but also the area affected. In relation to both the latter aspects interested persons must be invited to submit representations (section 5(2)). Moreover, the Board is expressly required to take into consideration the availability of alternative accommodation for people whose occupation will become unlawful by virtue of any proclamation (section 5(6)).

The language of section 5(2) and (6) is peremptory and it is accordingly submitted that non-compliance with their provisions would render the report of the Board invalid, or, at least, not a 'report ... under section 5' as is required by section 32. This would, in turn, render any proclamation based on the report invalid. Potential grounds for challenge to the validity of the proclamation in criminal proceedings are immediately apparent.[13]

In theory, review grounds should not be confined to those of a procedural nature. In declaring a group area by proclamation, the State President exercises an administrative discretion and the product is a form of delegated legislation.[14] Scrutiny by the courts in terms of the review grounds set out in *Kruse v Johnson*[15] should be an automatic consequence, so that invalidity of the relevant proclamation could constitute a special defence.

Before considering the decided cases in this regard, mention should be made briefly of procedural constraints on a challenge to the validity of a proclamation in the magistrate's court. In terms of section 110 of the Magistrates' Court Act 32 of 1944, a magistrate's court may not pronounce on the validity of (inter alia) a proclamation of the State President, and the presiding officer is expressly required to assume its validity. Where a ground of defence is that the proclamation is ultra vires, section 117 of the Criminal Procedure Act provides for the accused to be committed for a summary trial in the Supreme Court.

Once in the Supreme Court, I would argue that, in accordance with the general principles of criminal procedure, the state bears the onus of proving the validity of the proclamation. However, provided that it is valid on its face, the doctrine omnia praesumuntur rite esse acta (all acts are presumed to have been lawfully done) will place a heavy evidentiary burden on the accused to show grounds for review. (A contrary approach is suggested in *R v Abdurahman*[16] but questioned by Rumpff CJ in *S v Werner and Adams.*[17]) The state can be compelled to produce all the documents and reports preceding the proclamation.[18] A stay of proceedings pending a review of the State President's decision to issue the proclamation in terms of Rule 53 of the Uniform Rules of Court may provide a preferable procedure.

Turning to the decided cases, one finds, however, that the courts have failed dismally in their constitutional duty to protect the individual in the face of the wide powers accorded the executive under the Act. As Schoombee has pointed out,[19] the notorious decision of the Appellate Division in *Minister of the Interior v Lockhat*[20] has given the executive virtual immunity against judicial review in implementing the Act. In that case, property owners of the 'Indian' group challenged a proclamation affecting them on the grounds, inter alia, of the State President's failure to consider the availability of suitable alternative accommodation and the partial and unequal treatment to a substantial degree of different groups to which the proclamation gave rise.

For the first ground there was strong support in section 5(6) and other provisions of the Act and related legislation, as well as in decided cases under the Blacks (Urban Areas) Act 21 of 1923. For the second ground, there was ample authority, including decisions of the Appellate Division such as *R v Abdurahman*[21] for the rule of interpretation that a power to discriminate to the extent of partial and unequal treatment to a substantial degree would not be attributed by a court unless the relevant statute provided for it expressly or by necessary implication. No express authority was to be found in the Act.[22] Every government statement at the time of its enactment in Parliament insisted that there was no intention to discriminate.[23] While the court a quo had no difficulty in finding that such a result was not necessarily implied, the Appellate Division reversed the decision, finding that substantial inequalities were clearly contemplated by the legislature as a consequence of the Act and rejecting all the grounds of review, including that relating to alternative accommodation.

Criticism of the decision has been both widespread and apposite and it is unnecessary to repeat in detail.[24] Its legacy has been two-and-a-half decades of dereliction of duty by the courts which have invariably relied on *Lockhat* to reject challenges based on the unreasonable exercise of powers under the Act or the absence of alternative accommodation.[25]

During September 1980, *Lockhat*[26] was reconsidered in the Appellate Division when the cases of *S v Adams* and *S v Werner*[27] were heard together. In both cases a defence of necessity was raised; this is discussed below. In the latter, the validity of the relevant proclamation was again challenged. Professor Dugard argued the challenge both on the basis that *Lockhat* could be distinguished and on the basis that it was incorrectly decided. A number of new grounds were argued, including manifest injustice, interference with the fundamental right to family life and the presumption that Parliament intends to legislate in accordance with its international obligations (in this instance articles 55 and 56 of the Charter of the United Nations). (The heads of argument are reproduced in the report and are essential reading for any lawyer considering a review on this basis.) In a judgment more noteworthy for its brevity and cynicism than its jurisprudential merit, it was considered relevant that *Werner* had voluntarily moved to Johannesburg as a 'coloured', knowing of the shortage of 'coloured' housing and that he was free to return to the Cape at any time. Rumpff CJ reasserted that the legislature must have foreseen housing shortages for particular groups as an inevitable consequence of the Act and confirmed the correctness of *Lockhat.*

Any lawyer might be forgiven for throwing in the towel at this point. Yet it is submitted that the following small signs suggest that there is still room for creativity. For instance, Professor Dugard, while defending a so-called mixed marriage couple on charges under section 26, recently challenged the validity of a proclamation on the grounds that it ignored the commitment to Christian values contained in the preamble to the Constitution Act 110 of 1983 and that it was grossly unreasonable that subordinate legislation should have the effect of interfering with a marriage no longer prohibited by the now repealed Prohibition of Mixed Marriages Act 55 of 1949. In addition, the court in *Govender*[28] provided a structure within which a magistrate's administrative discretion was to be exercised.[29] What is more, the decision allows the alternative accommodation argument in by the back door (see pp 153-4). Another recent decision which is potentially of great significance in this regard is *Waks v Jacobs en die Stadsraad van Carletonville.*[30] Despite the clear provisions of the Reservation of Separate Amenities Act 49 of 1953 which allow a local authority to reserve parks for the exclusive use of a particular race group, with an express provision permitting the unequal treatment of race groups, the court set aside a decision to reserve all city parks for the white group on the grounds of unreasonableness. This stands in stark contrast to the decisions in *Lockhat* and its successors where although unequal treatment was not expressly allowed, a proclamation having this effect was found to be valid.

Premises within the group area

The state must prove that the premises allegedly illegally occupied fall within the proclaimed group area. Section 34 is designed to assist the state. It provides that the relevant Surveyor General may issue a certificate stating that the land it describes is situated within a group area defined in terms of section 23(1). The certificate is then deemed to constitute prima facie evidence of its contents in a court of law. The form of the certificate is prescribed by regulation.[31]

Various special defences have been taken on the basis of alleged flaws in certificates under this section and its predecessors. In *S v Motara*,[32] the defence's contention, that there was no evidence that the person who signed the certificate was authorized to do so by the Surveyor General, was rejected on the basis of a general provision allowing delegation to land surveyors in his or her office contained in Act 9 of 1927. (The certificate is depicted in the reported judgment.) In *S v Bhoolia*[33] it was contended that the surveyor exceeded his authority in certifying premises to be in a white group area when section 34 referred only to 'any group area'. It was suggested that there should be additional proof that it was an area of the *white* group. The argument failed. (A further argument based on the lack of correlation between the description of the property on the certificate and that in the title deed failed due to the absence of proof of such a difference.)

Occupation

No definition of occupation is contained in the Act. It has been pointed out that in ordinary usage the concept has a variety of meanings depending on its context. Fortunately in regard to this element the courts have been prepared to adopt a fairly restrictive interpretation. Thus early cases applied the meaning given to the term under so-called 'pegging' legislation (which restricted the land rights of 'Asiatics' before the introduction of the Act) in the matter of *Madrassa Anjuman Islamia v Johannesburg Municipal Council*,[34] that is, habitual physical presence or physical presence for a substantial period. Applying this definition it was held, correctly, that attendance at cinemas and sports gatherings did not constitute occupation.[35]

True to form, the legislature responded by introducing a provision whereby lesser forms of physical presence could be defined by the State President by proclamation as constituting occupation for the purposes of the Act. This is contained in section 1(4) and states:

> The State President may by proclamation in the *Gazette* declare that, subject to such exceptions as may be specified in the proclamation, any provision of this Act relating to the occupation of land or premises

shall apply also with reference to any person who is at any time present in or upon any land or premises, or in or upon land or premises situated in an area specified in the proclamation, or in or upon land or premises other than land or premises situated in an area so specified, for a substantial period of time or for the purpose of attending any place of public entertainment or partaking of any refreshments at a place where refreshments are served or as a member of or guest in any club, as if his presence constituted occupation of such land or premises.

The proclamation currently in force is R17 of 1986 dated 21 February 1986 (*GG* 10110) which provides that:

except in an area defined in a proclamation under section 19(1) of the said Act, the provisions of sections 17(1), 20(1) and 26(1) of that Act, in so far as they prohibit the occupation of land or premises and the allowing of such occupation, shall apply also with reference to any person who is at any time present in or upon any land or premises in the controlled area or in a group area, as the case may be, and to any person who allows such person to be so present for a substantial period of time or for the purpose of attending any place of public entertainment or partaking of any refreshment as a customer at a place where refreshments are served in a licenced restaurant, refreshment or tea-room or eating-house where the partaking of refreshment ordinarily involves the use of seating accommodation, or as a member of or guest in any club (save as a representative or guest of the state, a provincial administration, a local authority or a statutory body) as if his presence constituted occupation of such land or premises. [The reference to section 19 is a reference to 'free trading areas'.]

Section 1(4) is yet another example of the prevalence of executive discretion in the Act. Schoombee argues most convincingly that the general terms of the section dealing with presence 'for a substantial period of time' called for further specification in any proclamation issued under it and that the failure to do so in the above proclamation renders at least that portion void for vagueness.[36]

Not to be outdone by the legislature, a judicial attempt was also made to curtail the complete acceptance of the *Madrassa* definition. In *R v Asmal*[37] Broome JP criticized the restriction of occupation to habitual physical presence and included use of premises for storage purposes only as occupation without anyone being habitually present.

This decision was criticized in *R v Ghoor*[38] where, after a review of the decided cases, De Villiers AJ settled for the following definition:

habitual physical presence, or physical presence for substantial periods of time, flowing from some form or another of control, whether subordinate or overriding, over the land or premises in question.

Subsequent judgments have followed this definition.[39]

Finally, brief mention should be made of two provisions which have the respective effect of 'expanding' and 'contracting' the concept of occupation. Section 35 effectively penalizes the use of premises in a way not amounting to letting where permission for letting only has been granted.[40] A provision contracting the 'occupation net' is section 19 which allows relaxation of restrictions in 'free trading areas'.

A disqualified person

Membership of a group other than that for which the area has been proclaimed in terms of section 23 is the basis upon which a person is disqualified. The issue must finally be determined by the court in a grotesque and humiliating procedure in which it must debate upon and decide on which side of the apartheid divide the accused falls. It is an indictment of our courts that they have not, at the very least, regularly condemned the process, involving, as it does, invasion of fundamental rights to privacy, dignity, equality and an undisturbed family life, as well as the right to due process. (Something of an exception is to be found in the comments of Hiemstra J in *R v Nicholas.*[41]) The courts are guided in their enquiry by the views of prying, prejudiced neighbours and 'expert witnesses' such as school inspectors with years of experience in ferreting out pupils whose skin pigmentation does not match that of the educational institution concerned.[42]

The Act recognizes the following groups: white, 'coloured', black and any other group declared by the State President by proclamation (sections 1 and 12). Methods of discrimination are contained within the Act and no cross reference is made to the Population Registration Act 30 of 1950. The white group includes any person who 'in appearance obviously is a white person' as well as any person 'generally accepted' as a white person. Excluded from the white group are persons white in appearance but generally accepted to be of another group and white persons who marry or cohabit with a person of another group. The black group includes 'any person who in fact is or who is generally accepted as a member of an aboriginal race or tribe of Africa', a woman of any group who marries or cohabits with a man of the black group, and any white man who marries or cohabits with a black woman. The 'coloured' group includes any person who is neither of the white group nor the black group, a woman of any group who marries or cohabits with a man of the 'coloured' group, and a white man who marries or cohabits with a woman of the 'coloured' group. Thus, save in the case of a white man, it is the husband who determines the racial grouping of the wife.

Groups declared by proclamation will always be subsets of the 'coloured' and black groups (section 12(2)). The group may be declared for the purposes of the Act generally or for the purpose of particular provisions of the Act or for particular group areas (section 12(2)(b)). Examples are the Indian, Chinese and Malay groups.[43]

Once again, the intrusion of executive discretion has presented the possibility of defences based on the invalidity of the relevant proclamation. Once again the courts have not hastened to the assistance of the accused. The definition of Indian group includes 'a member of a race or tribe whose national home is in India or Pakistan'. In *S v Bhoolia*[44] expert anthropological evidence was led on the concepts of 'race', 'tribe', 'nation' and 'national home' to show that the definition was a contradiction in terms and accordingly void for vagueness. The court rejected this argument, relying essentially on the decision of Fannin J in *S v Naicker*[45] where it was held, inter alia, that under the Act the concept of race had a 'more popular, if less scientific, meaning' than the anthropological one. The fact that Proclamation 516 of 1964 allows a person to fall into more than one group and that it 'describes' groups rather than 'defines' and 'declares' them (the language of the Act) has also been held not to invalidate it.[46]

What emerges from the definitions is that while appearance is of central importance, the concept of general acceptance may override it. The equivalent words in the Afrikaans text for 'generally accepted' are 'gewoonlik deurgaan vir'. Adopting a 'common factor' approach in marrying texts, Shaw J held in *R v George*[47] that the broader meaning of 'usually passes for' is that to be given to the words 'generally accepted'. However, Fagan CJ in *Vilbro*[48] found the texts to be reconcilable without resorting to such a broader meaning. It is submitted that the latter decision is open to criticism in this respect and that the linking of the definition section with penal provisions justifies a restrictive interpretation. In construing the present Act the fact that unlike the Group Areas Act 41 of 1950 considered in *Vilbro* the Afrikaans text was signed should also be considered. Hiemstra J in *Nicholas*[49] emphasized that 'generally accepted' did not mean universally accepted and that the law 'perpetually strives to fit doubtful situations into a scheme that moves in the direction of a realized sense of right'.

Constructing a defence based on a denial of disqualification is rendered all the more daunting by the barrage of presumptions which must be straddled (section 45). These include presumptions that until the contrary is proved:

(a) a person who is in appearance obviously white, is a member of the white group;

(b) a person who in fact is or is generally accepted as a member of an aboriginal race or tribe of Africa, is a member of the black group;

(c) a person falling under neither of the above two presumptions, is a member of the 'coloured' group;

(d) a person is a member of that group of which that person is alleged in the charge sheet to be a member.

In practical terms this means that in a prosecution based on an allegation that a person of the 'coloured' group occupies premises in a white group area, the onus lies on the state to establish, beyond reasonable doubt, that the accused is not obviously a white person in appearance. If the state discharges this onus, the accused must then prove on a balance of probabilities that he or she is generally accepted as a white person.[50] The magistrate is encouraged to record his or her own observations as to the 'obviousness' of the accused's appearance, but may also hear evidence in this regard.[51] Some of the criteria which courts have considered in adjudicating general acceptance as a member of the white group are acceptance in the neighbourhood as white, registration as a parliamentary voter, attitudes of fellow employees, frequenting places of entertainment reserved for white persons and having children enrolled in schools reserved for white persons.[52] Mobility between groups is recognized and the date on which the question must be determined is the date of summons.[53]

Proper notice

Only persons who were in lawful occupation of a group area immediately prior to its proclamation and thereafter became disqualified are entitled to notice (section 26(1) read with section 23(2)) before their occupation becomes unlawful in terms of section 26(1) read with section 23(2). Notice must either be given in respect of an area, in the *Gazette* and one or more newspapers circulating in the area or, in the event that a person falls outside the area to which such a notice applies, by personal notice delivered or sent by registered post to the occupier or person allowing occupation (sub-sections 23(2) and (3)). The notice periods are 12 months for business premises and 3 months for others. For a person entitled to notice a defence could successfully be based on the absence of notice or to his or her non-compliance with the notice provisions.

Unlawfulness

Proof of the above elements together with proof of criminal intent would be sufficient to establish that a crime has been committed. In terms of section 90 of the Criminal Procedure Act, the state is not required to allege and prove any 'exception, exemption, proviso, excuse or qualification'. A number of these are to be found in section 26. For example, section 26(1), which principally defines the offence, ends with the words 'except under the authority of a permit', but this need not be alleged or proved.[54] However, should the accused adduce evidence in support of a defence that one of the exceptions is applicable to him or her, the state would, in terms of its overall duty to prove unlawfulness and guilt beyond reasonable doubt, bear the onus of disproving the allegation.[55]

Apart from permits (section 21 deals with the granting of permits) section 26(2) provides that it shall not be unlawful for otherwise disqualified persons to occupy land or premises in a group area:

(a) as a bona fide employee of the state;

(b) as a bona fide visitor for not more than 90 days in any calendar year;

(c) as a bona fide guest in an hotel;

(d) as a domestic servant, provided that the State President has proclaimed the area to be one to which the exception applies and only to the extent that there is compliance with any conditions set out in that proclamation;

(e) as a bona fide patient or inmate of a hospital or certain other institutions.

Further exceptions may arise out of proclamations issued by the State President in terms of section 26(3) whereby he may exempt groups or classes of disqualified person generally or in relation to land or premises in a particular group area on such conditions as he may determine. For example, in *S v McClusky*,[56] the court considered an exemption in terms of section 26(3) of bona fide employees not of the white group who occupied business premises provided that they were not employed in a managerial position and were under the fulltime supervision of the employer or other member of the white group. These conditions had been breached by the employees who were found to be in control of the premises without supervision. Their conviction was confirmed by the Appellate Division.

An attack on a condition in an exception which is grossly unreasonable or otherwise beyond the powers of the State President may form the basis of a defence. Thus in *S v Ockers*[57] it was held that a condition in a proclamation in terms of section 26(2)(c) (the exemption of domestic servants) requiring domestic servants also to obtain a permit in terms of section 21 was invalid.

General defences excluding unlawfulness would also be available to an accused. In *S v Adams*[58] a defence of necessity was based on the acute shortage of housing for members of the Indian group. Although it was accepted that this was the reason for the accused person's having taken up residence in a white area, the defence was rejected on the basis that there was no evidence of an *absolute* shortage of houses. Perhaps this could still be shown in different circumstances.[59] Although the defence also failed in the Appellate Division, Rumpff CJ overruled the finding of the court a quo that the accused bore the onus of establishing the defence of necessity because the charge related to a statutory offence.[60] This would be the case only if it was provided for expressly or by necessary implication in the relevant statute, which it was not here. Facts would naturally have to be placed before the court by either party, but no onus of proof rests on the accused. If, in *Adams*, the prosecution had been unable to prove beyond reasonable doubt the absence of a state of necessity, the accused would have been entitled to an acquittal.

Mens rea

Mens rea (criminal intent or fault) is not excluded, either expressly or by necessary implication, in the formulation of the offence in the statute. The question arises whether it takes the form of intention or whether negligence would be sufficient. The word 'allow' in section 26 suggests that mens rea in the form of intention and not merely negligence is required to establish the offence of *allowing* occupation. Negligence is not sufficient to establish the offence of occupation either. The criteria for establishing whether negligence will suffice set out in *S v Du Toit*,[61] do not apply in this instance. Moreover, it could hardly have been the intention of the legislature to require intention for 'allowing' but not for 'occupying'.

Intention must be proved in relation to each element of the offence.[62] Defences excluding mens rea may thus be available to an accused charged under section 26. A mistake of law or fact would constitute a defence, provided that it is genuine and, in the latter instance, essential.[63] The usual principles regarding onus of proof would apply.[64]

In *Vilbro*,[65] the accused considered themselves members of the white group. The court, however, found on the facts that they were not and their convictions were upheld by the Appellate Division. It is submitted that, in the light of subsequent authority, the case was wrongly decided and that a defence of mistake of fact was available to the accused. There was, at the very least, a reasonable possibility that the accused, in believing that they were members of the white group, lacked intention in relation to the element of disqualification. That their mistaken belief may have been unreasonable is not relevant.[66]

Other examples of a possible defence of absence of mens rea spring to mind. A newcomer to a town who does not realize that an area inhabited by many people of his or her group has in fact been proclaimed as a group area for another group might raise a defence of mistake of law.[67] Likewise a person who occupies an area mistakenly believing it to have been declared a group area of another group for *ownership* only. Mistake of fact might be raised by a person who was under a misapprehension as to the boundary of a particular group area.

Sentencing and eviction

The penalty for a contravention of section 26 is imprisonment for a period not exceeding two years, a fine not exceeding R400 or both (section 46(1)(a)). The court in convicting a person on a charge of occupation in terms of section 26 *may,* in addition to any penalty imposed, make an order for his or her ejectment and the ejectment of any other person of the same group proved to be living there, whether permanently or otherwise (section 46(2)(a)). In the landmark decision of *S v Govender*[68] the court was at pains to emphasize that an eviction order was *not* part of the sentence (see below).

Judicial attitudes to contraventions of the Act and sentencing have changed over time. Indeed, in a recent decision a magistrate in Pinetown declined to immediately sentence a person convicted under section 26. In postponing sentencing for three years the magistrate remarked that society no longer viewed the breach of the Act in the same way that it had done 20 years ago.[69] This attitude is in contrast to that reflected in the Group Areas Amendment Bill of 1988, which sought to increase the above penalties to five years and R10 000 respectively.

An important principle has emerged from the case law in relation to sentencing. It has been held that a suspended sentence of imprisonment is appropriate only where vacation of the premises forms the condition of suspension. In *S v Neuhoff*[70] the illegal occupation consisted of performing duties falling outside those permitted by a condition contained in a proclamation in terms of section 26(3) of the Act. No question arose of the accused being required to vacate the premises and the court therefore struck out the suspended period of imprisonment imposed by the magistrate.[71]

Where an ejectment order is made, the court has a discretion to determine the manner in which effect is given to the order. Where alternative accommodation is difficult or impossible to obtain, it has been held that the court should lean towards granting a lengthy period of time within which to vacate the premises.[72] This principle has to some extent been superceded by the decision in *Govender*[73] which has in effect virtually prevented ejectment orders from being granted where alternative accommodation is not available. Nonetheless, it is submitted that a lengthy period should always be granted as such an order will invariably disrupt the accused's life.

Prior to *Govender* lower courts would automatically order ejectment in terms of section 46(2) upon conviction. Referring to the fact that the 1966 Act substituted the word 'may' in section 46(2) for the word 'shall' in the equivalent section 34(2) of the 1957 Act, Goldstone J held that the legislature clearly intended to confer a discretionary jurisdiction as opposed to imposing an obligatory direction on the magistrate. A magistrate could not make an eviction order of his own accord but only at the request of the prosecutor after appropriate evidence was placed before the magistrate to enable him or her to conduct a full enquiry. Nor is there an onus on the accused to show why an ejectment order should not be granted.

The learned judge went on to specify some examples of considerations which might be relevant to a proper exercise of the magistrate's discretion including: the nature of the area concerned; the attitude of the neighbours; the policies and views of interested departments of state; the attitude of the landlord; the prospects of a permit being granted; the personal hardship which such an order would cause; and the availability of alternative accommodation.

In providing these guidelines the judge showed an understanding of and approach to administrative law not often seen among South African judges. The beneficial effects for the individual of a proper check on a wide administrative discretion (here the magistrate does not act in his judicial capacity) have been plain to see. What the courts failed to do in *Lockhat*[74] (and its successors) in rejecting the altenative accommodation argument has been achieved in *Govender*. The decision has been hailed as a primary reason for the current paucity of prosecutions under the Act. Predictably the 1988 Group Areas Bill sought to reverse the beneficial effects of the judgment by providing that upon conviction it was compulsory (and no longer discretionary) for an eviction order to be made by the magistrate. Having dropped the Bill, the government now appears to be willing to accept and live with the effects of *Govender*.[75]

The considerations mentioned by Goldstone J highlight a number of possible grounds for opposing an application for an eviction order apart from lack of alternative accommodation. A pending application for a permit or a favourable response to a survey of neighbours' attitudes are possible examples.

Part III: Private Enforcement

Recent trends in policy and legislation manifest an intention on the part of central government to shift the enforcement of unjust laws to local authorities and private individuals.[76] This has been particularly true in the area of land law (see, for example, the Prevention of Illegal Squatting Amendment Act 104 of 1988). Although the dropping of the Group Areas Bill of 1988 has to some extent prevented importation of the trend into the Group Areas Act, private enforcement has nonetheless become a far greater problem than prosecutions under the Act. This is particularly so in Johannesburg where the shortage of accommodation has resulted in large numbers of disqualified black tenants leasing flats in certain white group areas. Exploiting the high demand for accommodation and the insecure position in which the Act places such tenants, landlords charge exorbitant rentals for flats in shocking condition which they often refuse to maintain.[77]

Space does not permit a full discussion of the remedies available to assist tenants in such situations, limited though they are. Suffice it to say that careful scrutiny of the procedure adopted by a landlord for technical defences and the imaginative use of the Rent Control Act 80 of 1976 and the mandament van spolie might provide relief.[78] As is often the case with criminal prosecutions, merely putting up a tenacious defence, whatever the legal basis, may be sufficient to stop the proceedings and protect the tenant. Much of the tenant's ammunition is to be found among the advantages accorded by the law to possessors.

Perhaps the most important of these is the maxim in pari delicto potior est conditio defendentis seu possidentis (in equal guilt the position of the defendant or possessor is stronger; also described as the par delictum rule). Before examining the application of this maxim in the context of the Group Areas Act it is necessary to consider the status of a contract entered into in contravention of the Act.

It is a basic principle of our law that a thing done contrary to the direct prohibition of the law is void and of no effect.[79] A contract found to be illegal and void will not be enforced by our courts in terms of the maxim ex turpi causa non oritur actio (no action can be based on an illegitimate cause). However, before our courts will hold that a contract entered into in breach of a statutory provision is void, they must be satisfied that that was the intention of the legislature.[80] In *Savage and Lovemore Mining v International Shipping Co*,[81] the position was summarized as follows:

> [O]n the authority of Voet 1.3.16, that which is done contrary to the law is not ipso iure null and void where the law is content with a penalty laid down against those who contravene it. The law is content with such a penalty in many cases in which 'greater inconveniences and impropriety would result from the rescission of what was done than would follow the Act itself done contrary to the law'.[82]

The factors considered in discerning the intention of the legislature could be subsumed under the principle that the legislature intends to promote public policy. Both the *Metro* and *Savage and Lovemore* cases concerned activities regulated by permit and contracts entered into without the authority of an appropriate permit. In both cases the court refused to hold that the contracts were void and unenforceable. In the *Savage and Lovemore* case there was regard to the following factors among others:

- the legislature had not directly prohibited the activities concerned, but rather given the Minister the power to regulate them;
- other express penalties existed to penalize offenders;
- the purpose of the legislation was not frustrated by enforcing the contract;
- the breach of the relevant statute by the plaintiff was not wilful.

Applying these principles to a lease in contravention of the Group Areas Act, it might be argued that public policy would be in favour of upholding the contract. However, the direct prohibition of a lease of immovable property by a disqualified person in a group area for ownership (see definition of immovable property in section 1, read with section 27) would make it more difficult to persuade a court that the legislature did not intend to render offending leases void. For the tenant the advantage of the contract being enforcible would be that he or she could insist on compliance by the landlord with the duty to maintain the premises. The landlord on the other hand would be entitled to sue for arrear rental. If the contract was held to be void, the landlord would be non-suited in such a claim.[83] An important consequence of enforcibility for the landlord would be that he or she could sue for eviction upon lawful and proper termination of the lease.

Assuming a lease to a disqualified tenant is held to be illegal and unenforcible, is the landlord then entitled to sue for eviction in order to recover possession of the property parted with in terms of the illegal contract? It is in this context that the par delictum rule becomes relevant. The rule provides that where both parties are equally aware of the illegality of the contract, the party who has parted with property in terms of the illegal contract cannot sue for its recovery. The rule was inherited from Roman and Roman-Dutch law and derives from the principle that the courts should discourage illegality and immorality.

Its potential benefit for the tenant who is disqualified in terms of the Act is immediately apparent and it has certainly been used to protect tenants under illegal leases from ejectment.[84] The courts have recognized, however, that a completely rigid application of the rule would lead to injustice, but difficulty has been experienced in finding criteria to determine when it should be relaxed. The leading authority is the decision of the Appellate Division in *Jajbhay v Cassim*[85] where the plaintiff relied on the illegality of the lease in terms of the Johannesburg Malay Location Regulations in seeking the tenant's eviction. The approach of the court is summarized in the following portion of the judgment of Tindall JA (at 558):

> Our courts are not bound to enforce rigidly in every case the general rule in pari delicto potior est conditio defendentis but may come to the relief of one of the parties where such a course is necessary in order to prevent injustice or to satisfy the requirements of public policy.

However, the court declined to relax the rule and refused an eviction order, placing particular emphasis on the tenant's not being in arrears with his rental and his having received no notice.

Although the application of the law in this decision has been strongly criticized, inter alia for reverting to the terms of the illegal contract to decide whether relaxation was justified,[87] the principle it articulates has been accepted as a correct statement of the law and applied in subsequent cases.

A recent application of the *Jajbhay* principle in the context of black tenants living in white group areas in Johannesburg is the decision of Goldstone J in *Norvan Investments (Pty) Ltd v Vumase.*[88] The applicant landlord argued that the par delictum rule should be relaxed both on grounds of public policy and injustice. Concerning the former it was suggested that it was contrary to public policy to allow the continued contravention of a statute by allowing the disqualified tenants to remain in possession. This was rejected on the basis that the rule had often been applied in similar circumstances. In fact the Appellate Division has rejected this argument on the basis that public policy is adequately protected by the criminal law.[89]

In support of the injustice argument the applicant contended that, since the respondents were in arrears with their rental, their eviction was necessary to prevent injustice. In the absence of an application for the hearing of oral evidence, the court accepted the respondent's version that underpayment of rental was justified by the dilapidated and unhealthy condition of the building. In any event, the court pointed out that the applicant held sufficient funds in the form of a deposit to cover the arrear rental and eviction was refused.

As far as notice was concerned, the court treated as a preliminary issue the absence of a month's notice which would have been that required under the lease had it been legal. It would appear from the court's reasoning that if 'proper' notice had been given, eviction could have been granted 'at common law' without having to consider the par delictum rule. This approach is convincingly criticized by Cooper,[90] where he points out that 'the lessor's notice does not purge their relationship of its illegal origin nor terminate the lessee's occupation; therefore, potior est conditio possidentis [the position of the possessor is stronger]'. Rather, the question of whether notice was given in accordance with the illegal agreement is to be treated as a factor in weighing up public policy and the prevention of injustice. However, it is questionable whether the courts would ever refuse ejectment in a case where what would otherwise have been sufficient notice has been granted. In an obiter dictum in *Kelly's*[91] case, Tindall ACJ states categorically that reliance cannot be placed on the maxim to resist ejectment if notice required by the illegal lease is given. The idea of allowing the disqualified tenant to remain in possession in perpetuity was also rejected in *Jajbhay's* case.[92]

Nonetheless it is submitted that the wide criteria of 'public policy' and 'injustice' might in special circumstances allow for reliance on the maxim, despite 'proper notice', particularly bearing in mind that the rule was applied strictly in Roman law (save for a few exceptions). An example might be where it is shown that the sole motive for giving notice was the statutory illegality, and that a tenant who was not disqualified would have been allowed to continue in occupation.

It might also be argued, in circumstances where the Rent Control Act would have applied had the tenant not been disqualified, that the notice period provided for in that Act should be required before the rule can be relaxed. Tindall ACJ's rejection of this argument on the basis that 'the Rent Act contemplates legal not illegal leases' is patently illogical: in prescribing a month's notice the common law also contemplates legal leases, yet Tindall ACJ was prepared to accept that period.[93]

Conclusion

The focus of enforcement of the Act has largely shifted away from prosecutions to low-intensity enforcement by the police and private enforcement by landlords. This shift has coincided with, and perhaps been caused by, a change in attitude on the part of the courts and the government. Examples of the courts' new approach are the *Govender*[94] judgment and the views expressed by the Pinetown magistrate referred to above.

An indication of the government's new approach is to be found in the following statement by the Minister of Constitutional Development and Planning on 9 May 1989:

> In future it will be ensured that reported cases are handled with compassion, when dealing with offenders of the Group Areas Act, especially when the eviction of persons might be considered. The individual needs of the persons concerned, will as far as possible, be considered and attempts will be made to offer them suitable and acceptable alternative accommodation.

The underlying reason for this sudden compassion must be the government's desire to avoid the negative publicity group areas evictions occasion. Extensive publicity on group areas matters has in recent years been a result of extended community-based campaigns co-ordinated by organizations such as Actstop.

Because they are more difficult to monitor, the new forms of enforcement have the advantage for the government that they are less likely to give rise to publicity. The challenge facing community organizations is clear: All actions against disqualified tenants whether taking the form of police investigations or civil actions by landlords should be vigorously defended and publicly exposed. As has already been suggested, the best protection for disqualified tenants lies not in legal defences, but in publicizing their plight.

Notes

1 See Robertson at 124.

2 B24/1988 (GA).

3 *The Argus* 3 February 1989, *The Sunday Tribune* 10 March 1989.

4 Statement by Chris Heunis, Minister of Constitutional Development and Planning, on 9 May 1989, *The Citizen* 10 May 1989.

5 J J Schoombee 'Group Areas Legislation – The Political Control of Ownership and Occupation of Land' 1985 *Acta Juridica* 77.

6 *SA Barometer* vol 3 no 7, 21 April 1989.

7 *R v Slabbert* 1956 (4) SA 18 (T).

8 *Omar v Minister of Law and Order* 1987 (3) SA 859 (A).

9 See *S v Mandela* 1968 (4) SA 123 (C) at 129.

10 *The Star* 18 August 1989, *The Cape Times* 19 July 1989.

11 1986 (3) SA 969 (T).

12 *Sunday Star* 13 August 1989.

13 See, for example, *Scott v Hanekom* 1980 (3) SA 1182 (C) on notice in newspapers.

14 See L Dison & I Mohamed *Group Areas and their Development* (Durban: Butterworths 1960) 68.

15 [1898] 2 QB 91.

16 1950 (3) SA 136 (A).

17 1981 (1) SA 187 (A) at 222E - 223A. See also G M Burchell, R L Milton & J M Burchell *South African Criminal Law and Procedure* vol 1 2nd edn (Cape Town: Juta 1983) at 238-9; HWR Wade *Administrative Law* 6th edn (Oxford: Clarendon Press 1988) at 342.

18 *S v Yengeni* CPD 18 May 1989 Case no 551/89, unreported.

19 Above note 5 at 96.

20 1961 (2) SA 587 (A).

21 1950 (3) SA 136 (A).

22 Then Act 77 of 1957.

23 See Schoombee, above note 5, at 91.

24 See Schoombee at 96ff and cases cited there.

25 See, for example, *S v King* 1966 (1) SA 500 (A) at 506; *S v Mosoeu* 1961 (4) SA 518 (T), *Harnaker v Minister of the Interior* 1966 (4) SA 303 (A) and *Suliman v Minister of Community Development* 1981 (1) SA 1108 (A).

26 1961 (2) SA 587 (A).

27 1981 (1) SA 187 (A).

28 1986 (3) SA 969 (T).

29 Courts are sometimes more hesitant to do this in the case of a judicial officer, see *In re Racal Communications Limited* [1981] AC 374.

30 TPD 30 August 1989, Case no 5971/89, unreported.

31 See GN 819/1963 reg 10.

32 1963 (2) SA 579 (T), confirmed on appeal 1963 (4) SA 849 (A).

33 1969 (3) SA 606 (T).

34 1919 AD 439; [1922] 1 AC 500.

35 *Fen Sam Jackson v Conradie* 1955 (4) SA 266 (EC); *S v Brandsma* 1963 (1) SA 261 (N).

36 Above note 5 at 92ff.

37 1958 (3) SA 664 (N).

38 1960 (3) SA 42 (C).

39 *S v Essack* 1964 (1) SA 384 (T); *S v Mamajee & Co (Pty) Ltd* 1965 (1) SA 485 (T).

40 Schoombee, above note 5, at 94.

41 1958 (3) SA 761 (T) at 763.

42 See, for example, *R v Vilbro* 1957 (3) SA 223 (A).

43 Proclamation 516 of 3 April 1964, Schedules I to III.

44 1969 (3) SA 606 (T).

45 1966 (1) SA 594 (N) at 597.

46 *S v Ahmed* 1969 (2) SA 276 (C).

47 1954 (2) SA 243 (N).

48 1957 (3) SA 223 (A).

49 1958 (3) SA 761 (T) at 764.

50 See *R v Vilbro* 1957 (3) SA 223 (A) at 227G-H.

51 At 228-9.

52 See J A van S D'Oliviera 'Group Areas and Community Development' in *LAWSA* vol 10 (Durban: Butterworths 1980) at 345.

53 1958 (3) SA 761 (T) at 765A, but cf *R v Lucas* 1953 (2) SA 257 (N) at 258C-E.

54 *S v Tshwape* 1964 (4) SA 327 (C).

55 See Burchell, Milton & Burchell, above note 17 at 238.

56 1979 (2) SA 649 (A).

57 1974 (2) SA 523 (C).

58 1979 (4) SA 793 (T); 1981 (1) SA 187 (A).

59 See M Navsa 'Group Areas', unpublished paper presented at the Conference on Removals and the Law, UCT, April 1989.

60 *S v Adams* 1981 (1) SA 187 (A) at 220C-H.

61 1981 (2) SA 33 (C).

62 See Burchell, Milton & Burchell, above note 17, at 233.

63 Ibid 160ff, *S v De Blom* 1977 (3) SA 513 (A).

64 Burchell, Milton & Burchell, above note 17, at 227ff; *S v De Blom* 1977 (3) SA 513 (A) at 532E-H.

65 1957 (3) SA 223 (A).

66 See Burchell, Milton & Burchell, above note 17, at 174ff.

67 See Navsa, above note 59, at 9.

68 1986 (3) SA 969 (T).

69 *Natal Witness* 29 July 1989.

70 1971 (3) SA 935 (T).

71 See also the authorities referred to in *S v Neuhoff* at 936.

72 See Dison & Mahomed, above note 14 at 53.

73 1986 (3) SA 969 (T).

74 1961 (2) SA 587 (A).

75 *The Argus* 3 February 1989, and statement by Heunis, above note 4.

76 See Haysom in this volume at 111.

77 *Weekly Mail* 26 May 1989 and 23 June 1989.

78 For an explanation of this remedy, see O'Regan in this volume at 172-3.

81 1987 (2) SA 149 (W).

82 At 205.

83 *Hatch v Koopoomal* 1936 AD 190.

84 See, for example, *Kelly v Wright and Kok* 1948 (3) SA 522 (A).

85 1939 AD 537.

86 At 558.

87 See the authorities cited in Farlam & Hathaway *Contract: Cases, Materials and Commentary* 3rd edn by G Lubbe & C Murray (Cape Town: Juta 1988) 295.

88 WLD 12 May 1988 Case no 5262/89, unreported.

89 See *Kelly v Wright and Kok* 1948 (3) SA 522 (A) at 529 ff.

90 See WE Cooper *The South African Law of Landlord and Tenant* (Cape Town: Juta 1973) 15-16.

91 1948 (3) SA 522 (A).

92 1939 AD 537 at 557.

93 *Kelly v Wright and Kok* 1948 (3) SA 522 (A) at 528.

94 1986 (3) SA 969 (T).

CATHERINE O'REGAN

The Prevention of Illegal Squatting Act *

Since the mid-1970s, one of the most commonly used legal mechanisms for forcibly removing communities has been the Prevention of Illegal Squatting Act 52 of 1951. In 1988 the Act was amended to further facilitate such removals despite widespread public outcry. Striking features of the amended Act include the substantial penalties for non-compliance with the Act; the granting of unfettered summary powers to local authorities and landowners to demolish buildings; and the exclusion of legal remedies through the ousting of the jurisdiction of the courts. In this article, I will analyse the provisions of the Act, as amended, under three headings: the powers given to remove squatters; the summary powers of demolition given to landowners and local authorities; and the powers to establish 'approved' informal settlement areas.

Part I: Powers of Removal

There are two types of removal powers in the Act: criminal provisions and administrative procedures. They will be dealt with separately.

Criminal provisions

The Act contains an array of criminal provisions. The key provision is in section 1 which provides that:

> Save under the authority of any law, or in the course of his duty as an employee of the government or of any local authority, no person
>
> (a) shall enter upon or into without lawful reason, or remain on or in any land or building without the permission of the owner or the lawful occupier of such land or building whether such land is enclosed or not.

This provision has remained largely unchanged since it was introduced in 1951. The section criminalizes activities far beyond the scope suggested by the title of the Act. In *R v Phiri*[1] De Wet J held that even a 'casual

Resident of Weiler's Farm
(Gill de Vlieg, Afrapix)

trespasser' would be in breach of section 1. Accordingly he held that the Act

> goes further than to control squatting ... in its plain meaning, it also penalises persons who enter into or on land without a lawful reason even if there is no question of squatting in issue at all.[2]

Section 1 is very similar to the criminal provision contained in section 1 of the Trespass Act 6 of 1959.[3] Indeed, people residing on land without the permission of the owner can be charged both in terms of section 1 of the Trespass Act, and section 1 of the Prevention of Illegal Squatting Act. This happened recently in the Noordhoek squatters criminal prosecution, the first prosecution (of which I am aware) to take place since the amendment of the Act in 1988.

The section creates two separate offences, entering upon land without a lawful reason and remaining on land without permission. Schreiner ACJ explained the need for two offences:

> Reasons for using the word remain and for making two offences may be found in the fact that the mischief of squatting, though it became acute, no doubt, as a result of movements of large numbers and housing shortages after the last war, would to some extent exist even where the squatter had lived all his life on the property or had been there before Act 52 of 1951 came into operation or had previously been allowed to enter and stay there.[4]

Despite its far-reaching scope, section 1 did not, prior to its amendment in 1988, prove to be an effective technique for forcibly removing entire communities. For example, during 1976 approximately 1 000 Crossroads residents were prosecuted under this section, but the community remained at Crossroads.[5] Criminal prosecutions in terms of section 1 did not succeed in forcibly removing whole communities for a range of reasons. Firstly, using section 1 to effect the removal of an entire community required a large-scale prosecution programme. The state is often reluctant to undertake such programmes because they inevitably overload the courts, the police and other state institutions.

Secondly, in order to remove people by using section 1, the state had to be able to prosecute squatters successfully. In fact, proof of the offence set out in section 1 was often difficult for the state. Three elements gave rise to particular difficulty: the requirement that the state show that the occupation of the land was without the landowner's consent could not be met by the state where it could not prove who owned the land (as happened in *S v Peter*[6]); the need to prove that the accused person's entry was unlawful (see *S v Mampura*);[7] and the need for evidence that the land fell within the ambit of the Act. (The state encountered difficulties in obtaining convictions in the past because it failed to lead this evidence. Previously, section 11 of the Act, which was repealed in 1986, provided that its provisions would apply only to areas that the State President by proclamation declared to fall within its scope.)

However, thirdly, even obtaining a conviction did not automatically lead to the removal of the convicted person. Section 3 of the Act provided that a magistrate had a discretion as to whether to order the eviction of a person convicted under the section. In *S v Govender*[8] the magistrate's discretion to make an eviction order in terms of a similar provision in the Group Areas Act was circumscribed. Goldstone J held that, in exercising his discretion under the Group Areas Act, the magistrate should have taken into account a wide range of factors:

> Many considerations may be relevant to the court's discretion, for example, the nature of the area concerned; the attitude of the neighbours; the policy and views of the Department of Community Development or any other interested landlord; the prospects of a permit being issued for continued lawful occupation of the premises; the personal hardship which such an order may cause and the availability of alternative accommodation.[9]

As the magistrate had not taken such considerations into account, Goldstone J upheld the appeal against the order. The Prevention of Illegal Squatting Act contained a discretionary power of eviction given to magistrates similar to that contained in the Group Areas Act and it was argued that similar considerations should be taken into account by magistrates before making eviction orders.

Fourthly, convicted persons could appeal against sentence, a process which could take up to a year and would automatically suspend the operation of the sentence pending the appeal.

However, amendments to the operation of section 1 in the 1988 Act, have meant that in the future it may provide a more effective technique for forcibly removing at least small communities of squatters. This is for three reasons: Firstly, section 1(2) now provides that:

> If in the prosecution of a person for a contravention of subsection (1) it is proved
>
> (a) that he entered upon or into land or a building of any other person, it shall be presumed that that person entered upon or into the land or building without lawful reason;
>
> (b) that he remained on or in any land or building of any other person, it shall be presumed that that person so remained without the permission of the other person, unless the contrary is proved.

This section creates rebuttable presumptions which will facilitate the task of the state in proving the elements of the charge and place the burden of proof on the accused to prove the lawful reason or permission. This change has been much criticized, for it is contrary to the fundamental principles of our common law.

The change in onus may not be complete. Where the charge is one of 'remaining on the land', the subsection does not create a rebuttable presumption that the accused person has remained on the land without the permission of the lawful occupier of the land, and the state will consequently still have to prove there is no lawful occupier of the land other than the owner, or alternatively that any lawful occupier of the land has not given permission to the accused person to remain on the land.

Secondly, section 11B of the Act now provides that an appeal against a criminal conviction will no longer have the effect of suspending the criminal conviction. Once again this amendment is contrary to the general principles of our law.

The third relevant amendment is contained in section 3(1) which now provides that a magistrate upon convicting a person in terms of section 1 shall order the eviction of that person. The guidelines for the exercise of the judicial discretion set out in *S v Govender*[10] are therefore no longer relevant. The removal of the discretion is also contrary to general principle as it is the courts, not Parliament, that should have discretionary power to decide on appropriate sentences.

Accordingly, section 1 of the Act may result in more removals from land than previously, for the technical difficulties faced by the state in obtaining convictions have been greatly reduced, and the effect of a conviction has been altered to ensure that eviction will follow. However, the administrative difficulties created by a large-scale programme of prosecutions may still mean that section 1 will not be an effective mechanism for the removal of squatters, where large numbers of people are present on the land. In addition, political pressures may well hamper the use of section 1. This is illustrated by the recent Noordhoek prosecutions which have been suspended while negotiations take place regarding the establishment of an informal settlement area or township for Africans in the southern Peninsula.

In addition to section 1, there is another provision containing criminal penalties which could result in forced removals. Section 4 of the Act is aimed at curbing what has been called 'squatter farming': a practice whereby people are allowed to reside on land in breach of section 1 or an order made in terms of section 5 in return for the payment of site fees or other consideration. Where a person is convicted of a contravention of section 4, the court must now make an order ejecting the occupants of the land concerned. By linking the offence to a breach of section 1, however, the scope of the section is sharply limited, for squatters who have permission to reside on land will, by definition not be in breach of section 1 as we have seen.

A further criminal provision which may result in forced removal is that contained in section 6F. This is discussed in the following section as section 6F is largely concerned with an administrative removal process.

Administrative procedures

Section 5

Before the 1988 amendments, section 5 of the Act gave a magistrate administrative powers to make orders to remove persons from land and to demolish any structures in circumstances where the magistrate was satisfied that 'the health and safety of the public generally' would be endangered if such a removal did not take place. It too appears not to have proved a successful measure for removing persons.

During the 1940s, several applications were made to the Johannesburg magistrate in terms of a War Measure[11] for the issue of a removal order against the Moroka squatters, but magistrates proved extremely reluctant to make removal orders. Furthermore, although the War Measure contained no express provision requiring that affected parties be given an opportunity to make representations to the magistrate, the Supreme Court in *Mofokeng v Minister of Native Affairs*[12] held that 'persons must be given an opportunity of answering the statements which have been made to their prejudice before the order is made'. Accordingly, Ramsbottom J set aside a magistrate's order evicting Mofokeng and 200 families from their homes.

Subsequently, in the 1951 Act, the government introduced a provision that notice should be given to persons affected by the order. No statistics exist on the use of the provision, but there are at least two reported examples of its use, in Umlazi and in Pretoria, both of which appear to have been successful.[13] However, the provision was used without success in an attempt to remove the Crossroads community in mid-1976.

The 1988 amendments have altered this provision to give a magistrate the administrative power to move persons where it has been proved to his or her satisfaction either by an owner or legal occupier that persons have entered upon the land of that owner or occupier without consent and are refusing to depart, or by an administrator or local authority that persons have 'entered and are congregating upon any land ... whether with or without the consent of the owner or occupier'. The requirement that the magistrate must be satisfied that the health and safety of the population is under threat has accordingly been removed. The notice provision, however, remains.

As the procedure is clearly an administrative procedure, no appeal lies from the decision of the magistrate, but, of course, where the magistrate fails to exercise the administrative discretion in a proper fashion, an affected party may launch proceedings to review the decision. In such circumstances, the new section 11B provides that, as with appeals, the review proceedings will not operate to suspend the implementation of any order made by the magistrate.

These amendments appear to give magistrates a wide discretion to make orders to remove persons in terms of section 5. Little guidance is now given by the section as to what factors the magistrate should take into account when deciding whether to issue a removal order or not, and the discretion seems almost unfettered. However, the amending Act introduced a new section 11A which provides that the Minister of Constitutional Development and Planning may, by notice in the *Gazette*, 'determine the general policy in regard to the prevention of illegal squatting which shall be adhered to in the Republic'. Although the section expressly requires only the Administrator and local authorities to abide by this policy, a magistrate too may well be obliged to take any such policy into account in exercising the discretion in terms of section 5. To date no such policy has been established.

In addition, it may be that, as Budlender has argued, the discretion must necessarily be limited by the 'general policy and purposes of the Act'.[15] However, the general policy underlying the Act is not manifest from the wording of the Act and the Act contains no definition of squatting.

Nevertheless, this lack of guidance may make it more difficult to effect removals than an initial reading would disclose. The section specifically provides that the magistrate shall give those under threat of removal an opportunity to make written and oral representations to him. Any such inquiry could be extremely cumbersome, as each person threatened with removal would be entitled to present such evidence as he or she considers necessary. Consequently, the procedure may be time-consuming, expensive and possibly not particularly effective.

Indeed, a local authority seeking an order under this section has already faced these difficulties. The Prevention of Illegal Squatting Amendment Act was promulgated on 8 February 1989 and on 20 February 1989 the municipality of Kraaifontein in the Cape applied to the Kraaifontein magistrate in terms of section 5 for the removal of 125 people from a piece of land known as Bloekombos. After several months of preparation and some days of argument, the magistrate dismissed the application on 12 June 1989 on the ground that the Kraaifontein municipality had failed to show that it was either the owner of the land, or the local authority with jurisdiction over the land. After three months, the argument had been concerned entirely with preliminary technical points rather than any substantive issues. Detailed substantive affidavits prepared by the threatened community were never handed to the magistrate, as the application was disposed of on technical grounds. It is impossible to assess how long a full hearing on the substantive merits would have taken.

Accordingly, the amendment of section 5, although clearly intended to facilitate the forced removal of squatters, may not prove as successful as the drafters had hoped.

Section 6F

This far-reaching and much criticized new section provides for the removal of persons living on land situated outside the jurisdiction of local authorities who are not employed by the owner or occupier of that land, even where those people are present on the land with the consent of the owner or occupier. The section appears to be designed to replace the provisions originally contained in chapter IV of the Development Trust and Land Act 18 of 1936 which were repealed by the Abolition of Influx Control Act 68 of 1986. Since then, there have been few express provisions governing the forced removal of black persons from white farms, although the provisions of the Group Areas Act 36 of 1966 also limit the right of blacks to reside in white rural areas. The rise of the Conservative Party in the rural areas, particularly in the Transvaal and the Orange Free State, together with a shrinking white population and a burgeoning black population on the white farms may well have caused the government to introduce a mechanism whereby unemployed residents on white farms could be easily and forcibly removed from those farms.

Section 6E of the Act provides for the establishment of 'local committees' in areas falling outside the jurisdiction of local authorities. A local committee must order an investigation into the occupation of land where the local committee 'has reasonable grounds to believe' that land is being occupied by persons not employed by the owner or legal occupier of that land. Persons not employed by the owner or legal occupier would appear to include retired workers and members of a farmworker's family who would ordinarily have a right to remain on the land, even though they are not employed.

Where the committee finds that the land is being so occupied, section 6F(2) provides that:

> it shall cause the owner or legal occupier ... to be served with a notice in writing in which the finding of the committee is set out and the legal occupier is directed to eject those persons from the building ... concerned in the manner mentioned in the notice within a period of 30 days or after the date on which the notice has been served on him.

It should be noted that the committee is obliged to issue such a notice once it has been satisfied that unemployed persons are residing on the land and that the committee may direct the manner in which the person is to be evicted.

A landowner who is aggrieved by the notice served upon him or her may, in writing, submit an objection to the committee within 14 days of the notice being served upon him or her (section 6F(3)). This objection shall be considered by the committee whose decision thereafter shall be final (section 6F(4)). A landowner who fails to comply shall be guilty of a criminal offence for which the maximum penalty is a fine of R10 000 and/or imprisonment for a period of five years.

A crucial question here is whether the local committee may require a landowner to evict a person without first obtaining a court order. The 30-day time limit imposed appears to suggest, at first reading, that this may be the case. However, a further reading shows that this is not so. Section 6F(6)(a) provides that:

> If a person referred to in subsection (1) does not vacate the building, structure or land concerned within the period mentioned ... at the request of the owner of lawful occupier, the committee may order that person in writing to vacate the building structure or land within a period mentioned in that order.

This section makes clear that all section 6F(2) envisages is that the local authority may require the landowner (or legal occupier) to issue a request to the relevant persons to vacate the property. Thereafter, any person who fails to comply with the local committee's order shall be guilty of an offence and, upon conviction, the court shall order the summary ejectment of that person from the land.

Accordingly, a local committee may not require a landowner forcibly to eject a person without first obtaining a court order, and so a landowner need only issue a request to the persons concerned. Where such a request has not been complied with, the committee has the power to issue an order ejecting the persons. It would appear, however, that the order issued by the committee ejecting the persons must be subject to the audi alteram partem principle for the following reasons.

The powers enjoyed by the local committee are very similar to those enjoyed by a magistrate in terms of section 5, although there is no express provision that a local committee may issue an order of eviction only after having heard the representations of affected parties. However, under the original War Measure, magistrates were also not expressly required to hear representations made by the affected parties, but in *Mofokeng v Minister of Native Affairs*, Ramsbottom J held that the principle of audi alteram partem (hear the other side) must apply to the magistrate's powers in terms of the Measure:

> It is clear that the making of an order may have the most serious consequences for the persons affected .... Every family in a community may be forcibly removed from the place where it has established its home, and its dwelling may be demolished without compensation.[17]

Similar considerations apply to the local committee's powers in terms of section 6F(6)(a). Of course, the general applicability of the maxim audi alteram partem has been rendered uncertain in some cases by confusing dicta. Nevertheless, it appears that the rule established in *R v Ngwevela*[18] by Centlivres JA should be observed:

The maxim should be enforced unless it is clear that Parliament has expressly or by necessary implication enacted that it should not apply or that there are exceptional circumstances which would justify the Court's not giving effect to it.[19]

Even if it is held that the local committee must comply with the requirements of the maxim audi alteram partem, little substantive protection will be provided to persons who are not employed by the owner or legal occupier of the land on which they live. Section 6F appears to make it clear that in such cases the local committee shall order their ejectment.

The implications, and perhaps the origins, of section 6F are indicated by a memorandum issued by the South African Agricultural Union to its members in November 1988.[20] The memorandum proposed that members of the union compile a list of all those persons living, but not employed, on their farms and on neighbouring farms. The clear suggestion underlying the memorandum was that after the enactment of the Prevention of Illegal Squatting Amendment Act such lists would assist local committees in forcibly removing unemployed squatters from white farms.

To date, there seems to have been no action in terms of section 6F, but there is no doubt that it is a powerful tool to effect the forced removal of unemployed persons living on farms.

Part II: Powers of Demolition

The administrative procedures discussed above which give administrative bodies the power to remove people also give those bodies the powers to demolish dwellings. However, in addition to these powers, section 3B of the Act has, since it was introduced in 1976,[21] given landowners and local authorities powers of summary demolition. These powers have apparently been the most commonly used in the Act so far, but they have also been the subject of extensive litigation.

Section 3B

Section 3B gives landowners, local authorities and provincial officials powers of summary demolition, but crucially, not powers of summary eviction. This distinction is important, for squatters not only reside in, and therefore have possession of structures, but they also reside on, and have possession of land. Section 3B gives landowners and officials powers only to demolish structures, not to evict people from land.

Section 3B(1) reads as follows:

> Notwithstanding the provisions of any law to the contrary –
>
> (a) but subject to any law under which he is compelled to demolish or remove any building or structure, the owner of the land may without an order of court demolish any building or structure erected or occupied on the land without his consent, and remove the material from the land;
>
> (b) an officer of a local authority designated by the council of the local authority for this purpose, may without an order of court and at the expense of the owner of the land, demolish any building or structure which –
>
> > (i) can be used for occupation by persons;
> >
> > (ii) does not comply with the requirements of any legal provision under which a plan or description is to be approved by the local authority before the building or structure may be erected; and
> >
> > (iii) is situated within the area of jurisdiction of the local authority on land which is not the property of the local authority;
>
> and remove the material from the land.

According to the ordinary principles of our common law, landowners and local authorities do not have the right to demolish buildings without a court order. Where people are unlawfully deprived of possession without a court order, the law provides a remedy, the mandament van spolie. The mandament is a common-law remedy which provides that possessors who can show that they have been unlawfully deprived of possession will have possession restored to them. In order to obtain relief, applicants need to show that they were in peaceful and undisturbed possession; that their dispossession by the respondents was unlawful and that the respondents are able to restore possession to them.

Section 3B is a provision which, in certain circumstances, deprives squatters of the right to claim a mandament van spolie in respect of the summary demolition of their homes. Because section 3B gives powers of summary demolition only, however, all *evictions* from land may give rise to the grant of a mandament van spolie, if the requirements for the mandament are met. In *Ntshwaqela v Chairman, Western Cape Regional Services Council,*[22] the respondents had forced the applicants to leave their homes by threatening them with the summary demolition of their homes and their arrest. The applicants sought a spoliation order, saying that they had been deprived of possession through duress. The respondents argued that their actions had not constituted duress as they were entitled to threaten arrest and demolition in terms of the Prevention of Illegal Squatting Act. Howie J held that:

> Accepting that the police were in possession of sufficient information to justify arrests under the Act and that the owners themselves were empowered under the Act to demolish structures erected without their consent, I do not agree ... that the squatters were merely warned of possible arrest and demolition ....
> ... On analysis, therefore, as regards retention of possession, there was in fact no choice at all.
> To say the squatters vacated the land voluntarily is to fly in the face of the evidence. Applicants departed against their will without consenting to do so.[23]

On appeal, this conclusion was upheld by the Appellate Division in an as yet unreported judgment.[24]

The extent to which section 3B excludes the mandament van spolie will depend on a careful analysis of the section. However, it will be strictly interpreted, for it is a fundamental principle of our law that:

> [P]ersons are not entitled to take the law into their own hands to enforce their rights. There is a legal process by which the enforcement of rights is carried out. Normally speaking, it is carried out as a result of an order of court being put into effect through the proper officers of the law ...; in most civilized countries there exists the same principle that no person enforces his legal rights himself. For very obvious reasons that is so; if it were not so, breaches of the peace, for instance, would be very common.[25]

The question of consent

An important question that has come before the courts is what the nature of the consent referred to in section 3B(1)(a) is. In the recent Appellate Division decision, *George Municipality v Vena*,[26] the demolition of certain buildings was attacked on the ground that the landowner had consented to the erection and occupation of the buildings. Milne JA held that the requirement of consent did not require written or formal consent. Indeed,

> [S]ection 3B(1)(a) is, in my view, capable of meaning that
> (a) the owner's consent to erection may be given before, during or after the erection and may be given in any manner whatsoever, that is to say, expressly or impliedly, orally or in writing or by conduct;
> (b) the consent may be in very general terms eg for 'a dwelling' or 'a shack for X and his family to live in'. That would probably be the kind of consent usually given under this subsection.[27]

It appears that once a landowner has consented to the erection or occupation of a dwelling, he or she may not withdraw the consent and rely on section 3B(1)(a) to demolish the house, unless it was clear from the consent originally given that it was for a fixed period of time or could be withdrawn on notice. As Berman J held in *Luwalala v Port Nolloth Munisipaliteit*:

> It is not without significance that the words 'erected or occupied' are in the past tense. It could never have been the intention of the legislature to permit the owner of land, who at some time in the past consented to a building being erected thereon and to its occupation by another, and who now revokes that consent, to enter upon it and without a 'by your leave' set about demolishing it. That this must be so is in accordance with the need for the narrow construction referred to above; to interpret it otherwise is to recognize the right of an owner of leased property, upon the expiry of his tenant's lease, to demolish the subject matter of that lease over the occupier's head without obtaining an order for his ejectment – a right which the law-giver did not intend to accord under the Act which relates to 'squatters' .... The Act does not apply to a dwelling which was erected by the owner where the person occupying the dwelling never had the owner's consent to do so.[28]

Notice

Section 3B(2) expressly provides that no prior notice of the demolition is required. Originally, a period of notice was required, and failure to give the requisite notice resulted in the grant of a mandament van spolie.[29]

Ouster clause

The application of section 3B has been further complicated by an ouster clause. It was the granting of spoliation orders to dispossessed squatters that led Parliament to enact an ouster clause, section 3B(4)(a) in 1977. This clause was amended in 1988 to read as follows:

> It shall not be competent for any person to ask for any order, judgment or other relief in any civil proceedings of whatever nature in any court that are founded on the demolition or intended demolition or the prevention of the demolition under this section of any building or structure, or on the removal or intended removal or the prevention of the removal of any material or contents thereof from the land on which the building or structure is situated, and it shall not be competent for any court to grant or give such order, judgment or other relief unless such person first satisfies the court on a balance of probabilities that mala fide action has been or is to be taken.

How effectively does this ouster clause exclude spoliation claims? In *Luwalala v Munisipaliteit van Port Nolloth*,[30] Berman J held that the earlier version of this section could operate to oust the court's jurisdiction only where the threatened action was action that fell within the ambit of section 3B:

> the jurisdiction of the court is ousted only where relief is sought from it which is founded on the demolition or intended demolition or the prevention of any demolition of any building or structure under *section 3B*.[31]

This interpretation would seem to be correct, although there has been some confusion regarding the operation of ouster clauses. However, in *Minister of Law and Order v Hurley*,[32] Rabie CJ held, relying on *Schermbrucker v Klindt NO*,[33] that:

> It is a well-recognized rule in the interpretation of statutes, it has been stated by this court 'that the curtailment of the powers of a court of law is, in the absence of an express or clear implication to the contrary, not to be presumed'. The court will, therefore, closely examine any provision which appears to curtail or oust the jurisdiction of courts of law.[34]

The initial question to be answered, therefore, in determining whether the ouster clause contained in section 3B(4) will operate to oust the jurisdiction of the court, is whether the action taken was actually taken in terms of section 3B. If it was not, the ouster clause will not exclude civil proceedings.

If this interpretation is not upheld, squatters will have to show bad faith on the part of the demolishers in bringing about the demolition. This may not be as difficult as it would appear. For example, where there have been ongoing negotiations regarding the presence of the squatter community on the land, and the demolition has taken place without notice, it may well be that the bad faith requirement will have been met.

In conclusion, despite the extravagant ouster clause, it is still not clear when squatters will be deprived of relief under the mandament van spolie for the summary demolition of their homes. It also appears from the judgments that judges will strictly interpret the provisions of section 3B to reduce the powers of summary demolition. Accordingly, section 3B may still not provide the state with a speedy and straightforward tool for effecting forced removals.

Part III: Approved Informal Settlement Areas

Since its introduction, the Prevention of Illegal Squatting Act has contained provisions governing the establishment of temporary approved informal settlement areas, which, until the 1988 amendments, were called 'emergency camps'. Indeed, the War Measure upon which the Prevention of Illegal Squatting Act was based[35] made provision for the establishment of emergency camps and several such camps were established in the late 1940s.

In circumstances where communities have been threatened with removal, they have at times responded by actively seeking the establishment of an emergency camp as happened in the case of Crossroads in the mid-1970s.

Emergency camps or transit areas

Section 6 of the 1951 Act contained provisions empowering local authorities to establish emergency camps 'for the purpose of the accommodation of homeless persons'. The regulations issued by the local authority for the administration of such camps had to be approved by the Minister of Justice or Native Affairs and published in the *Government Gazette*. In 1976, the Act was amended to provide that only Bantu Affairs Administration Boards would have power to establish emergency camps for occupation by African people. In 1986, the power to establish emergency camps was once again returned to local authorities, although the Minister of Constitutional Development and Planning also obtained the power to direct local authorities to establish emergency camps.

The emergency camp provisions do not appear to have been used widely, although seventeen emergency camps for the housing of 'coloured' persons have been established in the Gordonia area. Crossroads was declared an emergency camp by the Cape Divisional Council in 1976, but the regulations governing the camp (never published in the *Government Gazette*) were repealed by the Divisional Council in 1978. More recently, Weiler's Farm in the Losberg district and Oukasie, the old township outside Brits, were declared emergency camps.

In 1988, Parliament abolished the provisions governing emergency camps and made provisions to govern the establishment, regulation and abolition of informal settlement areas, to be known as 'transit areas'. Section 6(11) of the Act now provides that any emergency area established under the previous provisions shall be deemed to be a transit area established under the new provisions. It is clear from the provisions of the legislation that transit areas are to be temporary informal settlement areas.

Although, in *Africa v Boothan,*[36] it was held that a local authority had jurisdiction to establish an emergency camp only over land which it owned, section 6(2) gives local authorities power to expropriate land in order to establish a transit area. In addition, section 6(4) provides that no compensation shall be payable in respect of an expropriation where the land

> is occupied by homeless persons, unless the owner or lawful occupier of such land can prove that it is so occupied without his permission.

Clearly, this provision is aimed at discouraging landowners from allowing squatters to live on their land. It is unlikely that a local authority will be able to rely on this provision without causing extensive public outcry.

Section 6A: Designated areas

In 1986, the Abolition of Influx Control Act amended the Prevention of Illegal Squatting Act to introduce a second type of informal settlement area, the so-called 'designated area'. Section 6A(1) reads as follows:

> The Minister of Constitutional Development and Planning may by notice in the *Gazette* designate a portion of land defined in the notice as land on which persons who are unable to find accommodation may ... settle or reside.

The difference between designated areas and transit areas seems to be that designated areas are to constitute more permanent areas for informal settlement than transit areas.

In terms of the amended Act, it is provincial administrators who now enjoy the power to establish and issue regulations to govern designated areas (sections 6A(3) and 6A(10)). As with transit areas, the Act makes provision for the expropriation of land to facilitate the establishment of designated areas (section 6A(2)).

In the case of both transit areas and designated areas, Parliament has provided that neither ordinary township planning rules, nor the Group Areas Act and the Slums Act shall apply (sections 6(4), (5), (9) and (10)). Transit areas and designated areas may provide local authorities and administrators with a flexible tool for managing urbanization. They may also, however, provide threatened communities with a way to seek an alternative to forced removal.

Conclusion

This legal analysis of the Act suggests that despite the clear attempt by the government to render forced removals in terms of the Prevention of Illegal Squatting Act 'judge-proof', the powers provided are still not absolute. Indeed, there are repeated and striking indications that where possible, in this area of the law anyway, judges may seek to limit the powers given to state officials and landlords.

Notes

* This article was originally published as part of an article in the (1989) 5 *South African Journal of Human Rights*. It is reprinted with the kind permission of the editors. I am indebted to Kobus Pienaar for making available his unpublished paper on the Prevention of Illegal Squatting Act presented at the Law and Removals Conference in April 1989.

1 1954 (4) SA 708 (T).

2 At 710A.

3 See Keightley in this volume at 182.

4 *R v Zulu* 1959 (1) SA 263 (A).

5 See *S v Peter* 1976 (2) SA 513 (C).

6 Ibid.

7 See *S v Mampura* 1964 (3) SA 477 (T).

8 1986 (3) SA 969 (T).

9 At 971.

10 See note 8.

11 Proclamation 76 of 1944 which was the precursor to the Prevention of Illegal Squatting Act. See O'Regan 'No More Forced Removals? An Historical Analysis of the Prevention of Illegal Squatting Act as Amended' (1989) 5 *South African Journal on Human Rights* 361 for a discussion of this measure.

12 1949 (3) SA 784 (T).

13 See *Zungu v Acting Magistrate, Umlazi* 1962 (3) SA 782 (O) and *Thubela v Pretorius* 1961 (3) SA 153 (T) and 1961 (4) SA 506 (T).

14 See O'Regan note 11 above.

15 See Budlender at 77 in this volume.

16 See note 12 above.

17 At 792-3.

18 1954 (1) SA 123 (A).

19 At 131.

20 See *The Star* 9 November 1988.

21 By Act 92 of 1976.

22 1988 (3) SA 218 (C).

23 At 224-5.

24 *Adminstrator of the Cape of Good Hope v Ntshwaqela* 30 November 1989, Appellate Division.

25 *Sithole v Native Resettlement Board* 1959 (4) SA 115 (W) at 117D-F.

26 1989 (2) SA 263 (A).

27 At 272F-G.

28 CPD 12 January 1989, Case no 10458/88, unreported.

29 See *Fredericks v Stellenbosch Divisional Council* 1977 (3) SA 113 (C).

30 See note 28 above.

31 At 27-8 of typescript judgment.

32 1986 (3) SA 568 (A).

33 1965 (4) SA 606 (A).

34 At 584A.

35 Proclamation 76 of 1944 as amended by Proclamation 67 of 1947. See note 11 above.

36 1958 (2) SA 459 (A).

RAYLENE KEIGHTLEY

The Trespass Act

Trespass may be defined as the 'unlawful intrusion over the boundaries actual or ideal of another's land'.[1] This notion of trespass is well recognized in legal systems which accord recognition to and protection of the sanctity of ownership and related rights in land. The legal prohibition of acts of trespass is not intended to protect such rights from actual or measurable harm as other legal remedies exist for this purpose. Instead, the designation of trespass as an unlawful act recognizes that the mere unwanted presence of a person on another's land is sufficient to warrant the sanction of the law. For this reason, trespass covers a wide variety of situations. Laws prohibiting acts of trespass can accordingly be used for a multitude of different purposes.

In South Africa, where 87 per cent of the land has been reserved for ownership by 13 per cent of the population, this is of particular significance. The criminalization of acts of trespass by the Trespass Act 6 of 1959 ('the Act') serves to buttress this widescale denial of access to the land for a large sector of the population. Despite the non-political formal nature of the Act, there is no doubt that it is used for political purposes. Many unreported cases reveal its extensive use in rural areas. In these cases the Act has not been used to prevent people from gaining access to land for criminal purposes. Instead it has secured the removal of people from land where their presence has, for one reason or another, become inconvenient to the owner or 'lawful occupier' of the land or to the state.

The Act has, for example, been used extensively against squatters. One recent example of this is the prosecution of the Noordhoek squatters on the Cape Peninsula. The land on which the squatters are living belongs in part to a private owner and in part to the Western Cape Regional Services Council. The squatters were originally forcibly removed from the land in December 1987. In 1988 they obtained an order from the Cape Supreme Court declaring their removal unlawful. The squatters accordingly returned to the land where they suffered harassment from municipal police and were again threatened with eviction. The community, however, stayed firm in its resolve to remain on the land. In April 1989, fourteen of the squatters were charged under the Trespass Act, inter alia. These prosecutions clearly represent yet a further attempt to force the squatters into leaving the land.[2]

It is in this sense then that the Trespass Act plays such a vital role in the struggle for land rights in South Africa. Trespass charges usually arise within the context of a broader dispute over access to land. Very often the Act is used in conjunction with other statutes, such as the Prevention of Illegal Squatting Act 52 of 1951, or in conjunction with other attempts by the state to remove people from land. Although the Act contains no provisions which empower the courts to order the eviction of anyone convicted of trespass, the practical effect of arrest and conviction under the Act is often to drive those convicted off the land. This effectively enables the landowner or lawful occupier to secure the removal of people without the inconvenience and expense of instituting civil proceedings. In addition, by reason of the Act's outwardly non-political nature, it very often allows such removal to take place without unwanted attention from the media and human rights organizations.

The use of the Act within the context of land disputes raises certain difficulties for lawyers. First, trespass charges must be seen within the context of the broader dispute. A variety of political, sociological, administrative and economic factors shape every dispute. These must be taken into account by lawyers in framing defences to any charges under the Act as the strategy adopted in court will be circumscribed by them. Secondly, a successful defence to a trespass charge will probably not bring an end to the broader dispute as other strategies are likely to be adopted in an attempt to secure the removal of those charged. These difficulties are of great practical importance and they should be borne in mind throughout the examination of the Act which follows.

The nature of the statutory crime of trespass

The Trespass Act is categorized in *LAWSA* as one of a number of statutes concerning prohibited presence on land.[3] Also dealt with under this section in *LAWSA* are the Prevention of Illegal Squatting Act 52 of 1951, the Reservation of Separate Amenities Act 49 of 1953 and the Group Areas Act 36 of 1966. Thus despite its apparent characterization as an ordinary criminal statute, it is closely connected with legislation that has been created specifically to advance government policy in relation to the racial acquisition and use of land.

The Trespass Act itself is very short, comprising only four sections in all. Section 1 (1) creates the offence of trespass in the following terms:

> Any person who without the permission –
> a) of the lawful occupier of any land or any building or part of a building; or
> b) of the owner or person in charge of any land or any building or part of a building that is not lawfully occupied by any person,
> enters or is upon such land or enters or is upon such building or part of a building, shall be guilty of an offence unless he has lawful reason to enter or be upon such land or enter or be in such building or part of a building.

It should be noted that whereas the Act outlaws presence on and in both land and buildings without consent, within the context of disputes over access to land the Act is invariably used to punish presence on land rather than in buildings. For this reason reference will be made throughout this chapter to presence on land alone.

A number of points arise for discussion in relation to section 1(1) of the Act.

(i) The absence of permission

In respect of the absence of permission the Act effectively creates two separate offences depending on whether the land in question is lawfully occupied or not.

In terms of section 1(1)(a), an offence is committed if the entry or presence on land which is lawfully occupied occurs without the permission of its lawful occupier. Thus in *S v Mdunge*,[4] where a farm was owned by a father but managed by his son, it was held that it was the permission of the son, as lawful occupier, and not that of the father, as owner, that was relevant in respect of a charge under section 1(1)(a) of the Act.

In order to be a 'lawful occupier' a person must, it seems, be in the position of exercising some rights of control over the land.[5] In *S v Davids*[6] it was held that these rights of control must be greater than those exercised by a 'mere tenant, bywoner or labourer'. Thus, it would not avail a squatter on farmland to secure the permission of farm labourers, who are occupying the land lawfully, as they are not lawful occupiers under the Act.

In terms of section 1(1)(b), it is an offence to enter or to be on unoccupied land without the permission of the owner or person in charge. The owner of land is best identified by way of title deed but the production of such a document is not always necessary to establish the identity of the owner.[7]

A 'person in charge' of unoccupied property is one to whom some degree of authority to control the property has been delegated.[8] In a case pre-dating the Act,[9] it was held that 'a policeman or any other passer-by who might think the accused person's presence unwelcome to the occupier' is not a person in charge. However, where the owner has called on the police to exercise control, the police would be regarded as person(s) in charge and could accordingly object to a person's presence.

It is incumbent on the state to allege and prove that the land in question is occupied or unoccupied and that the necessary permission of the specified person in each case has not been obtained by the alleged trespasser. Thus in *S v Lekwena*[10] the accused were charged under section 1(1)(b) with entering a 'Bantu Reservation' without the permission of the headman who, it was alleged, was the person in control of the land. The accused argued that the charge sheet failed to allege, and that the state had failed to prove, that the land was not lawfully occupied. The accused argued further that there were in fact approximately 300 families living on the land in question. The court held that in the circumstances the state had failed to prove that the land was not lawfully occupied and the appeal against conviction succeeded.

Similarly, where the state incorrectly alleges and proves that a particular person failed to give permission it will have failed to prove a necessary element of the offence. For example, where, in respect of occupied land, the state alleges and proves that the owner's consent was absent, and the owner is not the lawful occupier of the land, the accused may escape conviction on a charge under section 1(1)(a) of the Act. The state may also, of course, cite the wrong person as the owner or occupier. This has particular importance in disputes concerning land owned or controlled by administrative organs of government or by groups of companies. In these situations, it is often very difficult to determine exactly which is the relevant body having ownership or control of particular land. There is always the possibility that the wrong administrative body or company has been cited as the owner or lawful occupier of the land and that the accused will have a valid defence to the charge on this ground.

It should be noted, however, that where the charge sheet is defective in one or another of these respects but the state's evidence nevertheless proves the relevant requirements under the Act, it is likely that the court will merely order an amendment of the charge sheet.[11] Thus a purely technical defence based only on a defective charge sheet is not likely to assist the accused.

As far as the consent itself is concerned, exactly what is required to constitute 'permission' is unclear and none of the reported cases on the Act appear to have turned on this issue. However, it appears that even qualified permission might be sufficient.[12] Presumably, whatever permission is granted must bear some relation to the entry or presence that subsequently takes place. In other words, it is questionable whether, if a person obtains permission from a farmer to visit friends on his or her farm, this would extend to permission to be on the farm for the purpose of holding a union meeting amongst the farmworkers. The answer would probably depend on the particular facts of the case.

(ii) The absence of 'lawful reason'

If a person has 'lawful reason' to be on the land, the fact that he or she is there without the necessary permission will not be sufficient to secure a conviction. The purpose of allowing entry onto property without permission but with lawful reason is to provide for the necessities of ordinary social intercourse.[13] Thus, it has been held that a person will have lawful reason to be on land if he or she is 'engaged in innocent pursuits...[and has] no reason to anticipate objection on the part of the owner or occupier'.[14]

Despite this apparently simple formulation of lawful reason, however, it is difficult to arrive at a clear understanding of the concept. This is in part due to the fact that the courts have, in many cases, tended to confuse lawful reason with the element of mens rea (criminal intent) in trespass cases. In *S v Brown*[15] the courts noted that this confusion arises because the facts necessary to establish lawful reason are often identical to those necessary to establish mens rea. Thus, if it can be established that a person had a lawful reason to be on another's land, then, on the same facts, it can also be established that he or she did not have the necessary mens rea to commit the offence of trespass.

Milton & Fuller[16] point out that there is a clear distinction between 'lawful reason' and mens rea in that the former requires an actual lawful entry or presence whereas the latter only requires a bona fide belief in a lawful entry or presence. In practice, however, there are difficulties in distinguishing between the two. Most of the decided cases have tended to decide the issue on the basis of the absence of mens rea rather than on the existence of a 'lawful reason'.[17] This would appear to be the more predictable approach for the courts to adopt, taking into account the difference in the burden of proof in relation to each of these two elements, which is discussed on the following pages. However, it has not facilitated an adequate exposition of the element of 'lawful reason' which remains a problematic aspect of the offence.

(iii) Entry and presence

As far as the actus reus or wrongful act is concerned, the Act requires only that a person 'enters or is upon ... land'. This means that an entry alone may fall foul of the Act and it is not required that a person remain on the land for any extended length of time before a conviction can be secured. Thus, the threat of laying charges under the Act may be used as a method of preventing people from gaining physical access to land. Furthermore, where access is gained, the landowner or lawful occupier can immediately lay charges under the Act and so force people to leave before they have become established there. An example of this type of situation would be where labour tenants are charged with trespass after they fail to vacate farmland once the labour tenancy agreement is purportedly terminated by the farmer.[18]

The kind of presence prohibited by the Act, viz. the mere act of being on land, may be contrasted to some extent with the kind of presence prohibited by the Prevention of Illegal Squatting Act, which prohibits the act of 'remaining' on land. The Trespass Act accordingly applies in situations where the presence of people is temporary and only of short duration. It also, however, applies in situations where the presence is more permanent. In this respect too, therefore, the Trespass Act is of wide application and it can be used to suit a variety of situations. In the Noordhoek squatters case, for example, not only were trespass charges laid against the squatters themselves, but members of the press and others who visited the squatters to lend their support were also threatened with trespass charges.[19]

Actual personal presence of the accused on the land must be established. Thus, in *S v Brown*[20] it was held that the mere purchase of a house in a 'coloured' area without the necessary permission of the municipality did not amount to a trespass in terms of the Act. Although the state led evidence that the accused had arranged for a builder to effect repairs to the house, it had failed to prove a single instance of personal presence on the property by the accused himself. The conviction was accordingly set aside.

(iv) The requirement of mens rea (criminal intent)

It has been clearly established by a number of decisions that mens rea is an element of the offence created by the Act. Thus, in *R v Venter*[21] it was held that 'when a trespasser on any person's ground is there because of what he believes to be a right to be on that ground, the Crown cannot succeed on a charge under this section'. The issue of mens rea turns on the bona fide belief of the accused in the lawfulness of his or her presence on land belonging to another.[22]

The case law on the Act reveals a number of instances where the absence of mens rea has served as the basis for an acquittal. In *S v Nkopane*[23] a new employee of a mining company holding mining rights on a particular farm was acquitted on a charge of trespass under the Act. The court held that he had no reason to believe that he was trespassing on the property by using a particular footpath, even though the farmer alleged that the footpath was out of bounds to mine employees. In *S v Lekwena*[24] the court itself raised the point that the accused, who had been born in the district concerned, probably had reasonable grounds for believing that they were entitled to be on the land in question, which had been designated a reserve area, without the necessary permission of the Bantu Commissioner. As such, the accused lacked the necessary mens rea for the offence. The case *R v Mbeki*[25] concerned an African who knocked at the door of a house owned by whites on what he believed was a lawful errand. He did not understand the instructions issued to him by the houseowner's wife to leave the premises and, therefore, did not obey them. He was charged with committing an offence under the Act but was acquitted on appeal on the basis that he lacked the necessary mens rea to commit the offence.

Some of these cases clearly illustrate the point made earlier concerning the overlap between mens rea and 'lawful reason'. In both the *Nkopane* and *Mbeki*[26] cases, while the accused clearly lacked mens rea, their presence on the land or premises in question could equally be regarded as having been for a 'lawful purpose'.

(v) The burden of proof

The Act creates one clear exception to the general principle that the state bears the burden of proving all the elements of an offence.[27] This exception relates to the element of an unlawful entry or presence or, to use the words of the Act itself, the absence of a 'lawful reason'. In this regard the burden of proof rests on the accused to prove on a balance of probabilities that his or her entry or presence was for a lawful reason and hence not unlawful.[28] It is accordingly incumbent on the state merely to prove a technical trespass, in other words, entry or presence without the requisite permission, after which the burden of proof shifts to the accused to establish that in any event he or she had lawful reason for entering or being on the premises.[29] Thus, in the *Mcunu*[30] case, the state established that the accused had not had the permission of the owner of residential premises to be in the servants' quarters of the residence. The accused then argued that he had entered the premises in order to call for his girlfriend who was visiting there at the time. It was argued that this constituted a 'lawful reason' for his presence on the property. The court assumed, without deciding, that this would have constituted a lawful reason, but held that on the evidence presented to the court the accused had failed to prove that this was in fact the reason for his presence on the property.

In *S v Nkopane*[31] and *S v Ziki*[32] the courts seemed to suggest that the mens rea requirement under the Act provided a second exception to the general principles of criminal law regarding the burden proof. In both cases the court placed the burden of proof on the accused to establish the absence of mens rea, although no reasons were given for placing this burden on the accused.[33] The more recent decision in *S v Brown*[34] questions the correctness of this view on the basis of the Appellate Division decision in *S v Fouche*.[35] On this basis, and bearing in mind the general principles of criminal law, it is probably correct to state that the burden of proving that the accused had the requisite mens rea to commit an offence under the Act rests on the state. It is possible that the original confusion concerning the burden of proof in relation to mens rea arose out of the failure by the courts to distinguish clearly between mens rea and 'lawful reason'.

In relation to the other elements of the offence, the burden of proof clearly rests on the state. Thus, the state must allege and prove that the land is occupied or unoccupied, as the case may be;[36] it must prove who the owner or lawful occupier of the land is; the absence of permission by the relevant person must be proved; and, finally, the state must prove entry by or the presence of the accused.

(vi) Sanctions in terms of the Act

Section 2 provides that anyone convicted of an offence under the Act is liable to a fine of up to R2 000 or to a period of imprisonment not exceeding two years, or both.

The sentences meted in trespass cases can be relatively harsh. In *R v Mcunu*[37] for example, the accused was sentenced to two months' imprisonment without the option of a fine for visiting the servants' quarters of a residential property without permission. The court on appeal held that although the sentence was severe it was not shockingly severe and therefore refused to interfere. It is important to note that the court in this case took into account the fact that the accused had previous convictions, including a prior conviction under the Act. This type of precedent does not augur well for people who are charged under the Act as part of a broader dispute over access to land. Repeated convictions in such cases are quite common and this gives rise to the possibility that the removal of the accused from the land will eventually be effectively secured by the imposition of a period of imprisonment.

Even in cases where a prison sentence is avoided, the outcome of a conviction and sentence might still be to secure the removal of the accused from the land. Firstly, the sentence is frequently suspended on condition that the accused leaves the land in question. In *S v Brown*[38] the sentence of

R40 or 80 days imprisonment was suspended on condition that the structure owned by the accused was removed from the land. In an unreported case in 1983 involving Hout Bay squatters, the sentences of between R60 or 60 days and R90 or 90 days were suspended on condition that the accused vacated the land by a given date. Such sentences place people in a no-win situation: either they obey the conditions of the suspension of sentence and lose their struggle to stay on the land, or they refuse to obey the conditions of suspension, in which case, sooner or later, they are likely to end up in prison, thus losing the struggle in any event.

Secondly, the mere fact that charges under the Act are repeatedly laid against the accused might cause sufficient disruption and hardship in their lives as to wear down their resistance to the extent that they eventually leave the land of their own accord. This has been the experience amongst labour tenants in the south-eastern Transvaal who have been subject to such harassment.[39]

A particularly disturbing feature of charges being laid under the Act is the experience in some cases of the accused being refused bail on the basis that their release on bail will result in the repeated commission of the offence. Thus, in the Hout Bay squatters' case, the court held that were the accused to be released on bail, they would return to their homes on the land in question and would once more be liable for arrest on the same charge. Bail was accordingly refused. It is therefore possible that prior to any sanctions being imposed in terms of the Act, the accused might be forced to leave the land.

These instances all show that apparently minor sanctions can have far-reaching consequences for those prosecuted. What is also illustrated is that despite the absence of eviction provisions in the Act, it is frequently used for the very purpose of effecting evictions.

Possible defences to charges under the Act within the context of disputes over access to land

Where trespass charges arise as part of a broader dispute over land, as for example in the use of the Act against squatters, a successful defence to the charges will not necessarily end the matter. It will, however, certainly represent an important moral and political victory for the accused persons which may in turn have important implications for the eventual outcome of the dispute.

Cases in which the Trespass Act has been used in land rights disputes have not been systematically documented. For this reason, many of the defences discussed below are merely suggestions as to the kinds of legal strategies that might be adopted in such cases. The efficacy of any of these defences will, of course, depend on the circumstances involved in each case.

(i) Tactical defences

Given that disputes over access to land require very careful strategizing from both sides, lawyers representing those threatened with losing access to land must inevitably consider not only strictly legal arguments but also tactical arguments.

It is not uncommon for trespass charges to be withdrawn when lawyers become involved in these disputes. For this reason it may be advantageous for lawyers to advance arguments at an early stage to support the withdrawal of the charges. In this regard, reference could be made to the attitude of the superior courts which have, in a number of cases, criticized the use of the Trespass Act to settle what are essentially civil disputes. In *S v Ziki*[40] the court held that:

> [T]he case illustrates the impropriety of attempting to settle a civil dispute by means of criminal prosecution. If the [complainant] succeeds in an action for ejectment of [the accused] it will attain the object which it no doubt sought by the institution of this prosecution.

Similar sentiments were voiced in *S v Brown*[41] and *R v Venter.*[42] It is interesting to note that in all of these cases, the appeals against the convictions succeeded. The success of a strategy which attempts to rely on the unwillingness of criminal courts to be used to settle civil disputes would, however, depend on the broader issues involved in a particular dispute.

(ii) Legal defences

(a) Defences based on the existence of permission

An accused who can show that he or she in fact had the necessary permission to enter or to be on the land in question obviously has a valid defence. However, it is unlikely for this to be adduced by way of simple facts in complicated land disputes. For this reason it might be difficult to prove the existence of express consent.

In certain cases it might be possible to raise the defence of implied consent. This argument could be advanced in situations where the accused has been on the land for a considerable period of time without any objection from the owner or lawful occupier. The failure to raise any objection to the accused person's presence might constitute implied consent to such presence.

Indirect support for this position appears in the judgment of the Appellate Division in *George Municipality v Vena.*[43] Regarding the meaning of 'consent' in section 3B(1)(a) of the Prevention of Illegal Squatting Act, the court held that the owner's consent could be given before, during, or after the structure in question had been erected, and that it could be given 'in any manner whatsoever ... expressly or impliedly, orally or in writing or by conduct'.[44] The court thus recognized that consent can take many forms. A similar argument could be raised in the context of the Trespass Act although much will depend on the particular facts of each case as not every failure to object will give rise to implied consent.

In addition, where the accused person's presence on land was originally authorized by a contract which has been unilaterally terminated by the owner or lawful occupier, a conviction for trespass would normally not be competent. In such cases it could be argued that once permission to be on the land is granted, it can be withdrawn only by way of a valid termination of the contract giving rise to it. Should such termination be invalid for any reason, the permission itself will not have been withdrawn. Thus, in the unreported decision of *S v Hadebe*[45] the accused, who was a labour tenant on the complainant's farm, was charged with trespass when she failed to vacate the farm after receiving one month's notice of the termination of the labour tenancy agreement. The court held that the notice was insufficient and in fact amounted to no notice at all. The accused was accordingly acquitted of the charge.[46]

(b) Defences based on the existence of a 'lawful reason'.

From the discussion of 'lawful reason' above, it is clear that to succeed with a defence based on lawful reason it is not necessary for the accused to go so far as to show that he or she had a right to be on the land. Innocent pursuits in respect of which no objections from the owner or occupier are anticipated will not be regarded as prohibited acts of trepass.

What are accepted as innocent pursuits must, to some extent, be influenced by the fact that in South Africa land is largely owned by white people and alleged trespassers are usually black people. Social intercourse between the different race groups is very limited and it may therefore be difficult for a black person accused of trespassing on white-owned land to convince the court that his or her presence on the land was for a lawful reason. This will be so particularly in cases where the trespass charges arise as a result of an already existing dispute over access to land.

Despite these difficulties, there are circumstances in which the defence of the existence of a lawful reason may well succeed. Thus, where the presence of the accused on land is by virtue of an agreement with the owner or lawful occupier and the trespass charges arise out of the purported termination of that agreement, the accused might raise lawful reason as a defence. This defence would be available where the termination of the agreement is invalid as the presence of the accused on the land would not then be unlawful. In this situation, the accused could either raise a defence based on the existence of permission or a defence based on the existence of lawful reason. In view of the difference in the burden of proof in respect of these two elements, it would be prudent in such cases to argue, firstly, that the state has failed to prove the absence of permission, and, in the alternative, that the accused has lawful reason to be on the land.

(c) The absence of mens rea as a defence

Where any defence based on the existence of permission or lawful reason fails, an acquittal may nevertheless be secured on the basis that the accused lacked the necessary mens rea for the offence for example, where it appears from the evidence that he or she bona fide believed that he or she had the requisite permission to be on the land, or that such permission was not required.[47]

Where accused persons have been on the land for a long time without objection from the owner or occupier, and trespass charges are laid without warning, the defence of the existence of implied permission might of course be raised. If this fails, however, the accused might still escape conviction on the basis that they lacked the necessary mens rea for the offence. Without any objection communicated to the accused it would be difficult to conclude that they knew that they were committing an offence.

Similarly where the evidence shows that the accused bona fide believed that he or she had lawful reason to be on the land, the defence will succeed regardless of the fact that the accused fails to discharge the burden of proving lawful reason. This is an important point to bear in mind, given the difficulties involved in succeeding on a defence of lawful reason. As the state bears the burden of proving the existence of mens rea, a defence based on the absence of mens rea is more likely to succeed than one based on lawful reason.

The absence of mens rea offers some scope for successfully defending charges under the Act. The problem, however, is that, should the accused remain on the land after an acquittal on this basis, he or she is likely to again be charged under the Act. In the subsequent trial it will be difficult to convince the court that the accused still believed that he or she was entitled to be on the land.

Conclusion

Although the Trespass Act lacks many of the alarming features of other statutes concerned with control over access to land, its role within the context of land disputes should not be underestimated. It is a versatile piece of legislation which lends itself well to being used in all kinds of disputes. The effect of its successful use can be devastating for those who are charged under its provisions. On the other hand, for landowners intent on securing the removal of people the Act offers a simple and effective method of doing so. It is interesting to note that the Act is still being used to remove people who have settled on land despite the amendments to the Prevention of Illegal Squatting Act.

Given the ease with which trespass charges can be laid and the far-reaching consequences of such charges, it is reasonable to conclude that the Trespass Act will continue to be used in disputes over access to land. The significance of this for lawyers involved in land disputes is that the Act offers some scope for legal intervention. Unlike the Prevention of Illegal Squatting Act, for example, the provisions of the Trespass Act do not overwhelmingly favour the state. However, within the context of disputes over land, successful challenges to a charge under the Act will not be easy. It should also be noted that in many cases accused people do not have the benefit of legal assistance.

It is essential that legal challenges to the use of the Act in the context of forced removals be made. Without such challenges to this apparently ordinary piece of legislation, the process of depriving people of access to land will continue unabated.

Notes

1 J R Milton & N M Fuller *South African Criminal Law and Procedure* vol 3 (Cape Town: Juta 1971) 187.

2 Surplus People Project *Dossier on Noordhoek* (1989).

3 A J Middleton & S Stoker 'Statutory Offences' in *LAWSA* vol 6 (Durban: Butterworths 1981) 440.

4 1962 (2) SA 500 (N).

5 Milton & Fuller, above note 1 at 193.

6 1966 (1) PH H26 (N).

7 *S v Lechudi* 1945 (1) PH K31 (GW); Milton & Fuller, above note 1 at 195.

8 Milton & Fuller, above note 1 at 195.

9 *R v Mocang* 1942 TPD 91.

10 1965 (1) SA 527 (C).

11 *S v Mdunge* 1962 (2) SA 500 (N), *S v Brown* 1978 (1) SA 305 (NC).

12 Milton & Fuller, above note 1 at 193.

13 Milton & Fuller, above note 1 at 189.

14 *R v Jakwane* 1944 OPD 139 cited in Milton & Fuller, above note 1, at 190.

15 1978 (1) SA 305 (NC).

16 Above note 1 at 194.

17 See *S v Ziki* 1965 (4) SA 14 (E); *S v Nkopane* 1962 (4) SA 279 (O); *R v Mbeki* 1950 (2) SA 53 (E).

18 See Hathorn & Hutchison in this volume at 206.

19 See Surplus People Project *Dossier on Noordhoek.*

20 1978 (1) SA 305 (NC).

21 1961 (1) SA 363 (T) at 364.

22 Milton & Fuller, cited above note 1 at 194.

23 1962 (4) SA 279 (O).

24 1965 (1) SA 527 (C).

25 1950 (2) SA 53 (E).

26 1962 (4) SA 279 (O); 1950 (2) SA 53 (E).

27 Milton & Fuller, above note 1 at 190.

28 *R v Mcunu* 1960 (4) SA 544 (N); *R v Nkopane* 1962 (4) SA 279 (O).

29 See Milton & Fuller, above note 1 at 190.

30 1960 (4) SA 544 (N).

31 1962 (4) SA 279 (O).

32 1965 (4) SA 14 (E).

33 See Milton & Fuller, above note 1 at 194.

34 1978 (1) SA 305 (NC).

35 1974 (1) SA 96 (A).

36 *S v Lekwena* 1965 (1) SA 527(C).

37 1960 (4) SA 544 (N).

38 1978 (1) SA 305 (NC).

39 See Hathorn & Hutchison at 197-8 in this volume.

40 1965 (4) SA 14 (E).

41 1978 (1) SA 305 (NC).

42 1961 (1) SA 363 (T) at 364.

43 1989 (2) SA 263 (A).

44 At 272F-G.

45 TPD, Case no A1765/88, unreported.

46 See Hathorn & Hutchison in this volume at 205.

47 See *S v Lekwena* 1965 (1) SA 527 (C); *S v Nkopane* 1962 (4) SA 279 (O).

MORAY HATHORN AND DALE HUTCHISON

Labour Tenants and the Law

In South Africa, the term 'labour tenant' denotes a black person residing on white-owned land who undertakes to work for or supply labour to the landowner for part of the year (usually three to nine months) in return for the right to use a small portion of the land for his or her own purposes; for example, to erect a dwelling, grow crops and graze stock. As such, labour tenants are small-scale farmers in their own right who are in a sense both labourers and tenants of the white landowner. Their degree of independence is greater than that of ordinary labourers, but less than that of cash tenants or share-croppers.

The labour tenant system dates back to the days of colonial conquest and was once the most widespread form of farm labour in the northern parts of South Africa, especially in the Transvaal and northern Natal. Today the system is under attack and has been so for many decades, as a result of a state drive to eliminate it altogether. Despite this pressure, the system still survives in certain districts, including extensive areas of the south-eastern Transvaal and northern Natal.[1]

The purpose of this paper is two-fold: first, to describe briefly the attempts by the state to regulate and later to abolish the labour tenant system; and secondly, to examine the legal nature and consequences of the labour tenancy contract, in particular, the circumstances and manner in which it may lawfully be terminated by the landowner. The lawfulness of such termination is vitally important in practice because the continued existence of the contract provides the labour tenant with a defence not only to a civil claim for eviction, but also to criminal charges under the Group Areas Act, the Trespass Act or the Prevention of Illegal Squatting Act.

The legislative history: attempts to regulate and later to abolish the labour tenant system

The labour tenant system has been regulated by various statutes over the course of time, virtually all of which have since been abolished. Today the control is indirect, through prosecutions under the Acts just mentioned. Some knowledge of the earlier legislation is necessary for a proper understanding of the history of labour tenancy in South Africa, and of the case law which grew up around it.

The pre-Union squatter laws of Natal and Transvaal provided an early form of control over the occupation of white farmland by blacks, and regulated various aspects of the relationships between farmer and 'squatter' (a term which covered labour tenants). Section 3 of Natal Ordinance 2 of 1855, in particular, was frequently used by farmers to evict dismissed labour tenants, and gave rise to much litigation on the validity of such dismissal.[2] It provided that if an owner of land complained to a magistrate that 'natives' were unlawfully residing on his or her land, then two cases might arise: (i) if the 'natives' had no initial permission to be there, they could be summarily ejected; (ii) if they resided there 'under a lease, or other agreement, which has expired, or become void, through any act or omission of the said native[s]', they could be evicted only by order of the magistrate, and subject to their being given 'due time to collect and gather in the crops then growing on the land'. The Transvaal Law 21 of 1895 provided, inter alia, that three months' notice on either side was required to terminate the contract of labour tenancy, and that in any event, the tenants should have the right to harvest their standing crops.[3]

The Natives Land Act 27 of 1913, which prohibited blacks from entering into 'any agreement or transaction for the purchase, hire or other acquisition from a person other than a native' of any land outside the 'scheduled native areas', did not immediately affect the position of labour tenants for it treated them as farm labourers who were expressly permitted to reside on white farms. Indeed, the Act swelled the numbers of labour tenants for it forced many cash tenants and sharecroppers, whose way of life it destroyed, into labour tenancy.[4]

The Native Service Contract Act 24 of 1932 represented the first attempt by the state to place the labour tenancy contract on a proper legal footing. In section 1 it defined the contract as one

> whereby a native binds himself or binds his ward ... to render any services of whatever nature as a consideration for permission granted to such native or any member of his family or of the kraal or household to which he belongs to occupy or use any land, by any person who has the right to grant such permission.

Section 5 regulated various aspects of the contract, including its creation (no formalities required), duration (one year unless otherwise specified, subject to a maximum of three years), renewal (automatic for a further year, unless three months' notice given on either side) and termination (for example, on the grounds of the tenant's absence from the farm without permission for a period in excess of six months). It expressly recognized the right of the tenants on termination of the contract to tend, reap and remove their standing crops and to demolish and remove their structures erected on the land. In the event of the land being sold or alienated to a third person, the latter would assume the previous employer's position under the contract, but either party could within three months cancel the contract on giving three months' notice.[5] Most of these provisions later found their way into the 1936 Act discussed hereafter.[6]

By far the most significant statutory provision concerning labour tenancy in recent times has been the notorious chapter IV of the Native Trust and Land Act 18 of 1936. Enacted as a response to state concern about the number of black people congregating on white-owned farmland, chapter IV established an elaborate system for the registration and control of labour tenants and squatters. In terms of section 26, only certain categories of black people were permitted to reside on white-owned farmland, one such category being registered labour tenants and their dependants. Contravention of the section was made a punishable offence. Owners of land were required to register the labour tenants residing on their land and could be called before the labour tenant control board to show cause why the number of tenants on the land should not be reduced. The board could order the landowner to reduce the number within a specific period, and could terminate any contract of labour tenancy that extended beyond that period. Any 'native' unlawfully residing on the land could, after an enquiry by the local native commissioner, be summarily ejected by the police, using reasonable force if necessary.

These drastic measures provided the basis for the mass farm removals that were later to follow. Initially it seems that they were not strictly enforced, but after the National Party came to power in 1948 the position changed radically. The new government immediately embarked on a programme of eliminating squatting and of gradually transforming the 'wasteful' (because part-time) system of labour tenancy to one of full-time, wage-paid farm labour, in order to create a 'reserve army of labour for capitalist agriculture'.[7] To this end chapter IV of the 1936 Act had to be implemented vigorously and the provisions in that Act relating to additional land purchases 'were precisely meant to accommodate the displaced squatters resulting from the application of chapter IV'.[8] This policy apparently caused some conflict within the ranks of the Natal and Transvaal farmers, but it soon became clear that a majority of the farmers wanted even more active steps by the state to eliminate the 'inefficient and uneconomic' labour tenant system which, they claimed, 'had a handicapping effect on the application of more efficient farming methods' by not allowing the efficiency of labour to keep pace with the 'increasing mechanization of agriculture'.[9] In consequence, the Nel Committee of Inquiry into the Labour Tenant System was appointed. In its Report of 1961, the Committee recommended that legislation be introduced as soon as possible with a view to the total abolition of the labour tenant system within seven years. Recognizing that 'simultaneous total abolition ... might cause an uncontrolled position to arise', the Committee recommended abolition 'by means of proclamation to a particular farm, area, district or province according to circumstance'.[10] These recommendations were given effect to in the Bantu Laws Amendment Act 42 of 1964, which repealed the Native Service Contract Act of 1932 and substantially amended chapter IV of the Native Trust and Land Act of 1936.

The result of this legislation was the progressive and systematic abolition of the labour tenant system in most districts where it still existed, and the forced removal of squatters and labour tenants from farms in the 1960s and 1970s, all in terms of the various 'resettlement schemes' of the government.

> Between 1960 and 1970, 340 000 labour tenants plus 656 000 squatters and 97 000 squatters in "Black Spots" were estimated to have been removed. In addition, an estimated 400 000 labour tenants were removed between 1971 and 1974. By 1976 labour tenancy in South African agriculture had to all intents and purposes been abolished and farm labour was stabilized.[11]

The Surplus People Project estimates that of the 3,5 million people removed from their homes between 1960 and 1983 pursuant to the relocation policies of the government, about 1 129 000 had lived on white-owned farms.[12]

With its purpose largely achieved, chapter IV was repealed by the Abolition of Influx Control Act 68 of 1986. As a result, labour tenancy contracts are no longer governed directly by statute, but, as noted earlier, other statutes continue to exert an indirect form of control.

Despite the massive attempts to abolish it and the claims that these attempts have been successful, it would appear that the labour tenant system continues to exist in a number of districts in South Africa. Today the evictions continue, but under different laws. It is common practice for white farmers in the south-eastern Transvaal to give labour tenants one month's notice to quit the farm together with their dependants and possessions. When such notices are disregarded, the farmers lodge complaints with the police leading to prosecutions under the Trespass Act 6 of 1959 or, occasionally, under section 1 of the Prevention of Illegal Squatting Act 52 of 1951. As most labour tenants do not have legal representation, these cases often result in the conviction and subsequent eviction of the tenant. If the tenants return to the farm, as they usually do, the process is repeated until the cumulative effect of the fines and jail sentences imposed wear down their endurance and courage to the point where they decide to leave the farm.

It is of the utmost importance to recognize that the existence of a valid contract permitting the tenant to occupy the land provides a valid defence to a charge under the above-mentioned Acts, as well as to a (very rare) charge under section 20 of the Group Areas Act 36 of 1966, and to a civil claim for eviction. If, therefore, the contract was not lawfully terminated – for example, because of inadequate notice – the attempt to evict the tenant will not succeed, as demonstrated by two recent, unreported cases in the Transvaal which follow earlier cases dealing with the pre-Union squatter laws.[13] These cases will be considered below.

The contract of labour tenancy

Nature of the contract

From the description and definition given earlier it will be apparent that the contract of labour tenancy falls somewhere between a lease of land (locatio conductio rei) and a service contract, or contract of employment (locatio conductio operarum). It is not strictly a true lease since the rent does not take the form of money or a share of the fruits of the land;[14] nor is it an ordinary contract of employment, for the reward (merx) consists neither wholly nor partially in money, but rather in the right to occupy and use the land.[15] However, as pointed out by the late Mr Justice Van den Heever,

> [i]f we forget the Roman technicality, ... we could look upon [the labour tenancy] contract either as a lease of land, the merx being labour, or a locatio conductio operarum, the merx being the right to occupy land.[16]

The classification of the contract is important because of the naturalia or terms implied by law that accompany recognized categories of contract. For example, if the labour tenancy contract may be regarded as a form of lease, the labour tenant would enjoy the protection of the 'huur gaat voor koop' rule and the farmer would have a tacit hypothec over the tenant's possessions (invecta et illata). On the other hand, the contract would then fall within the scope of the transactions prohibited by the Natives (now Black) Land Act 27 of 1913, which is not and never has been the accepted view. Likewise, if the contract were to be regarded as a simple one of employment, it would in earlier times have been subject to the Master and Servant Laws, which again was never the case.

Where an agreement satisfies the requirements of two or more types of contract regulated by law, the agreement may either be relegated to the dominant type of contract (the absorption theory), or the naturalia of each type of contract may be applied to the relevant portion of the agreement in so far as that is possible or practicable (the combination theory), or the agreement may be considered to fall into a new category of its own, rendering the naturalia of the accepted contract types inapplicable (the sui generis theory). Our case law shows a preference for the absorption theory (for example, a partiarian agricultural lease is now generally accepted to be a lease, although in some respects it resembles a partnership);[17] though it has also adopted the sui generis theory at times (for example, in respect of a contract to supply board and lodgings).[18] In the case of labour tenancy, while the practice of the courts has not always been consistent, the tendency undoubtedly seems to be to follow the sui generis theory.

In Natal, the practice of the legislature and of the courts was to refer to the labour tenancy contract quite loosely as one of lease, and to exclude the operation of the Master and Servant Laws.[19] In the Transvaal, on the other hand, the courts regarded the contract as neither lease nor employment, but sui generis. For example, in *Mvubu v Herbst* 1924 TPD 741 at 749 and 752 Krause J stated:

> It is true that the relationship of master and servant is incidentally established, in the performance of the contract, but I do not think that breaches of the agreement, from whatever cause, are governed by the principles which are peculiar to that relationship .... [T]he contract between the parties is sui generis.[20]

And in the Cape case of *Crous v Crous* 1937 CPD 250 at 256 Davies J was adamant that the contract was not one of lease: '[H]e paid for the ground in services; that is not the contract of letting and hiring.'

The nature of the contract was not finally determined by the Appellate Division in the leading case of *De Jager v Sisana* 1930 AD 71. Since counsel for Sisana, the tenant, conceded in argument that the agreement was not a lease, 'though in some respects, analogous to a lease' (at 74), the majority judgment of Curlewis JA proceeds on that basis, and refers to the contract as one of service (at 76). The judgment of Wessels JA, which was not concurred in by the rest of the Bench, on the grounds that there was no need to decide the issues thereby raised, states quite emphatically (at 83) that the contract is not one of lease and that Sisana was not a tenant:

> There is no doubt some similarity between the case of a lease of land and the occupation of a squatter like the defendant. In both cases land is occupied – in the case of a lease in return for rent, in the case of a squatter in return for farm labour; but here the similarity ceases....

Wessels JA was equally emphatic that the relationship of the parties was not that of master and servant (at 86). In his view, the agreement amounted to an 'innominate contract' (at 84).

Cooper[21] is of the opinion that the classification of the contract should turn on the real intention of the parties which is to be inferred from the purpose of the agreement.

> So where a farmer lets land to B to farm in return for B rendering services the contract would be a locatio conductio rei, but if a farmer 'engages the services of' B as a labourer and B agrees to render services in the general farming operations carried on by the farmer and in consideration of his services B is entitled to land to be worked by him for his own benefit, with the right to cultivate the lands and to reap the crops sown by him, the contract will be locatio conductio operarum, because in the first example, the purpose of the contract was the letting and hiring of land and in the second one, the letting and hiring of services.

In his view, the contract in *De Jager's* case was clearly a locatio conductio operarum.[22]

The only firm conclusion that can be drawn from the aforegoing is that the contract of labour tenancy is not a lease. Whether it is an unusual species of locatio conductio operarum or an innominate contract sui generis is perhaps debatable. The courts incline to the latter view, and such an approach seems both justified and perhaps advantageous to the labour tenant: given the lack of specific recognition of the contract at common law and its close resemblance to both lease and employment, the courts may be obliged to treat the labour tenant for some purposes as a lessee and for others as an employee. In this way he might, for example, benefit from the recent developments in labour law while also enjoying at least some of the benefits accorded to lessees.

Creation of the contract: formalities

The contract of labour tenancy is created in the ordinary way by simple agreement between the parties. It seems that at no stage in its history have formalities been required.[23] However, if the agreement were to be classed as a lease, and if it were to endure for ten years or longer, it would fall subject to the provisions of the Formalities in Respect of Leases of Land Act 18 of 1969.

Reciprocal obligations of the parties

The essentialia or distinguishing characteristics of the contract are (i) an undertaking by the labour tenant to supply labour to the farmer for part of the year, (ii) in return for the right to use some of the land for his or her own purposes. In almost all cases these essentialia will be supplemented by ancillary terms, express or implied, spelling out the precise details of the relationship between the parties. Some of these terms are so well-established by custom or usage as to amount almost to naturalia, terms implied by law in the absence of contrary agreement.

The obligations of labour tenant are as follows:

(i) They must provide personal services or those of an able-bodied family member (or members) to the farmer for the specified period each year. If the period is not specified and the agreement is to the effect that the services will be rendered at odd intervals as and when required, tenants should not absent themselves from the farm for long periods without the consent of the farmer. The nature of the services to be rendered may be specified in the contract, in which case of course tenants cannot be called upon to perform other services, or they may be of a general character.

(ii) The tenants must use the land allocated to them only for their own private purposes as agreed upon in the contract. These purposes will almost always include the right to establish a residence, graze cattle or other stock and to cultivate the soil. Any limit on the number of animals permitted must obviously be observed.

The farmer must make the land agreed upon available to the labour tenants and allow them

(i) to reside on such land, together with their families and dependants;

(ii) to erect a dwelling or dwellings, including such structures as may be necessary to house animals and/or to store crops and agricultural implements;

(iii) to graze cattle or other stock on the land allocated them; and

(iv) to cultivate the land, that is, to plough it, to sow seed and later to reap the crops. The farmer should not interfere with such farming operations, whether by calling on the tenants to provide services at such times, or otherwise.[24]

Duration

The duration of the labour tenancy contract is determined by reference to the intention of the parties at the time of contracting. Earlier statutory provisions to the effect that no labour tenancy contract should run for more than three years (subject to renewal) and that in the absence of an agreed period the contract should be deemed to have been entered into for a period of one year, have since been repealed.[25] It follows that there is no longer any limit on the duration of the contract. In fact, most such contracts are of indefinite duration, many having passed from generation to generation. The courts have tended to treat such agreements as periodic leases or 'yearly tenancies', running from one year to the next without a definite terminal point.[26] In our law, a contract of unspecified duration is quite acceptable and not void for uncertainty.[27]

Renewal

In the case of a lease the following distinction is made: (a) Where the contract is for a specified period, it may be renewed either expressly or impliedly. An implied renewal is known as a tacit relocation and is concluded by the lessor permitting the lessee to remain in occupation after the termination of the lease and accepting rent for the continued use of the property.[28] The duration of a tacit relocation, in the absence of a contrary intention being expressed, is taken to be the period for which rent is payable. (b) In the case of a periodic lease, on the other hand, where the contract is of indefinite duration, the lease runs from period to period – month to month, year to year, and so on – and there is no question of renewal: the contract continues until it is terminated by proper notice given by either party.[29]

Similar principles apply to a contract of employment[30] and would thus undoubtedly apply also to a labour tenancy contract. Indeed, they were applied to such a contract in *Tshabalala v Van der Merwe* 1926 NPD 75 where Dove Wilson JP made it clear that most labour tenancies are of indefinite duration. Having stated that it was difficult to ascertain from the pleadings and evidence whether the agreement in question was originally of definite or indefinite duration, he continued:

> If we take it that this was originally an agreement for one year from 30 June to 30 June, followed by a series of tacit relocations on the same basis ... the question of the length of notice in such circumstances, does not arise. The use of notice in such circumstances, assuming that it is necessary, is not to terminate the contract, but to prevent, or guard against the danger of, tacit relocation, so that the tenant may not, by remaining on, set up a tacit renewal of the contract....
>
> But if, on the other hand, as the particulars of claim and the evidence, coupled with the usage, which it is common knowledge obtains almost universally in matters of this kind, would seem to suggest, the contract between the parties is to be regarded as one from year to year, the duration being left undefined, the essential feature of such a contract is that it endures until terminated by due notice (at 77-8).

Termination

The labour tenancy contract is of course subject to all the normal principles governing the termination of contracts and will thus be discharged, for example, by mutual agreement of the parties (which may be of immediate effect), by effluxion of time (in the unusual case of a tenancy for a specified period) and by cancellation on the grounds of a material breach of contract (for example, if the tenant refuses to render his services or if the farmer deprives the tenant of the use of the land). Two cases merit special attention: termination by the death of either party, and termination by giving reasonable notice.

(i) Death

The general principle of the law of contract is that a person's contractual obligations are transmissible to and bind his estate on death 'unless their nature involves a delectus personae or terms of the contract show that it was not intended that they should be transmitted'.[31] The death of either party to a lease agreement does not normally result in the automatic discharge of the contract.[32] In the case of a service contract, death of the employee terminates the contract but not the death of the employer;[33] and the same applies to a partiarian agricultural lease.[34]

The question, therefore, is whether the identity of either party to the labour tenancy agreement is so important to the other that death will terminate the contract. Discussing *De Jager v Sisana* (above), Van den Heever expresses the view that the tenant does have such a delectus personae:

> The squatter promising his services to the former owner has, it must be assumed, in mind the nature and intensity of his employer's industry. It is of the utmost importance to him whether his employer is an easygoing master, engaged, say, in cattle ranching, or a hard taskmaster engaged in intensive cultivation of crops or even in some manufacturing industry ....[35]

This is debatable. Where a labour tenant has lived all his life on a particular farm, for example, the expectation surely is that the tenancy is to endure irrespective of changes in the ownership of the farm. Where the tenancy is not of long duration, on the other hand, it probably does depend inter alia on the nature of the services required of the tenant whether or not the identity of the tenant or of the employer is of importance to the other party. Much will therefore depend on the circumstances of each case.

A strong argument can be made for the view that the death of neither party should automatically terminate the contract. The nature of the agreement is such that it often endures from generation to generation. It would in any event be terminable on reasonable notice. The services owed are often, if not usually, of an impersonal nature, the duty being to provide one or more able-bodied persons to supply the labour, rather than the services of the tenant himself. Moreover it is usually not just the tenant who is living on the land under the agreement, but his family and other dependants too. As such, the death of the tenant should not deprive his family of the right to remain on the land, provided they can still supply the requisite labour; a fortiori, the death of the farmer should also not terminate the contract.

(ii) Reasonable notice.

The general rule is that 'where an agreement is silent as to its duration, it is terminable on reasonable notice in the absence of a conclusion that it was intended to continue indefinitely'.[36] If the parties expressly or impliedly agree to be bound in perpetuity, that is, that there should be no unilateral right to cancel after giving due notice, the court will respect their agreement.[37] However,

> when parties bind themselves to an agreement which requires them to work closely together and to have mutual trust and confidence in each other... it is reasonable to infer that they did not intend to bind themselves indefinitely, but rather contemplated termination by either party on reasonable notice.[38]

It might perhaps be argued that in at least some labour tenancy contracts, the parties intend to bind themselves indefinitely, and that the agreement cannot be unilaterally terminated even on reasonable notice. Such an argument is unlikely to be successful, however, for as noted earlier, the courts have quite consistently construed labour tenancy contracts as yearly tenancies terminable on reasonable notice.[39] The vital question, therefore, is what constitutes reasonable notice in such a contract.

As might have been expected, the courts have stressed that what constitutes a reasonable notice depends on all the circumstances of the case, including the nature of the agreement, the use to which the land is put, custom, the length of previous occupation by the tenant, and the difficulty of finding suitable alternative premises.[40]

In Roman-Dutch law, apparently, a year's notice was required to terminate a yearly lease of rural property,[41] and this rule was applied to labour tenancy in *Puputa v Potterill* (1900) 21 NLR 201. In other cases, however, periods of three months (*Wood v Maqaqa* (1909) 30 NLR 29) and six months (*Tshabalala v Van der Merwe* 1926 NPD 75) have been accepted as reasonable; and the courts have generally expressed considerable doubt about the Roman-Dutch rule.[42] The matter cannot be regarded as settled, even though Cooper states unequivocally that 'there is no fixed ratio between the period of the lease and the notice period'.[43] In *Wood v Maqaqa* at 152 Tatham J thought 30 days' notice to a yearly tenant who had been in occupation for years was 'altogether inadequate', and went on to state the following:

> Whether three months' notice, indeed, would be adequate in all cases, I would not be prepared to say; certainly I regard three months as almost the shortest notice which ought to be given. One's knowledge of conditions of this country convince one that it is difficult for a native to find at a moment's notice new land upon which to settle. To remove his kraal takes some time when he has found the land. The right of occupation of the soil has from the earliest times been a source of social and political trouble, and it is incumbent upon the Court to see that the rights of tenants, as regards notice, especially in a country like this, are properly safeguarded when they are being turned off the land.

In two recent Transvaal cases notice periods of one month and two months were regarded as unreasonable.[44]

In accordance with the law of lease, it has been held that the notice of termination must be given so that it expires at the end of a period of the labour tenancy (usually 30 June) so that the tenant can reap his crops (*Wood v Maqaqa* at 32; *Tshabalala v Van der Merwe* at 83). In *Stidworthy v Peacock* 1908 EDL 130, however, where one months' notice to quit was accepted as reasonable, Juta AJ held that the plaintiff (who seems to have been a labour tenant) had no right to remain in possession until the crops planted by him had ripened and been gathered. Apart from the case of a colonus partiarius, said the judge, 'I know of no other arrangement by which a man is entitled to claim notice according to the seasons' (at 131). Although this decision was referred to with approval by Davis J in *Crous v Crous* 1937 CPD 250 at 252-3, it is harsh and inequitable and ought to be rejected in favour of the many other cases which adopt a more humane approach.

In our view there is much to be said for the view, in line with the Roman-Dutch rule and the decision in *Puputa's* case, that a reasonable period of notice in most contracts of labour tenancy is one full year, to expire after the tenant has harvested his crops. This is especially the case where the labour tenant is elderly and has nowhere else to go. Indeed, in many such cases even a year's notice seems altogether unreasonable. Take the case of Mr Johannes Mtjali who had lived and worked all his life on a farm in the Wakkerstroom district. At the age of 73 he was too old to perform useful work himself and his children had migrated to the cities, leaving him without any means of supplying labour to the farmer. In October 1988 he was given one month's notice to quit and in due course was prosecuted under the Trespass Act. Fortunately he was acquitted on the ground that a month's notice was unreasonable in the circumstances, but the question arises whether even a year's notice would have been reasonable. We think not. Aged farmworkers are extremely vulnerable and face indescribable hardship if evicted. The Riekert Commission recommended that once farmworkers passed working age they should be allowed to continue to live on their employer's land after retirement.[45] In line with this recommendation, it would not be too difficult in circumstances such as those in which Mr Mtjali found himself, to find a tacit agreement between the parties that the labour tenant should be allowed to retire and live out the remainder of his days on the farm. Even in the absence of true consent to such an arrangement by the farmer, a term or contract to that effect may be established on the basis of estoppel or quasi-mutual assent (that is, on the reasonable reliance by the tenant on the impression created by the farmer).

Another factor which may be highly relevant in determining the reasonableness of the notice period is the ease or difficulty with which alternative premises may be found. Labour tenants are seldom able to find suitable premises elsewhere. Clear evidence of a failure to find alternative accommodation despite a diligent search would point towards the notice period being unreasonable, and was taken into account by the court in the cases of *Maqaqa* and *Stee Nene*. It would always be sensible, therefore, to lead supplementary evidence on this point. Suitable alternative premises would, it is submitted, be such as are capable of properly accommodating the labour tenant, his dependants and his possessions, and should include land for cultivation and the grazing of his stock.

The notice of termination must of course be communicated to the tenant, must be clear and unequivocal,[46] and cannot be withdrawn without the consent of the tenant.[47] A notice which stipulates an unreasonable period or is equivocal, is of no legal effect at all.[48]

Improvements

Section 5(7) of Act 24 of 1932 (later section 38 *bis* (6) of Act 18 of 1936) provided as follows:

> If on the termination of a labour tenant contract from whatever cause the labour tenant has any crop standing on the land which he was entitled to cultivate by virtue of such contract, he shall be entitled to tend such crop till it matures and thereafter to reap and remove it.

Section 5(8) of the Act further provided that labour tenants might demolish or destroy any structure erected by them on the land and remove any material therefrom, except where the 'employer' had supplied such material free of charge.

Now that these provisions have been repealed, the labour tenant's right to remove improvements to the land (including crops) or to claim compensation for such improvements will be governed entirely by the common law. Here again, it is of vital importance to know whether or not the labour tenant may properly be classed as a lessee, for at common law the rights of a lessee in respect of improvements are very much less than those of other lawful occupiers.

Prior to 1658 in Holland, lessees of rural tenements enjoyed the same rights to compensation for improvements as a bona fide possessor (i.e. one who possesses the property in the mistaken belief that he is the owner of it). These rights include the right to remain in occupation until compensated for necessary and useful expenditure incurred on the property, and the right to remove any improvement, in appropriate cases, provided this can be done without injury to the property.[49] The abuse of these rights by lessees led to severe restrictions being placed thereon by placaeten of 1658 and 1698. These placaeten have been received into South African law and have been applied to both urban and rural tenements.[50]

Briefly, the position of a lessee is now as follows:[51] He or she is entitled to compensation only for improvements in the form of annexures, provided they were made with the consent of the lessor. The compensation is limited to the value of the materials attached, and the right thereto accrues only once the lease has terminated and the lessee has vacated the property; in other words, lessees have no lien or right of retention. The lessee may remove materials attached to the lessor's property, but only during the currency of the lease; on termination, therefore, he or she forfeits all claims in respect of unauthorized attachments. The lessee has a claim for compensation in respect of ploughing, tilling and sowing, and the cost of seed, and during the currency of the lease he or she may remove his crop; but once the lease has terminated he or she may not go onto the land to harvest and remove his crop. In *Hansen & Latelle v Crafford* (1909) 26 SC 426 it was however held that if a tenant or occupier of land has sown or planted crops before receiving notice of termination, or after receiving such notice if he or she has reasonable ground for believing that they will mature before the end of the contract, he or she is entitled to claim such crops as his or her own and to go upon the land for the purpose of reaping them when ripe. This decision was followed in *Japhtha v Mills' Executors* 1910 EDL 150 at 156-7[52] but rejected in a number of other cases.[53]

The position in modern law of other lawful occupiers is very much stronger.[54] Although special rules apply to certain categories such as fiduciaries, usufructuaries and precarists, the general position is that the courts have extended to lawful occupiers the remedies available to the bona fide possessor, with this qualification: an equitable deduction may be made in respect of the occupier's use and enjoyment of the land.[55] Although none of those cases concerned labour tenancy, it is submitted that the labour tenant is a lawful occupier who is not a lessee and therefore that he or she too will enjoy the remedies of a bona fide possessor as regards improvements. Nor, it is submitted, would the qualification mentioned above apply in his case, for he or she has already paid with labour for the use of the land.

This conclusion is reinforced by dicta to the effect that the harsh and sometimes inequitable provisions of the placaeten should be given a narrow field of application.[56] In *Rubin v Botha* 1911 AD 114 at 118, for example, De Villiers CJ stated that:

> Where ... the relation of lessor and lessee does not exist between the owner and occupier by reason of the agreement of lease proving null and void, there is no valid reason why the basis of compensation applicable to lessees should be applied to improvements by the occupier.

A fortiori, the placaeten should not be held to apply to the labour tenancy relationship.

Successors in title

Can the labour tenant insist on remaining in occupation when the land is transferred to a new owner? The position on the death of the previous owner has been considered above; here we consider the rights of the tenant as against a particular successor such as a purchaser of the property.

As a general rule, of course, a contract is personal to the parties to it and thus cannot impose obligations on third persons. In the case of a lease, however, a lessee in possession of the property or with a registered title has a real right which protects his occupation against all third persons, including a purchaser who acquired the property in ignorance of the lease. This is as a result of the 'huur gaat voor koop' rule.[57] The new owner takes the place of his predecessor as lessor under the lease. Even where the lease is not registered, and the lessee is not in possession, so that the 'huur gaat voor koop' rule cannot operate, the lessee enjoys some protection under the general doctrine of notice: any particular successor who acquired the property with notice of the lease is bound to respect the rights of the lessee.

The question arises whether either of these doctrines can apply in the case of a labour tenant. In the early case of *Natal Creamery Ltd v Mahakana* (1912) 33 NLR 587 at 590 Broome J stated obiter that the 'contract of the former owner would devolve on his successors in title', but the matter was fully discussed for the first time in *De Jager v Sisana* 1930 AD 71. In the court a quo the judge declined to decide whether or not the 'huur gaat voor koop' rule applied, but he held that the doctrine of notice was applicable:

> Where a purchaser of land acquires it with the knowledge that another person is legally in occupation of any part of it he can get rid of that person only by putting an end to the contract upon reasonable notice, in the absence of any ground for terminating it without notice (at 80).

On appeal it was held by Wessels JA in his minority judgment that the contract was not a lease and therefore the 'huur gaat voor koop' rule was not applicable. Moreover, as the labour tenancy contract was personal to the parties and conferred no real right in the land itself on the labour tenant, the purchaser of the property was entitled to evict the tenant, even though he had bought the land with knowledge of the labour tenancy contract; in other words, the doctrine of notice was also not applicable. The only remedy of the tenant in such circumstances, said the judge, was to claim damages from the previous owner (the seller) for breach of contract.

Delivering the majority judgment, Curlewis JA preferred not to decide these issues, but thought that there might be some force in the contention that the doctrine of notice could be extended to such a case (at 74). Assuming that that principle applied to labour tenants, however, it could not assist Sisana in the present case for he was unwilling to render service to the new owner:

> But just as a lessee is bound to pay his rent to a new owner who in his turn is bound to recognize the lease, so by analogy a squatter who claims on the ground of equity that the new owner must recognize his right of occupation is bound in equity to render to the new owner the consideration in labour which was still due under his agreement with the previous owner for the right of occupation (at 76-7).

In *Crous v Crous* 1937 CPD 250 the court preferred the view of Wessels JA that neither the 'huur gaat voor koop' rule nor the doctrine of notice could apply in the case of a labour tenancy, holding that the new owner was entitled to evict the labour tenant even before he or she had reaped the crops. This approach is unacceptably harsh. Even if it be conceded that, there being no proper contract of lease, the labour tenant is not entitled to the protection of the 'huur gaat voor koop' rule, he or she ought at least to be protected against successors in title who acquired the land with knowledge of his or her tenancy. The simple justice of affording the tenant this minimal protection was expressly recognized by the majority in *De Jager's* case. The willingness of the majority to extend the doctrine of notice in this way (the doctrine usually protects only those with iura in personam ad rem acquirendam) has been hailed by Van der Merwe & Olivier[58] and should be fully exploited in future cases.

It remains to note that the equity of protecting the labour tenant against even successors without notice was recognized by the legislature in section 5(6) of Act 24 of 1932 (later section 38 *bis* (5) of Act 18 of 1936, now repealed):

> If the control of any land which a native is entitled to occupy or use by virtue of a labour tenant contract passes from the employer to some other person, the latter shall assume all rights and liabilities as employer under such contract, which shall continue as if no change of the parties thereto has taken place.

The section went on to provide that either party could within three months terminate the contract by giving three months' notice to that effect.

Conclusion

> It is a sad reflection on human nature that laws should always have tended to entrench power and privilege against the serving and deserving classes who are usually unorganized and mute.

These words of Van den Heever[59] are particularly apposite in the case of labour tenants. Having made a very significant contribution to the development of South African agriculture, they were rewarded with harassment, intimidation and a battery of laws designed to force them from the land, all in the interests of the ruling elite. With their roots going so deep in the native soil, however, many have succeeded in clinging tenaciously to the land. Their desperate fight to resist eviction evokes sympathy and admiration. Lawyers should do all in their power to assist them to remain on the land. While labour tenancy may be regarded as exploitative and a relic of feudalism, it is the only system in modern South Africa which enables black people to farm with a measure of independence on land which the legislature prohibits them from owning.

Notes

1 See Claassens in this volume at 43.

2 *Sigonswana v Tar* (1884) 5 NLR 135; *Baleka v Kemp* (1885) 6 NLR 54; *Puputa v Potterill* (1900) 21 NLR 201; *Wood v Maqaqa* (1909) 30 NLR 29; *Natal Creamery Ltd v Mahakana* (1912) 33 NLR 587; *Makala Zikalala v Groenewald* (1922) 43 NLR 150; *Tshabalala v Van der Merwe* 1926 NPD 75.

3 Article 8. See also Law 11 of 1887 and, on these laws, *Maynard v Chasana* 1921 TPD 243 and *Mvubu v Herbst* 1924 TPD 741.

4 C Bundy *The Rise and Fall of the South African Peasantry* 2nd edn (Cape Town: David Philip 1980) 190, 231.

5 On this Act, see *R v Magudulela* 1939 TPD 239; *R v Mokwena* 1947 (2) SA 686 (T); *Matjila v Moore* 1948 (3) SA 1001 (T); *Malemone v Dreyer* 1949 (2) SA 824 (T).

6 Section 38 *bis* of Act 18 of 1936, inserted by s 31 of Act 42 of 1964 which repealed the Native Service Contract Act of 1932.

7 M Morris 'State Intervention and the Agricultural Labour Supply Post-1948' in F Wilson, A Kooy & D Hendrie (eds) *Farm Labour in South Africa* (Cape Town: David Philip 1977) 68.

8 Ibid.

9 Ibid 70, quoting from a Report of the Department of Bantu Administration and Development UG 51-1960.

10 Ibid 70.

11 Ibid 71.

12 The Surplus People Project Report *Forced Removals in South Africa* vol 1 (Cape Town 1983) xxiv.

13 See *S v Hadebe* (TPD Case No A1765/88, unreported); *S v Stee Nene* (TPD Case No A176/89, unreported).

14 W E Cooper *The South African Law of Landlord and Tenant* (Cape Town: Juta 1973) 39.

15 *Wille & Millin's Mercantile Law of South Africa* 18th edn by J F Coaker & D T Zeffertt (Johannesburg: Hortors 1984) 349.

16 F P van den Heever *The Partiarian Agricultural Lease in South African Law* (Cape Town: Juta 1943) 42.

17 See *Du Preez v Steenkamp* 1926 TPD 362; Van den Heever op cit; Cooper at 325-8.

18 See *Rent Control Board v Beach Villas (Pty) Ltd* 1944 AD 16.

19 See the cases in note 1 above.

20 See the comments of Krause J in *Mvubu v Herbst* (note 3 above) at 749. See too *Maynard v Chasana* (note 3 above) at 246-7. In *R v Hees* 1938 TPD 333 at 338, however, Murray J described the agreement as a 'bona fide contract of service'.

21 Above note 14 at 43.

22 At 45 note 66.

23 See for example *Maynard v Chasana* at 247; cf s 5(2) of Act 24 of 1932 and s38 *bis* (2) of Act 18 of 1936 (both sections having since been repealed).

24 See, generally, *Mvubu v Herbst* (note 3 above).

25 Sections 5(1) and 5(3) of Act 24 of 1932, replaced by s 38 *bis* of Act 42 of 1964, discussed earlier.

26 See for example *Puputa v Potterill, Wood v Maqaqa, Natal Creamery Ltd v Mahakana, Makala Zikalala v Groenewald* and *Tshabalala v Van der Merwe* (all note 1 above); compare *S v Hadebe* (note 13).

27 *Trident Sales (Pty) Ltd v A H Pillman & Son (Pty) Ltd* 1984 (1) SA 433 (W) at 436.

28 Cooper above note 14 at 319-20.

29 Ibid 60.

30 Compare *Tiopaizi v Bulawayo Municipality* 1923 AD 317 at 322.

31 Per Boshoff JP in *SA General Electric Co (Pty) Ltd v Sharfmann* 1981 (1) SA 592 (W) at 596.

32 Cooper above note 14 at 297-8.

33 *Boyd v Stuttaford & Co* 1919 AD 101 at 114-15.

34 Van den Heever, above note 16 at 44-5; Cooper, above note 14 at 330.

35 Ibid 42-3.

36 Per Smalberger AJA in *Putco Ltd v TV & Radio Guarantee Co Ltd* 1985 (4) SA 809 (A) at 827.

37 *Trident Sales* case above note 27.

38 *Putco* case, ibid.

39 See the cases cited in note 26; also *S v Stee Nene* (note 13).

40 See especially *Wood v Maqaqa* (1909) 30 NLR 29 at 32 and *Makala Zikalala v Groenewald* (1922) 43 NLR 150 at 152-3.

41 See the authorities cited in *Hunt v Eastern Province Boating Co* (1883) 3 EDC 12 at 25 and in *Theron NO v Joynt* 1950 (3) SA 758 (O) at 762.

42 Compare *Tiopaizi v Bulawayo Municipality* 1923 AD 317 at 327; *Ntsobi v Berlin Mission Society* 1924 TPD 378 at 380; *Theron NO v Joynt* (above) at 762-3.

43 Above note 14 at 61.

44 See note 13 above.

45 *Report of the Commission of Inquiry into legislation Affecting the Utilization of Manpower (excluding the legislation administered by the Departments of Labour and Mines)* (Riekert Commission) RP32/1979 at 186 para 4300.

46 Compare *Matjila v Moore* 1948 (3) SA 1001 (T).

47 Cooper above note 14, at 62.

48 *Tiopaizi v Bulawayo Municipality* 1923 AD 317; *S v Hadebe* (note 13 above).

49 See generally C G van der Merwe *The Law of Things* (Durban: Butterworths 1987) para 93; J G Lotz 'Enrichment' in *LAWSA* vol 9 (Durban: Butterworths 1979) paras 84-8.

50 See *Syfrets Participation Board Managers Ltd v Estate and Co-op Wine Distributors* 1989 (1) SA 106 (W) and cases there cited.

51 See generally Cooper, above note 14 at 299-305.

52 See too *Burrows v McEvoy* 1921 CPD 229 at 236.

53 See Cooper above note 14 at 303 note 22, whose own view is that the *Crafford* decision is wrong; compare A J Kerr *The Law of Sale and Lease* (Durban: Butterworths 1984) 305-9.

54 See Van der Merwe above note 49 paras 97-101, Lotz above note 49 at 92.

55 See the cases cited by Van der Merwe above note 49 para 97 note 1.

56 Compare W de Vos *Verrykingsaanspreeklikheid in die Suid-Afrikaanse Reg* 3rd edn (Cape Town: Juta 1987) 254.

57 On which see Cooper, above note 14, chapter 19.

58 N J van der Merwe & P J J Olivier *Die Onregmatige Daad in die Suid-Afrikaanse Reg* 5th edn (Pretoria: J P van der Walt & Seun 1985) 270.

59 Above note 16 at 4.

CLIVE PLASKET

Homeland Incorporation: The New Forced Removals

The shift in state policy from the forced removal of communities to the forced incorporation of land into homelands[1] was probably considered by the state to be a reform. For the communities who were reprieved from removal and instead placed under sentence of incorporation, however, the spirit of reform was academic: instead of being moved to the dumping ground, the dumping ground was being brought to them. As a result the nature and intensity of struggles to avoid removals in the first half of the 1980s was reproduced in the second half of the decade in relation to incorporation, but with at least one difference: acts of incorporation resulted in more intense violence than removals ever did.[2]

For lawyers acting for communities threatened with incorporation, the shift in policy has had similar consequences. It has involved coming to terms with legislation different to that used to effect forced removals, but against a background of the same obstacles, similar state strategies and executive powers as awesome and unconfined. The legal response to incorporation, usually based on judicial review, often results in the facts of the struggle being lost or obscured. In judicial review cases, the correctness or fairness of the decision to incorporate is irrelevant, the legal issue being confined to the regularity of that decision.[3]

The legislation

Parliament has provided for two types of incorporation. The first, in terms of the National States Constitution Act 21 of 1971, provides for territorial consolidation of non-independent homelands. The nature of the empowering provision in this statute has allowed for successful challenges.[4]

The second form of incorporation is authorized by the Borders of Particular States Extension Act 2 of 1980. This Act is disarmingly simple and bland. The lack of embellishment, especially in the empowering provision, makes an exercise of power in terms of this statute very difficult to challenge.

The National States Constitution Act

The principal purpose of the National States Constitution Act 21 of 1971 is to 'provide for the establishment of legislative assemblies and executive councils in black areas' and for 'the declaration as self-governing territories of areas for which legislative assemblies have been established'.[5] Once a legislative assembly has been formed by presidential proclamation, the power to determine a homeland's borders vests in the State President of South Africa.

Under section 1(1) the State President may 'modify' the area of a homeland's jurisdiction and under section 1(2) the area may 'consist of various black areas' and be 'amended from time to time by the State President by proclamation in the *Gazette*'. The exercise of these powers is reliant on consultation by the Minister with the territorial authority, in the first instance, and with the executive council of the area in the second.

The Act contains procedural and substantive limitations on the State President's exercise of power to which the courts have been willing to hold him. Three jurisdictional facts (or preconditions for a valid exercise of power) can be discerned. These are that a valid proclamation in terms of section 1(1) of the Act must have been promulgated creating a legislative assembly for the homeland; consultation on the incorporation must have taken place between the Minister and the 'cabinet' of the homeland; and the State President must have acted, when promulgating the proclamation, on the recommendation of the Minister.[6]

The most important (and decisive) limitations on the State President's power to incorporate are linked to the purpose and policy of the legislation. This necessarily involves an enquiry into 'the nature of the area to be incorporated in order to determine its character vis-a-vis the inhabitants therein and their similarity to or dissimilarity from the inhabitants of the black area for which the relevant Legislative Assembly has been created'.[7]

The leading case on this limitation is *Mathebe v Regering van die Republiek van Suid Afrika*[8] in which it was held that the purported incorporation of Moutse into kwaNdebele was invalid. The basis on which the matter was argued was that Moutse was inhabited by North Sotho speakers and the attempt to make them part of a South Ndebele homeland was not authorized by the empowering legislation.

A unanimous Appellate Division upheld this argument. The crux of the judgment was that the Act and related legislation create a hierarchical system of administration for Africans, which has as its dominant theme 'national association' i.e. separation on the basis of ethnicity.[9] The attempt to incorporate Moutse was not for this purpose but rather for 'administrative convenience'.[10] As a result, the State President had acted beyond his powers because he had attempted to use section 1(2) for an unauthorized purpose:

> Thus, in my opinion, the State President used his powers in terms of section 1(2) of the National States Constitution Act for a purpose for which they were not granted, that is, to join the district of Moutse, in spite of the ethnicity of most of its inhabitants, to kwaNdebele. It thus follows that, in my opinion, the attempted action of the State President was invalid, and that Proc R277 of 31 December 1985 is null and void.[11]

The use of the apartheid argument against its own proponents has been criticized. It has been pointed out that in some instances the *Mathebe* judgment has been used by conservative people as 'authority' for the proposition that Moutse should be re-incorporated into Lebowa.[12] In defence, however, it must be pointed out that legal intervention to challenge the validity of an incorporation is more or less the last desperate bid on the part of a community which has exhausted all other remedies or has been taken by surprise. In the face of hostile legislation, lawyers are required to find any ground of review which will enable the matter to come before court.

Without wishing to understate the problem, it should be borne in mind that the *Mathebe* case succeeded. The residents of Moutse now have the opportunity to resolve this issue. Had the case been lost, the savage repression which characterized kwaNdebele's administration of the area would, no doubt, have continued.[13]

In many respects, the case of *Lefuo v Staatspresident van die Republiek van Suid Afrika*[14] is more important than *Mathebe*. This matter succeeded in setting aside the proclamation which purported to incorporate Botshabelo into QwaQwa. The court based its judgment on the ground that there was no similarity in political development between QwaQwa and Botshabelo. This is clearly a more extensive principle than the principle of ethnicity relied upon in the Moutse judgment. In the *Lefuo* case the ethnicity argument was not decisive because most inhabitants of Botshabelo are South Sotho, and therefore ethnically similar to the residents of QwaQwa.

Malherbe J considered the historical links (or lack of them) between the areas and noted that while QwaQwa had developed through the prescribed constitutional stages to self government, Botshabelo had not: it was 'an artificial town ... which came into existence less than a decade ago as a catchment area particularly for urbanized surplus Blacks.'[15] The lifestyle and culture of the two communities were quite different.

Malherbe J also found that it was relevant that QwaQwa had no historical claim to Botshabelo, that no notification of the incorporation had been given to Botshabelo residents and, although the ethnicity argument was not decisive, that some 120 000 non-South Sothos would be included in Qwa-Qwa if the incorporation was valid.[16] His conclusion, in granting the application was:

> that the attempted amendment of the area of QwaQwa by the publication of Proclamation R169 of 1987 is not compatible with the intention of the Legislature as it is expressed in the enabling provision as it could not have been done to promote the political development of the inhabitants of Botshabelo in terms of their ethnicity. It therefore follows that the application must succeed.[17]

The Borders of Particular States Extension Act

The Borders of Particular States Extension Act 2 of 1980 creates the power to excise areas from South Africa and to incorporate them into a 'sovereign and independent state' provided that the area to be incorporated appears in the schedule to the Act.[18]

The State President does not have to incorporate every area which appears in the schedule: he is granted a discretion whether to do so or not. This discretion is particularly wide and does not contain the types of limitations which have been found to be relevant to an exercise of power in terms of section 1(2) of the National States Constitution Act. The empowering provision simply says that the State President 'may from time to time by proclamation in the *Gazette* determine' that an area will be incorporated.[19]

Once the proclamation excising and handing over an area has been promulgated, the state to which it has been given must accept it in some way. In the case of Bophuthatswana, the Bophuthatswana Border Extension Act 24 of 1980 provides that areas in the schedule to the Act automatically form part of Bophuthatswana, while non-scheduled areas require an act of acceptance, by proclamation in the *Gazette.*[20] Both forms of acceptance depend on a valid South African proclamation.[21]

Only one challenge to the incorporation of land into an 'independent' homeland has come before the courts. The case of *Sebogodi v State President of the Republic of South Africa*[22] challenged the incorporation of the village of Braklaagte, near Zeerust, into Bophuthatswana. The facts of the case and the events subsequent to the validity of the incorporation being upheld, illustrate in clear and stark terms the nature of the state's policy and its disregard for the consequences of its actions.

Braklaagte was purchased by the ancestors of its present inhabitants in 1907. It is now home to about 9 000 people.[23] The residents first heard that their land had been sentenced to incorporation in 1986. They took immediate steps to inform the Minister of Education and Development Aid that they did not want to be incorporated and requested a meeting with him to motivate their opposition. A delegation from the community was eventually given a hearing on 15 December 1988 at which a lengthy memorandum was handed to the Minister and oral representations were made. It was brought to his attention inter alia that the community feared repression and persecution at the hands of the Bophuthatswana authorities if incorporation proceeded.

On 27 December 1988 a letter from the Minister was served on the community's attorneys. It said that a final decision to incorporate Braklaagte had been taken in 1984 and an agreement to this effect had been entered into between the State President of South Africa and Bophuthatswana in 1985. It was impossible for the government to 'rescind or renegotiate' the decision and Braklaagte would be incorporated from 31 December 1988.[24]

An urgent application was launched to interdict publication of the proclamation, pending a determination of its validity. Unfortunately, the relevant *Government Gazette* had been printed and was being distributed. A rule nisi was issued, however, calling on the respondents to show cause why the proclamation should not be set aside.[25] As no interim relief was obtained, the proclamation had legal force and the state relied on this to commence the implementation of the incorporation, even though this breached the spirit, if not the letter, of the rule nisi.

As stated above, challenges to incorporation often hinge on a narrow legal point. *Sebogodi's* case was no exception. The question was whether the respondents had exercised their discretion properly. It was argued that they had not for a number of reasons. The applicant's main argument was that the decision to incorporate Braklaagte into Bophuthatswana was reached before the government had the lawful authority to take such steps. (The decision was taken in 1984 and confirmed with Bophuthatswana in 1985 whereas the Borders of Particular States Extension Act was amended to cover Braklaagte only in 1986.) The incorporation should have been reconsidered afresh after the amendment to the Borders of Particular States Extension Act. It was not and instead a policy established before 1986 was rigidly followed.

In a second argument, the applicants contended that even if the government was entitled to rely on the 1984 decision, the representations made to it by the community raised important new issues which should have provoked a reconsideration of that decision. Instead, evidence showed that the government considered itself bound to its earlier position. This was, the applicant argued, clear from the Minister's letter which had said that the decision could not be 'rescinded or renegotiated'.

Van der Merwe J rejected these arguments and dismissed the application. He held that as excision and incorporation is an 'involved process',[26] it was understandable and correct that the respondents took the view that their decision could not be 'lightly tampered with or ignored'.[27] He concluded that the respondents had not misdirected themselves by fettering their discretion and following a fixed and set policy.[28]

Conclusion

In spite of the success in challenging the incorporation of both Moutse and Botshabelo into homelands, this is an area in which legal intervention is seldom possible and frequently depends on contesting government omissions rather than asserting positive rights not to be incorporated.

Sebogodi's case is typical – it depended on one issue and failed. Other cases will raise other possibilities for legal action. For instance, the village of Leeuwfontein, which is adjacent to Braklaagte, was incorporated into Bophuthatswana in the same proclamation as Braklaagte but the residents were not given notice of the intended incorporation or a hearing prior to the publication of the proclamation. Incorporation, which amounts to a mass deportation, clearly affects the rights of those affected by it and it is possible to argue that the fact that no prior notice or hearing was given invalidates the proclamation in so far as it relates to Leeuwfontein.[29]

Another possible challenge to incorporation could be based on unreasonableness: the Braklaagte community warned that they would be persecuted after incorporation and their worst fears were realized a mere ten days after the judgment was given against them in *Sebogodi's* case. The Leeuwfontein community experienced exactly the same repression.[30] To throw another community to Bophuthatswana with the knowledge that they too may suffer from the same fate may amount to such gross unreasonableness that the inference may be drawn that the State President failed to apply his mind to the matter.[31]

Creative use of the courts and reliance on blunders on the part of the state are not a recipe for successful opposition to the policy of incorporation. The problem obviously lies in the existence of the policy and the statutory mechanisms for its execution. These will never be removed through judicial combat. While lawyers have sometimes played a decisive role, it is the struggles of rural people and the political pressure that those struggles generate which will defeat the policy.

Notes

1 See Claassens in this volume at 41ff.

2 The purported incorporation of Moutse into kwaNdebele provides a particularly vivid example of this violence. The area was invaded by vigilantes who abducted, assaulted and killed hundreds of Moutse residents. See Nicholas Haysom *Mabangalala: The Rise of Right Wing Vigilantes in South Africa* (Johannesburg: Centre for Applied Legal Studies 1986) 71-9. Then the residents of the area were subjected to severe repression at the hands of the police and 'kitskonstabels'. The police even tried to prevent residents from leaving Moutse to attend the hearing of the Appellate Division in which the incorporation was set aside. See CIIR *Now Everyone is Afraid* (London: CIIR 1988) 144-53. More recently, the residents of Braklaagte and Leeuwfontein were subjected to assaults and many were arrested after the areas were incorporated into Bophuthatswana. See *The Star* 28 March 1989; 30 March 1989; 4 April 1989; *Vrye Weekblad* 31 March 1989; *Weekly Mail* 31 March 1989; *New Nation* 5 April 1989 and *SA Barometer* vol 3 (13) 14 July 1989 at 203-6.

3 On the limited nature of judicial review and a comparison between review and appeal see L Baxter *Administrative Law* (Cape Town: Juta 1984) at 305-7 and 706-7.

4 The Alteration of Boundaries of Self-Governing Territories Bill 76-89(GA) which now appears to have been abandoned by the state was intended to provide a wider power to incorporate which would have superceded the powers presently contained in the National States Constitution Act.

5 This is the long title of the Act.

6 *Government of the Republic of South Africa v Government of KwaZulu* 1983 (1) SA 164 (A) at 199H. This case involved the reverse of the usual process of incorporation. The State President had purported to excise the district of Ingwavuma from kwaZulu with the intention of later ceding it to Swaziland.

7 *Lefuo v Staatspresident van die Republiek van Suid Afrika* 1989 (3) SA 924 (O) at 943H. This decision was upheld on appeal (2 March 1990).

8 1988 (3) SA 667 (A).

9 At 691B-F.

10 At 698B-699A, 699D-F.

11 At 700D (the editors' translation from the Afrikaans).

12 The area was excised from Lebowa by means of a proclamation made in terms of the National States Constitution Act. It was later 'confirmed' by section 16 of the Laws on Co-operation and Development Act 102 of 1983. See *Government of Lebowa v Government of the Republic of South Africa* 1988 (1) SA 344 (A). This case involved an interpretation of s 16 of the Act and the court held that the section successfully excised Moutse from Lebowa. It did not deal with the validity of the incorporation into kwaNdebele. The importance of the method of the excision is that if the state now wants to incorporate Moutse into

either kwaNdebele or Lebowa, it will have to do so through parliamentary legislation.

13 See note 2 above. See also Claassens in this volume at 43.

14 Above, note 7. Lefuo was successful on appeal (AD 2 March 1990).

15 At 941B (the editors' translation from the Afrikaans).

16 At 941G.

17 At 941-2, (the editors' translation from the Afrikaans).

18 Section 1(1).

19 Section 1(1).

20 Section 1 (scheduled areas); section 3 (non-scheduled areas).

21 Section 1(1) says: 'The land consisting of the territories described in the Schedule to this Act shall, on the date when any such land ceases to be part of the Republic of South Africa by virtue of the provisions of the Borders of Particular States Extension Act, 1980... become a part of the Republic of Bophuthatswana....'. Section 3(1) says: 'The President may from time to time by proclamation in the Gazette accept on behalf of the Government of the Republic of Bophuthatswana any other land which in terms of any law of the Republic of South Africa ceases to be part of the Republic of South Africa.'

22 TPD 14 April 1989 Case no 19332/88, unreported.

23 For a brief history of the village see the judgment from 3-6.

24 *Sebogodi* at 11-13.

25 *Sebogodi* at 1-2.

26 At 23.

27 At 24.

28 At 24-5.

29 The principle of natural justice expressed in the maxim audi alteram partem (hear the other side) applies where rights may be preducially affected. See Baxter *Administrative Law* note 3 above at 569-87.

30 See note 2 above.

31 Unreasonableness in the administrative law sense is notoriously difficult to establish. See *National Transport Commission v Chetty's Motor Transport* 1972 (3) SA 726 (A) at 735. The test for unreasonableness which our courts follow is that postulated by Stratford JA in *Union Government v Union Steel Corporation Ltd* 1928 AD 220 at 236-7: 'There is no authority that I know of, and none has been cited, for the proposition that a court of law will interfere with the exercise of a discretion on the mere ground of its unreasonableness. It is true the word is often used in the cases on the subject, but nowhere has it been held that unreasonableness is sufficient ground for interference; emphasis is always laid upon the necessity of the unreasonableness being so gross that something else can be inferred from it, either that it is "inexplicable except on the assumption of mala fides or ulterior motives" ... or that it amounts to proof that the person on whom the discretion is conferred, has not applied his mind to the matter.'

DAVID UNTERHALTER

Legitimate Expectation and the Law of Chiefs

The exercise of power flows from the conquest of land. This proposition may seem antediluvian in an age in which market transactions and complex forms of capital have come to dominate economic life. And our concerns tend to reflect this modernism. Yet the majority of South Africans have in the twentieth century been required to obey laws that are rooted in a history of land conquest, dispossession and consequent political domination.

Two sets of legislation, above all others, bear this historical stamp. First, the Natives Land Act[1] and the Native Trust and Land Act[2] in essence exclude Africans from acquiring land save for the acquisition of land in scheduled and released areas as defined in these enactments. These two acts take as their premise that land ought to be acquired and held on the basis of race and according to a principle of division that seeks to secure the holdings of land established by conquest.[3] Secondly, territorial division and exclusion had as their necessary concomitant the exercise of governmental authority over Africans in the scheduled and released areas. The Native Administration Act,[4] today the Black Administration Act, provides in section 1 that the State President is the Supreme Chief of all blacks in the Republic of South Africa. Section 25 provides for a system of governance by Proclamation in the areas included in the schedule to the Black Land Act 27 of 1913. Thus rule by administrative decree was entrenched, and with the clear intent that the exercise of absolute power was required to rule a subject people. Speaking in the House of Assembly, Deneys Reitz saw in the Supreme Chieftainship 'a reversion to the "great white chief" business' and he claimed that it revealed 'a typical slave state mentality'.[5]

The title Supreme Chief suggests a position of benevolent despotism. It certainly appears to have no respectable anthropological pedigree.[6] The position in fact has been used in the twentieth century in a despotic fashion with little evidence of benevolence. Great powers, however concentrated, must be effectively exercised. That requires functionaries, and it was to be expected that the tribal system and that figure of traditional authority, the chief, would be used for this purpose. Not surprisingly, section 2(7) of the Black Administration Act (the Act) lends substance to the appellation 'Supreme Chief' by giving extensive powers to the State President to decide upon the appointment, deposition and authority of the chief. Section 2(7) reads as follows:

> The State President may recognise or appoint any person as a chief of a Black tribe and may make regulations prescribing the duties, powers, privileges and conditions of service of chiefs so recognised and appointed .... The State President may depose any chief so recognised or appointed.

The Act intended that the chief should be a local functionary, carrying out those functions required to secure control of the areas within his jurisdiction and to provide for the routine administration of these areas, but only on the basis that a chief shall enforce within his area all laws and orders of the government relating to the administration of blacks. Those regulations require a chief to act as an all-purpose public servant, subject always to the powers of the government to whom he owes his office. The Act thus relegates the position of chief to one of subordinate official charged with securing in turn the control of his people.

The best planned legislative schemes are wont to produce unintended consequences. Chiefs appointed in terms of the Act (and the kindred enactments that have developed out of the government's bantustan policy) have not always proved to be docile functionaries. The powers of appointment and deposition given to the State President in sections 2(7) and 2(8) of the Act have led in essence to two species of conflict.

The first was predictable enough. The powers of appointment given to the State President do not require that these powers must be exercised according to tribal customary practice. Thus people with some expectation of elevation to a chieftainship in virtue of traditional practice have had their expectations thwarted by a wide discretion to make appointments according to other criteria. Those thwarted expectations are not just a matter of individual disappointment; appointments that offend against traditional practice are often construed by members of a tribe as unwarranted interference in the affairs of the tribe.

The second species of conflict has arisen because chiefs have sided with their people against measures taken by the government. These measures, often adopted in pursuance of the government's apartheid policy, have been considered detrimental to the interests of the tribe, and chiefs have identified with their people rather than the government, thereby placing their occupancy of the chieftainship in jeopardy. Thus in the 1950s chiefs were deposed and often banished for the support they gave to their people's resistance to cattle-culling and land-betterment schemes.[8]

These two species of conflict have tended to overlap. In *Kenana v Mangope* 1978 (2) SA 322 (T) the applicant, a deposed acting chieftain of the Amandebele-a-Motlane tribe, sought an order directing that the Chief Minister of the Bophuthatswana government be interdicted from preventing the applicant from exercising her office as acting chieftain. Among the issues that led up to these proceedings was the complaint that the question of the chieftainship was a domestic matter and that no outsider, including the government of Bophuthatswana, had any right to meddle in the internal affairs of the tribe. Furthermore, the applicant had addressed a letter to the Secretary of the Department of Bantu Administration and Development (as that position was then called) in which a resolution of the applicant's tribal authority was referred to. In terms of that resolution, the tribe sought to sever its connection with the government of Bophuthatswana.

The Act sought to make chiefs functionaries of the state. A chieftainship is a public office created by statute. That is a reversal of the position of the chief in traditional society, in which the role of the chief was to represent his or her people according to the dictates of customary practice, because the chief under the Act acts as an official answerable to the state rather than as a figure of authority answerable to his or her people. This reversal, effected by the Act, has plainly made the appointment, suspension and deposition of chiefs subject to the principles of administrative law. The wide powers conferred upon the State President under the Act to appoint, suspend and depose chiefs have quite often been used against chiefs who have incurred official displeasure or proved troublesome. That has in turn led to challenges in the courts by chiefs dissatisfied with the exercise of the State President's powers.

The latitude of the State President's powers under the Act has afforded little scope for review proceedings. However, one thread which runs through this area of the law is the invocation of the principles of natural justice. That is a claim that the State President must act fairly in the exercise of his powers under the Act to appoint, suspend and depose chiefs. The claim has met with mixed results in our courts. Here I shall examine those results and give some attention to the implications of the Appellate Division's recent approval of the concept of legitimate expectation in *Administrator of the Transvaal v Traub* (1989) 10 *ILJ* 823 (A).

The power to appoint, suspend and depose chiefs

The powers of the State President to appoint and depose chiefs derives from section 2(7) of the Act. This section permits the State President to appoint 'any person as a chief of a black tribe'. The drastic consequences of this power were stated by Hoexter ACJ in *Buthelezi v Minister of Bantu Administration* 1961 (4) SA 835 (A) where it was said:

> There is nothing in the Act which gives the son of the deceased hereditary chief any claim whatever to the chieftainship; on the contrary, the object of the legislation appears to have been to put an end to hereditary chieftainship.[9]

Before appointing or deposing a chief, the State President is, however, required to consult the appropriate territorial authority, if one has been established in terms of the Black Authorities Act 69 of 1951.[10]

Section 2 does not refer to the suspension of a chief. That section does, however, empower the State President to make regulations prescribing the duties, powers, privileges and conditions of service of chiefs and headmen. These regulations are contained in Proclamation 110 of 1957.[11] Regulation 30 deals with the suspension of a chief. In *Sekhukhune v Minister of Native Affairs* 1958 (2) SA 425 (T), Rumpff J considered an application to declare certain orders of suspension of an acting chief made under regulation 30 to be null and void. The suspension was declared void because the applicant had not been given a hearing. Shortly after this judgment was delivered, the State President amended regulation 30 of Proclamation 110 to read as follows:

> The Minister, the Secretary or the Chief Native Commissioner for the area concerned may at any time *without any trial* suspend any appointed chief or headman from his office (my emphasis).[12]

Although section 2 of the Act remains the principal enactment providing for the appointment and deposition of chiefs, the pursuance by the South African government of its Byzantine legislative schemes to effect balkanization in the form of 'black homelands' has led to the multiplication of authorities charged with the appointment and deposition of chiefs.

In the first place, section 3 of the National States Constitution Act 21 of 1971 gives legislative powers to the legislative assemblies in the self-governing territories. Those powers include the recognition, appointment and deposition of chiefs.[13] KwaZulu, for example, now has its own enactment, the kwaZulu Chiefs' and Headmen's Act 8 of 1974 which replaces Proclamation 110. Chiefs are still appointed in terms of section 2 of the Black Authorities Act but that power now rests with the kwaZulu cabinet.

The other major development has been the creation of independent states by the South African legislature. For example, the creation of Bophuthatswana as an independent state in terms of the Status of Bophuthatswana Act 89 of 1977 removed the authority of the South African authorities to exercise their powers in Bophuthatswana. The Legislative Assembly of Bophuthatswana was made competent to make laws for Bophuthatswana. The Legislative Assembly did just that. In Bophuthatswana, the appointment of chiefs is now governed by the Bophuthatswana Traditional Authorities Act 23 of 1978.

Observing natural justice

The powers given to the State President in section 2(7) of the Black Administration Act are wide, so wide indeed that the power to appoint a chief requires no deference to customary practice. The scope of this power has been confirmed by our courts on a number of occasions. In *Sibasa v Ratsialingwa and Hartman* 1947 (4) SA 369 (T), Roper J said this:

> Under the very wide terms of the subsection it is legally competent for the Governor-General to appoint as chief of a tribe a stranger to the family in which the hereditary chieftainship lies, or even a non-member of the tribe.[14]

The drastic nature of the State President's discretion has caused much dissatisfaction. The one persistent claim that has been made by those adversely affected by the exercise of this discretion is that the principles of natural justice must be observed, and in particular, that a person must be heard before a decision is taken that is detrimental to his or her interests.

The claim that the exercise of the State President's discretion in section 2(7) requires that a fair hearing be given has been considered by our courts in a fashion consistent with an orthodox, if much criticized, construction of the principles of natural justice. The orthodox position runs as follows. There is a presumption that the exercise of statutory powers requires compliance with the maxim audi alteram partem.[15] The scope of the presumption is restricted in two ways. First, the classification of discretions as judicial, quasi-judicial and administrative determines whether a decision-maker is obliged, in exercising his or her powers, to observe the principles of natural justice. Secondly, the principles of natural justice are binding only in cases in which the administrative act in question affects the individual's existing rights, liberties or privileges.

The formula 'existing rights, liberties or privileges' has exercised a powerful hold upon judicial reasoning. Its attraction is based on a simple notion of proportionality. The duty resting upon a decision-maker to comply with the principles of natural justice is triggered by the gravity of the affected individual's interests. The power to disturb existing rights is an interest of sufficient weight to warrant procedural protection. Thus in *Laubscher v Native Commissioner, Piet Retief* 1958 (1) SA 546 (A), the lack of the appellant's antecedent right to enter trust property meant that a permit to enter the area could be denied without a hearing.

The decisions in our courts that have considered the power of the State President to appoint, suspend or depose chiefs have closely followed the orthodox position. In *Monakgotla v Minister of Native Affairs* 1959 (1) SA 686 (T), Monakgotla had been appointed the acting chief of the Bakubung tribe. On 5 September 1957, the Minister, acting under powers vested in him in terms of the Act, deposed Monakgotla as chief of the tribe. Monakgotla was given no opportunity to meet the allegations that had been made against him. Citing *R v Ngwevela* 1954 (1) SA 123 (A), Roper AJ held that Monakgotla was entitled to an opportunity to put his case. This conclusion was reached by recourse to both aspects of the orthodox position. First, Roper AJ characterizes the power to depose a chief as quasi-judicial in virtue of the responsibilities and status attaching to the position of a chief. Secondly, the chief's right to be heard follows from the effect that the power entrusted to the Minister may have upon his existing rights as a chief.

We are here concerned with three separate powers:

i) the power to appoint a chief;
ii) the power to suspend a chief;
iii) the power to depose a chief.

There is clearly a distinction to be drawn between suspension and deposition. A suspension brings about a temporary situation in which the holder of an office may not act, whereas a deposition brings to an end a person's tenure of an office.

It follows from the orthodox position, and particularly the 'existing rights, liberties or privileges' formula, that an opportunity to be heard need be afforded only to a chief (or acting chief) who is suspended or deposed. A person who fails to secure appointment as a chief cannot insist upon a right to be heard. An aspirant chief has no antecedent right to the office, whereas an incumbent has an existing right that cannot be interfered with without due regard to the principles of natural justice.

And thus have our courts determined the matter. In *Buthelezi's* case,[16] it was held that the appellant, the son of a hereditary chief, had no vested right to the chieftainship, and the Governor-General was thus entitled to appoint one Mangosuthu Buthelezi as chief without any notice to the appellant. As we have noted already, there is no duty resting upon the State President to hear a person whose claim to a chieftainship rests upon customary practice, because in terms of the Act, custom affords no basis for entrenching rights to a chieftainship.

The situation is otherwise in cases of deposition and suspension. In *Minister van Naturellesake v Monakgotla* 1959 (3) SA 517 (A), Beyers JA held that where a Minister or official had the power to make a decision which might affect a person's rights, there exists in law a presumption that the legislature intended that the official's authority was only to be exercised with due regard to the rules of natural justice, among these that the party affected should be heard. The applicant here had not been heard, audi alteram partem applied, and his deposition was thus void. In *Sekhukhune's* case[18] similar reasoning required that the suspension of an acting chief, afforded no opportunity of stating his case, was void. However, as already indicated, the suspension of a chief is now governed by the amended version of regulation 30 of Proclamation 110 of 1957.

Legitimate expectation

The orthodox position is committed to the view that when a statute empowers a public official to take a decision that may prejudicially affect an individual's existing rights, liberties or privileges, such an individual has a right to be heard before that decision is taken. The orthodox position is ultimately justified by the following chain of reasoning. Official compliance with the principles of natural justice inhibits administrative efficiency. The cost of compliance is not warranted in carrying out all administrative actions, for example, in matters of internal administration. Thus some principle of proportionality is required so that the cost of procedural protection is incurred only in cases of administrative action in which the interests of the individual at stake are sufficiently weighty. The 'existing rights, liberties or privileges' formula provides the criterion by which warranted procedural protection may be judged.

This criterion has however attracted much criticism. It was long ago pointed out by Bentham that the advantage of gaining cannot be compared with the evil of losing.[19] The postulates of the orthodox position are conservative. The individual, on this view, has a weighty interest in securing his existing bundle of rights and no redistribution of that bundle of rights should be effected by administrative action without allowing the individual an opportunity to be heard. Few would doubt this. As Bentham said, 'every man naturally expects to preserve what he has'.[20] The problem with the orthodox position is that it undervalues the worth to the individual of the advantage of gaining. In a modern society, many benefits, offices, licenses and permissions are distributed by public authorities. Indeed a significant proportion of any individual's resources derives (at least potentially) from public authorities in this way, rather than by way of private transactions. And thus it is argued that the orthodox position is unwarrantably skewed towards the procedural protection of existing entitlements, whereas an individual's interest in gaining a benefit to which he or she has no right is no less important.

The conservative bias of the existing rights formula has been breached in administrative law as a result of the judicial development of the concept of legitimate expectation. The concept has its origin in the judgment of Lord Denning in *Schmidt v Secretary of State for Home Affairs*,[21] and it has since blossomed in the House of Lords,[22] the Privy Council[23] and the common law world generally.[24] In South African law, the concept of legitimate expectation has now been firmly established as a result of the decision in the *Traub* case.[25] In *Traub*, senior house officers and interns at the Baragwanath Hospital were refused re-appointment (in the case of senior house officers) and appointment (in the case of interns) as senior house officers by the Director of Hospital Services. No hearing was given to the respondents. The reason for this refusal was that the respondents had signed a letter that appeared in the *SA Medical Journal* criticizing hospital policy in the Transvaal and the conditions at Baragwanath Hospital. In the court below, Goldstone J found that the refusal to appoint the respondents was invalid because they were not afforded a fair hearing before the decision was taken.[26]

In the Appellate Division, Corbett CJ, delivering judgment for a unanimous court, found that the respondents had no right to be appointed to the posts, and thus the refusal had no effect upon their existing rights.[27] According to the orthodox position, that finding ought to have closed off the respondents' right to a fair hearing. However, the court proceeded to consider the concept of legitimate expectation.

Drawing strongly upon English and Australian cases, the Appellate Division in *Traub* may be said to have liberated our administrative law from the orthodox position that our courts had adopted in construing the principles of natural justice. In the first place, Corbett CJ found that:

> an adherence to the formula of 'liberty, property and existing rights' would fail to provide a legal remedy, when the facts cry out for one; and would result in a decision which appeared to have been arrived at by a procedure which was clearly unfair being immune from review.[28]

Whilst sounding the usual cautionary note that the doctrine of legitimate expectation must be developed incrementally and with a proper regard for the danger of undue judicial interference, the basic commitment of the court in *Traub* is that the doctrine of legitimate expectation is a compendious title for the broad requirement that administrative decision-makers must act fairly, and that the circumstances in which they must do so are not restricted to cases of existing rights.

Secondly, *Traub* has killed off the classification of administrative acts according to the triad of judicial, quasi-judicial and administrative acts as a way of determining the reach of the principles of natural justice. Of the classification, Corbett CJ had this to say:

> [A] classification as quasi-judicial adds nothing to the process of reasoning: the Court could just as well eliminate this step and proceed straight to the question as to whether the decision does prejudicially affect the individual concerned.[29]

Although the court in *Traub* (tentatively) expressed the view that a person who applies for a post is probably not entitled to be heard before the authority concerned takes its decision, nevertheless special considerations in this case warranted the application of the doctrine of legitimate expectation. First, the positions applied for were a necessary step for a doctor wishing to ascend the professional hierarchy. Second, it was a long established practice that an application for the post of senior house officer, once recommended by the departmental head, was invariably granted by the Director of Health Services. Thus it was held that the respondents had a legitimate expectation of being appointed and if the refusal of their applications was in prospect, the Director of Health Services was required to give the respondents a fair hearing.[30]

Many will welcome the acceptance of the doctrine of legitimate expectation in our law. The doctrine however admits of ambiguity and the *Traub* decision falls somewhat short of providing a full account of the doctrine's application.

There is some ambiguity as to whether the legitimate expectation refers to an interest that requires procedural protection or whether it refers to an expectation that the principles of natural justice will be applied before a decision is taken. In *Traub* both species of expectations are countenanced.[31] Under the first species of expectation, the right to a fair hearing flows from a legitimate expectation that an interest which may be adversely affected by an administrative decision has sufficient weight to warrant procedural protection. The second species of expectation considers the legitimacy of an individual's expectation of a hearing.

There remains the issue of how we are to judge the weight of the interests that trigger the right to a fair hearing. The outcome in *Traub* suggests two kinds of reason that warrant the procedural protection of an individual's interests. The first reason is based upon reliance. A person may warrantably rely upon the fact that a regular administrative practice that can reasonably be expected to continue will continue. If it does not do so, such a person should be afforded a fair hearing.[32]

The second reason is based upon special detriment. It is well recognized that one justification for the requirement that a person must be given a fair hearing is that it improves the quality of decision-making. The interesting case is one in which the decision-maker would have reached a different decision had a fair hearing been given. This kind of error (which I call 'error cost') is an inherent feature of all administrative systems. What administrative law needs to establish is that, in the class of administrative actions that do not permit a right to be heard, the cost of conceding that right is higher than the cost of the errors resulting from a failure to do so. The great advantage of the legitimate expectation doctrine is that it does not define rigid classes which exclude the right to be heard, and thus it remains a flexible doctrine which may be used to compare these costs.

In my view, the key to the successful application of the doctrine of legitimate expectation is an enquiry into error cost. That cost is to be determined not first in economic terms (as when we calculate the economic cost of a refusal to grant a licence) but also in terms of moral cost. Not all errors are the same: we tolerate some more readily than others. There are certain kinds of administrative decisions in respect of which the errors that are made are randomly distributed over a large class of persons. We tend to say of these errors, the decision is tough but not unfair. Some decisions, however, involve errors that are not randomly distributed, or apply to a special class of person for whom the consequences of the error are potentially very harsh indeed. In the *Traub* case, the fact that the respondents were having special treatment meted out to them with very grave consequences for their careers, ultimately persuaded the court that the Director of Hospital Services ought at least to hear the respondents before taking a final decision. Where the possible detriment is great, and there is a chance of error, this special detriment triggers the right to a fair hearing.

There is one final aspect of the doctrine of legitimate expectation that I shall briefly consider here. Much has been said about the doctrine in terms of the substantive benefits that persons might reasonably expect to acquire. The principal enquiry here is to make an assessment of the consequences of a refusal of a benefit without a hearing for the person. Our concern for the relationship between procedures and outcomes is important. But it does not exhaust our concern for the value of procedural safeguards. We also value defined procedures, such as a fair hearing, just for their own sake. It is very difficult to obtain any broad agreement about the results of administrative decision-making. However, people can more easily agree about the fairness of a procedure. And that is important because people are more likely to have confidence in an administrative system that operates according to fair procedures even though the results are, in their view, unjustified. The recognition in *Traub* of a person's procedural expectation as a basis for requiring a hearing may well go some way to restore the presumptive application of the principles of natural justice to administrative decision-making. Given the independent value of procedural protection, that is a particularly welcome feature of the decision.

The appointment and suspension of chiefs revisited

Under the orthodox construction of the principles of natural justice, persons who fail to secure appointment as a chief, though they may have an expectation of doing so by virtue of their status according to traditional practice, have no right to a fair hearing. The doctrine of legitimate expectation will now, in my view, afford such persons some prospect of requiring that the decision to appoint a chief cannot, in these circumstances, be taken without first giving the hereditary heir an opportunity to be heard.

That conclusion may be reached according to the reasoning that was recognized in *Traub*. First, in those cases in which it has been the regular practice to appoint the hereditary heir, the power of the State President to appoint any person does not dislodge the justified reliance of a hereditary heir upon the maintenance of conventional practice. Reliance of this kind founds a basis for requiring that a fair hearing be given. Secondly, in those cases in which customary practice has been interfered with, the hereditary heir is not left without a claim to procedural protection. Here, the hereditary heir may rely upon the argument from special detriment. The violation of traditional norms inflicts grave harm upon a hereditary heir because it undermines his or her special status within the tribe and indeed shows contempt for the institutional values of the tribe.

There remains the question of suspension. That matter, it will be recalled, is dealt with in regulation 30 of Proclamation 110 of 1957. The regulation gives the Minister the power to suspend any chief from his or her office 'without any trial'. The regulation appears to exclude the presumptive application of the principles of natural justice that were found to apply in *Sekhukhune's* case. It may however be argued that a trial is not at all the same thing as a hearing. A trial requires a full consideration of all the relevant evidence and a determination in accordance with that evidence. In addition, a trial contemplates a very full set of procedural safeguards of which hearing the suspended chief is but one. While the panoply of a trial is excluded under regulation 30, given the distinction between a trial and a hearing, it does not follow that the regulation excludes that more humble procedural safeguard, the right to a hearing.

Notes

1 The Natives Land Act 27 of 1913, now the Black Land Act.

2 The Native Trust and Land Act 18 of 1936, now the Black Trust and Land Act.

3 An informative account of this process appears in D van der Merwe 'Land tenure in South Africa: A brief history and some reform proposals' (1989) 4 *TSAR* 663.

4 Act 38 of 1927.

5 Cited by D Welsh from the *House of Assembly Debates* in 'The State President's power under the Bantu Administration Act' 1968 *Acta Juridica* 81.

6 Welsh at 88.

7 Proclamation 110 of 1957.

8 See J Collinge 'Tampering with Tradition' (1989) 61 *Work in Progress* 24.

9 *Buthelezi's* case at 841.

10 Section 2(8) *bis* of the Black Administration Act.

11 *GG* 5854 of 18 April 1957.

12 The amendment of Proclamation 110 of 1957 was published as Proclamation 171 of 1958 in *GG* 6084 of 18 July 1958.

13 Schedule 1 item 27 of Act 21 of 1971.

14 At 387.

15 The presumption is paradigmatically stated in *R v Ngwevela* 1954 (1) SA 123 (A) at 131. Audi alteram partem means hear both sides.

16 Cited above.

17 Which upheld the decision of Roper AJ in *Monakgotla v Minister of Native Affairs*. See Haysom in this volume at 113.

18 Cited above.

19 Cited in E Halevy *The Growth of Philosophical Radicalism* (London: 1955) 40.

20 Ibid at 40 (note 19).

21 [1969] 2 Ch 149 (CA).

22 *Council of Civil Service Unions v Minister of the Civil Service* [1984] 3 All ER 935.

23 *Attorney General of Hong Kong v Ng Yuen Shiu* [1983] 2 All ER 346.

24 *Kioa v West* (1988) 60 ALJR 1131 (HC); *Chandra v Minister of Immigration* (1978) 2 NZLR 559.

25 *Traub's* case cited above in the text.

26 The case is reported as *Administrator of the Transvaal v Traub* 1989 (2) SA 396 (T).

27 (1989) 10 *ILJ* 823 (A) at 833.

28 *Traub* at 840.

29 *Traub* at 842.

30 *Traub* at 840.

31 *Traub* at 837.

32 See Lord Fraser in *Council of Civil Services* note 22 above at 943-4.

Resource Bibliography: Selected Secondary Materials

by Susan Ogterop, Laurel Angus & Kathy Eales

A. Forced Removals

General

BALDWIN, ALAN 'Mass Removals and Separate Development' (1975) 1 *Journal of Southern African Studies* 215.

BALDWIN, ALAN *Uprooting a Nation: The Study of 3 Million Evictions in South Africa* (London: African Publications 1974).

CLAASSENS, ANINKA *The Myth of 'Voluntary Removals'* (Cape Town: Second Carnegie Inquiry into Poverty and Development in Southern Africa paper no 74 1984).

DESMOND, COSMAS *The Discarded People: An Account of African Resettlement in South Africa* (Harmondsworth: Penguin 1971).

FREUND, BILL 'Forced Resettlement and the Political Economy of South Africa' (1984) 29 *Review of African Political Economy* 49.

HALLETT, ROBIN 'Desolation on the Veld: Forced Removals in South Africa' 1984 *African Affairs* 301.

HOOPER, CHARLES *Brief Authority* (Cape Town: David Philip 1989).

INNES, DUNCAN *Disqualified: A Study of the Uprooting of the Coloured People in South Africa* (London: Africa Publications Trust 1975).

JOFFE, HILARY 'Rural Resettlement in South Africa' (1977) 6 *Africa Perspective* 13.

KANE-BERMAN, JOHN 'Population Removal, Displacement and Divestment in South Africa' (1981) 7 *Social Dynamics* 28.

MAASDORP, GAVIN and PILLAY, NESEN 'Urban Relocation and Racial Segregation: The Case of Indian South Africans' (Durban: Department of Economics, University of Natal 1977).

MARÉ, GERRY *African Population Relocation in South Africa* (Johannesburg: South African Institute of Race Relations 1980).

MURRAY, COLIN 'Displaced Urbanization: South Africa's Rural Slums' (1987) 86 *African Affairs* 311.

NASH, MARGARET *Black Uprooting from 'White' South Africa: The Fourth and Final Stage of Apartheid* (Braamfontein: South African Council of Churches 1980).

PLATZKY, LAURINE and WALKER, CHERRYL *The Surplus People: Forced Removals in South Africa* (Johannesburg: Ravan 1985).

PLATZKY, LAURINE 'Relocation in South Africa: A Review' (1985) 1 *South African Journal on Human Rights* 270.

Resistance and Resettlement in Southern Africa (1984) 29 *Review of African Political Economy* (special edition).

SURPLUS PEOPLE PROJECT *Forced Removals in South Africa: Surplus People Project Report* vol 1-5 (Cape Town: Surplus People Project 1983).

UNTERHALTER, ELAINE *Forced Removal: The Division, Segregation and Control of the People of South Africa* (London: International Defence and Aid Fund 1987).

Case studies

BADAT, MOHAMED The Political Economy of Forced Removals and Relocation: the Case of Natal, 1948-1980 (BSocSci Hons thesis, University of Natal 1980).

BALDWIN, ALAN and HALL, ANTHONY *A Place called Dimbaza* (London: Africa Publications Trust 1973).

COLE, JOSETTE *Crossroads: The Politics of Reform and Repression, 1976-1986* (Johannesburg: Ravan 1987).

DESMOND, COSMAS *Limehill Revisited: A Case Study of the longer-term effects of African Resettlement* (Pietermaritzburg: Development Studies Research Group, University of Pietermaritzburg 1978).

GREEN, PIPPA and HIRSCH, ALAN *The Impact of Resettlement in the Ciskei: 3 Case Studies* (Cape Town: Southern Africa Labour and Development Research Unit 1983).

JAMES, DEBORAH *The Road from Doornkop* (Johannesburg: South African Institute of Race Relations 1983).

MACLENNAN, BEN *Glenmore: The Story of a Forced Removal* (Johannesburg: South African Institute of Race Relations 1987).

OLIVIER, N J J '(Gedwonge) Verskuiwings en die Magopas van Ventersdorp: die (voor)laaste aflewerings' (1986) 1 *South African Public Law* 121.

PERLMAN, John M *The State and the African Working Class in the Pretoria-Odi Area: Population Management and Class Restructuring* (Johannesburg: Southern African Research Service 1983).

SHARP, JOHN 'Relocation and the Problem of Survival in QwaQwa' (1982) 8 *Social Dynamics* 11.

SILK, ANDREW *A Shanty Town in South Africa: The Story of Modderdam* (Johannesburg: Ravan 1981).

TRUMP, MARTIN 'The Clearance of the Doornfontein Yards and Racial Segregation' (1979) 12 *Africa Perspective* 40.

WESTERN, JOHN *Outcast Cape Town* (Cape Town: Human & Rousseau 1981).

'Winterveld' (1979) 10 *Work in Progress* 50.

WHITE, LUCIE E 'To Learn and to Teach: Lessons from Driefontein on Lawyering and Power' 1988 *Wisconsin Law Review* 699

Legal issues

HAYSOM, NICHOLAS and ARMSTRONG, AMANDA *Population Relocation and the Law: Social Engineering on a Vast Scale* (Cape Town: Second Carnegie Inquiry into Poverty and Development in Southern Africa paper no 86 1984).

LOOTS, CHERYL 'The Right to be Represented by a Leader Duly Appointed according to Law: *Moses Ngema v Minister of Law and Order*' (1985) 1 *South African Journal on Human Rights* 265.

Removals and the Law: transcript of a workshop held in Grahamstown, July 1982 edited by Ian Donald, Laurine Platzky and Judith Shier. (Cape Town: Surplus People Project; Pietermaritzburg: Association for Rural Advancement 1984).

B. Land Tenure

BOONZAAIER, E 'From Communal Grazing to "Economic" Units: Changing Access to Land in a Namaqualand Reserve'(1987) 4 *Development Southern Africa* 479.

CROSS, C R & HAINES, R J (eds) *Towards Freehold? Options for Land and Development in South Africa's Black Rural Areas* (Cape Town: Juta 1988).

DAVENPORT T R H and HUNT K S (eds) *The Right to the Land: Documents on Southern African History* (Cape Town: David Philip 1974).

DAVENPORT, T R H 'Some Reflections on the History of Land Tenure in South Africa, seen in the light of attempts by the State to impose Political and Economic Control' 1985 *Acta Juridica* 53.

KERR, A J 'Bantu Law Rights over Land Registered in the Name of Another' (1969) 86 *South African Law Journal* 15.

KERR, A J *The Customary Law of Immovable Property and of Succession* 2nd edn (Grahamstown: Rhodes University 1976).

LETSOALO, ESSY M *Land Reform in South Africa* (Johannesburg: Skotaville 1987).

MQEKE, R B 'Land Tenure in the Ciskei: A Synopsis and Evaluation of the Report of the Swart Commission' (1984) 13 *Speculum Juris* 29.

ROBERTSON, MIKE 'Land Law in South Africa until 1936' (1984) *University of Natal Law Review* 81.

ROBERTSON, MIKE 'Black Land Tenure: Disabilities and Some Rights' in A Rycroft (ed) *Race and the Law in South Africa* (Cape Town: Juta 1987) 119.

VOSLOO, L J 'Occupation and Ownership of Land in South Africa' (1968) 2 *De Rebus* 13.

C. Homelands

BUDLENDER, GEOFF 'A Common Citizenship?' (1985) 1 *South African Journal on Human Rights* 210.

BUDLENDER, GEOFF 'Constitutional Issues in KwaNdebele' in G Kruger and P Rainey (eds) *KwaNdebele – The Future?* (Pretoria: Lawyers for Human Rights 1988) 93.

BUDLENDER, GEOFF 'On Citizenship and Residence Rights: Taking Words Seriously' (1989) 1 *South African Journal on Human Rights* 37.

CORDER, HUGH and MURRAY, CHRISTINA 'Homelands Incorporation: The Courts Overruled' 1989 *De Rebus* 529.

DUGARD, JOHN *The Denationalization of Black South Africans in Pursuance of Apartheid: A Question for the International Court of Justice* (Johannesburg: Centre for Applied Legal Studies, University of the Witwatersrand 1984).

HORRELL, MURIEL *The African Homelands of South Africa* (Johannesburg: South African Institute of Race Relations 1973).

LIPTON, MERLE 'Independent Bantustans' (1972) 8 *International Affairs* 1.

The Moutse Issue (Pretoria: Department of Foreign Affairs 1986).

TURPIN, C C 'The Right of Ejectment' (1957) 74 *South African Law Journal* 145.

VENTER, F 'Bantoeburgerskap en Tuislandburgerskap' (1975) 38 *Tydskrif vir Hedendaagse Romeins Hollandse Reg* 239.

YAWITCH, JOANNE *Betterment: The Myth of Homeland Culture* (Johannesburg: South African Institute of Race Relations 1982).

D. Influx Control

BUDLENDER, GEOFF 'Ending Racially Discriminatory Legislation: Influx Control' (1986) 2 *Tydskrif vir Regswetenskap* 51.

BUDLENDER, GEOFF 'Reform in Perspective' in *Quarterly Countdown* (Johannesburg: South African Institute of Race Relations August 1989).

BUDLENDER, GEOFF and DAVIS, DENNIS 'Labour Law, Influx Control and Citizenship: The Emerging Policy Conflict' 1984 *Acta Juridica* 141.

COHN, WILLIAM 'Influx Control and Black Resistance in Apartheid South Africa' (1986) 3 *Trans Africa Forum* 53.

CORDER, HUGH 'The Rights and Conditions of Entry into and Residence in Urban Areas by Africans' 1984 *Acta Juridica* 45.

DU PLESSIS, WILLEMIEN and OLIVIER, NIC 'The Identification Act 72 of 1986' (1986) 1 *South African Public Law* 272.

HINDSON, DOUG *Pass Controls and the Urban African Proletariat in South Africa* (Johannesburg: Ravan 1987).

HORNER, DUDLEY (ed) *Labour Preference; Influx Control and Squatters: Cape Town entering the 1980s* (Cape Town: South African Labour and Development Research Unit Working Paper 50 1983).

Influx Control Policy (1986) 11(8) *South African Labour Bulletin* (special edition).

SCHOOMBEE, HANNES and DAVIS, DENNIS 'Abolishing Influx Control – Fundamental or Cosmetic Change?' (1986) 2 *South African Journal on Human Rights* 208.

E. Urban Areas – Housing and Administration

Black Urban Law 1984 *Acta Juridica* (special edition)

HUGO, GERT 'Urban Development and Town Planning' 1974 *De Rebus* 269.

MAASDORP, GAVIN and HUMPHREYS, A S B *From Shantytown to Township: An Economic Study of African Poverty and Rehousing in a South African City* (Cape Town: Juta 1975).

MORRIS, P and VAN DER HORST, S 'Urban Housing' in S van den Horst (ed) *Race Discrimination in South Africa: A Review* (Cape Town: David Philip 1981) 90.

OLIVIER, M 'Swartes in Stadsgebiede' 1983 *De Rebus* 343.

OLIVIER, NIC 'Property Rights in Urban Areas' (1988) 3 *South African Public Law* 23.

RAUTENBACH, I M 'Plaaslike Owerhede – Quo Vadis?' (1986) 1 *South African Public Law* 9.

YOUNG, AMANDA 'Housing Policy and Housing Shortage in Cape Town: 1942-80' (1982) 21 *Africa Perspective* 9.

F. Squatting

General

OBUDHO, R A and MHLANGA, C (eds) *Slum and Squatter Settlements in sub-Saharan Africa – Toward a Planning Strategy*' (New York: Praeger 1988).

O'REGAN, CATHERINE 'No More Forced Removals? An Historical Analysis of the Prevention of Illegal Squatting Act' (1989) 5 *South African Journal on Human Rights* 361.

Case studies

REYNOLDS, PAMELA *Childhood in Crossroads – Cognition and Society in South Africa* (Cape Town: David Philip 1989).

YAWITCH, JOANNE 'Women and Squatting: A Winterveld Case Study' in P Bonner (ed) *Working Papers in Southern African Studies* vol 2 (Johannesburg: Ravan 1981).

Legal issues (including Spoliation)

BUDLENDER, GEOFF 'Recent Developments in "Squatting Law"' (1990) 1 *Urban Forum* (forthcoming).

BUDLENDER, GEOFF 'South African Legal Approaches to Squatting' 1988 *De Rebus* 160.

LEWIS, CAROLE 'The Prevention of Illegal Squatting Act: The Promotion of Homelessness?' (1989) 5 *South African Journal on Human Rights* 233.

RISSIK, P U 'Transvaal Squatters' Law and the Master and Servants Act' (1921) 38 *South African Law Journal* 137.

ROOS, JOHAN 'On Illegal Squatters and Spoliation Orders' (1988) 4 *South African Journal on Human Rights* 167.

ROOS, JOHAN 'On Illegal Squatters and Spoliation Orders II' (1989) 5 *South African Journal on Human Rights* 395.

TAITZ, JEROLD 'A Spoliation Order is a Robust and Unique Remedy' (1982) 99 *South African Law Journal* 351.

TAITZ, JEROLD 'Spoliation Proceedings and the "Grubby-handed" Possessor' (1981) 98 *South African Law Journal* 36.

VAN BLOMMESTEIN, F 'Demolition Orders and the Audi Alteram Partem Rule' (1962) 79 *South African Law Journal* 7.

VAN DER BYL, D G 'Trespassers will be Prosecuted – No longer a Wooden Falsehood' (1955) 72 *South African Law Journal* 125.

VAN DER WALT, A J 'Defences in Spoliation Proceedings' (1985) 105 *South African Law Journal* 172.

G. Group Areas

AVINS, A 'Racial Separation and Public Accommodations: Some Comparative Notes between South African and American Law' (1969) 86 *South African Law Journal* 53.

BECK, ANDREW 'Contracts and the Group Areas Act: an Interesting Reversal' (1987) 104 *South African Law Journal* 252.

CACHALIA, YUSUF 'The Ghetto Act' (1957) 12(1) *Africa South* 39.

CHRISTIE, R *Group Areas and Property Market Economies* (Johannesburg: South African Institute of Race Relations Topical Briefing 1987).

COMHAIRE, J L L 'Urban Segregation and Racial Legislation in Africa' (1977) 15 *American Sociological Review* 50 .

COWLEY, CECIL '"Occupy" in terms of the Group Areas Act' (1960) 77 *South African Law Journal* 425.

DISON, L R and MOHAMMED, I *Group Areas and their Development* (Durban: Butterworths 1960).

D'OLIVIERA, J A VAN S 'Group Areas and Community Development' in W A Joubert (ed) *The Law of South Africa* vol 10 (Durban: Butterworths 1980).

GUNN, G H 'The Group Areas Act in relation to Race Zoning' (1951) 15 *Public Health* 258.

HENOCHSBERG, E S *An Explanation of the Group Areas Act, 1950* (Durban: Butterworths 1950).

HIEMSTRA, V G *The Group Areas Act* (Cape Town: Juta 1953).

HORRELL, MURIEL *Group Areas: The Emerging Pattern with Illustrative Examples from the Transvaal* (Johannesburg: South African Institute of Race Relations 1966).

JOHNSON, C J 'The Group Areas Act: Stage I' (1951) 68 *South African Law Journal* 286.

MCLENNAN, JOHN S 'Illegal Contracts and Group Areas' (1986) 1 *Natal University Law & Society Review* 185.

OMAR, I 'The Group Areas Act: A Historical and Legal Review' 1989 *De Rebus* 515.

SCHOOMBEE, H 'Group Areas Legislation – The Political Control of Ownership and Occupation of Land' 1985 *Acta Juridica* 77.

VAN DER VYVER, J D 'Qu'ils Mangent de la Brioche!'(1981) 98 *South African Law Journal* 135.

VAN REENEN, T H *Land. Its Ownership and Occupation in South Africa. A Treatise on the Group Areas Act and the Community Development Act* (Cape Town: Juta 1962).

H. General

Periodical Publications which regularly contain relevant material

Quarterly Countdown Johannesburg: South African Institute of Race Relations (four issues a year).

Race Relations Survey Johannesburg: South African Institute of Race Relations (published annually).

South African Journal on Human Rights Cape Town: Juta (published 3 times a year). See particularly the 'Human Rights Index' in each issue.

South African Review Johannesburg: Ravan

Transvaal Rural Action Committee occasional publications.

J. Bibliography

FREUND, BILL 'Forced Resettlement and the Political Economy of South Africa' (1984) 29 *Review of African Political Economy* 49.

KALLEY, JACKIE *South Africa under Apartheid: A Select and Annotated Bibliography* (Pietermaritzburg: Shuter and Shooter 1987)

MARÉ, GERRY *African Population Relocation in South Africa* (Johannesburg: South African Institute of Race Relations 1980).

PLATZKY, LAURINE and WALKER, CHERRYL *The Surplus People: Forced Removals in South Africa* (Johannesburg: Ravan 1985) contains a list of resources on relocation at 401.

Index

Index of Cases